TWENTIETH-CENTURY AMERICA

A Primary Source Collection from
The Associated Press

VOLUME 4

The Cold War at Home and Abroad 1945-1953

By the Writers and Photographers of
THE ASSOCIATED PRESS

GROLIER EDUCATIONAL CORPORATION

Twentieth-century America

at

James Shenton, Columbia University
CONSULTING LIBRARIAN: Sara Miller, Rye Country Day
    School, Rye, New York

**GROLIER EDUCATIONAL CORPORATION,
GROLIER PUBLISHING COMPANY**
PUBLISHER: Mark Cummings
VICE PRESIDENT, MARKETING: Beverly Balaz
VICE PRESIDENT, MANUFACTURING: Joseph J. Corlett
DIRECTOR OF REFERENCE PUBLISHING, MANUFACTURING:
    Christine L. Matta
SENIOR EDITOR: James Churchill
PRODUCTION MANAGER: Pamela J. Terwilliger
PRODUCTION ASSISTANT: Ann E. Geason
INDEXERS: Pauline Sholtys, Linda King, AEIOU Inc.

THE ASSOCIATED PRESS
PROJECT DIRECTOR: Norm Goldstein
HISTORICAL CONSULTANT: Robert Jakoubek

PROJECT COORDINATOR: Kathryn Kleibacker, Kleibacker and
    Associates
AUTHORS AND EDITORS: John Barbour, Robert J. Dvorchak,
    Rick Hampson, Charles J. Hanley, Larry McShane, Jerry
    Schwartz
CHIEF NEWS LIBRARIANS: Randy Herschaft , Barbara Shapiro
NEWS LIBRARIANS: Mary Ann Cataldo, Steve Carlson, Sukey
    Pett, Chris Schenkel, Jeffrey Tishman, Arnold Wilkinson
CHIEF PHOTO LIBRARIANS: Kevin Kushel, Chuck Zoeller
PHOTO DARKROOM SUPERVISOR: Tim Donnelly
PHOTO RESEARCHER: Debra Hershkowitz
PHOTO PRINTERS: John Carucci, Doug Jefferies, Jim Ryan

DESIGN
Combined Books, Inc.

Library of Congress Cataloging-in-Publication Data

Twentieth-century America: a primary source collection
    from the Associated Press / by the writers and
    photographers of the Associated Press.

    Includes index.

    ISBN 0-7172-7494-2 (alk. paper)
    1. United States—History—20th century—Sources.
    I. Associated Press
E740.5.T84   1995
973.921—dc20   95-12550
                                                        CIP

Printed in the U.S.A.

                    2 3 4 5 6 7 8 9

Atom bomb actual explosion, July 2, 1946.

CONTENTS

BULLETIN
  An alert to editors that this is a priority story. (The rare **FLASH** is used only to report a development of transcendent importance. An **URGENT** is secondary to a **BULLETIN**.)

BULLETIN

EISENHOWER ELECTED

NEW YORK, NOV. 4 (AP)—Gen. Dwight D. Eisenhower, swept to a smashing victory by American voters, promptly pledged tonight that as president he will never give "short weight" to his new responsibilities.

Addressing a wildly cheering crowd at his campaign headquarters, the Republican president-elect told his audience he had sent his Democratic opponent, Gov. Adlai E. Stevenson of Illinois, the following telegram:

"I thank you for your courteous and generous message. Recognizing the intensity of the difficulties that lie ahead, it is clearly necessary that men and women of good will of both parties forget the political strife through which we have passed and devote themselves to the single purpose of a better future. This, I believe, they will do."

Eisenhower's telegram was in reply to one he received a short time earlier from Stevenson, conceding the election.

The general's appearance in the packed grand ballroom of the Commodore Hotel touched off a thunderous ovation which went on for several minutes before he was able to speak.

Smiling happily, Eisenhower waved to the crowd again and again.

The general said that it was "trite to say that this is a day of dedication rather than triumph" and added that he was "indeed as humble as I am proud of the decision" of the American people.

Stating that he recognized the weight of the responsibility of his new office, Gen. Eisenhower pledged:

"I shall never in my service in Washington give short weight to this responsibility."

The general, when he was finally able to get in a word, after his ballroom reception, read Stevenson's concession telegram to the crowd.

Eisenhower then told the audience:

"We can't do the job ahead of us except as a united people. Let us unite for the better future of our children and grandchildren."

Maj. Gen. Song You Chan, commander of the ROK Capital Division, one of South Korea's most battle-tested units, looks very pleased as he bids goodbye to President-elect Eisenhower, who is about to take off in his light plane. The president-elect had visited the division, which only recently was pulled out of the line after months of hard fighting.

He again expressed his thanks to the people all over the country, as he put it, who worked for his election.

(Nov. 4, 1952)

Editor's Note

The following story—released from censorship after Dwight D. Eisenhower's departure from Korea—was written by Associated Press correspondent Don Whitehead, who accompanied the general on his tour. It was a return to familiar scenes for Whitehead, who covered Korea as a war correspondent two years ago.

IKE IN KOREA
By Don Whitehead

WITH EISENHOWER IN KOREA, DEC. 5 (AP)—U.S. President Elect Dwight D. Eisenhower is safely out of Korea and en route home tonight after three action-packed days of seeking a way to peace in this frozen land of war and misery.

Whether this unprecedented mission will prove

CAPTION or cutline
  Provides all necessary information referring to the AP photograph.

Dates have been added to the bottom of stories to facilitate reading in these volumes; AP's daily wire stories generally do not carry dates.

EDITOR'S NOTE
  Sometimes a publishable summary of a feature, but most often an advisory to editors on the story to follow and not for publication. (In this book, it is often used to advise readers about events or circumstances not included in the text.)

SLUGLINE or header
  Gives editors a brief note on the subject of the story to follow.

BYLINE
  Identifies the AP writer and is sometimes followed by specialty underlines such as **AP Special Correspondent** or **AP Newsfeatures Writer**. The standard underline for full-time AP employees is **Associated Press Writer**.

DATELINE
  Denotes place of origin and date of transmission.

LOGO (logotype)
  Identifies the story as an Associated Press transmission.

About This Book

Compiling an original source history of the 20th century had seemed a forbidding task.

But THE ASSOCIATED PRESS has been covering and disseminating the news since 1848 and has amassed a treasure trove of stories and photographs in its files.

The stories in these volumes are reprinted just as they were originally transmitted by AP to its member newspapers, edited occasionally only for consistency of style or for length. Connecting these stories is material written especially for these volumes—**Editor's Notes**—to place the events in their time and to provide some perspective.

On occasion, a story will be preceded by a **BULLETIN** or some other advisory originally sent on the wires to alert editors to the significance of what was to follow. (In the past, before computers and satellite transmission replaced the clackety-clack of teletypes and telephone lines, a **bulletin**—or **flash** or **urgent**—was accompanied by ringing bells to alert editors.)

Most of the AP stories have been preserved on microfilm. More recently, they have been archived in computer databanks.

Many files from the beginning of the century are no longer available in AP files. However, a number of these stories have been culled from individual newspaper archives and used here if they were identifiable as written by AP. (In early days, many newspapers did not credit the AP for the stories they printed.) The now familiar AP logotype—often called a "bug"—seen in the datelines of all Associated Press stories, originated in 1917.

It was then that a court decision established the property right of news and prohibited others from using AP stories after they had been printed by AP subscribers. In order to assure that no one could plead ignorance of the origin of the stories, AP put its "mark" on them—the (AP) logo.

It wasn't until 1925 that AP started using individual bylines. This was several years after Kirke Simpson's stories on the Unknown Soldier. When Simpson's articles were sent from Washington in 1921, requests for the name of the author were answered by a leased-wire message. The message did not authorize the use of Simpson's name as a byline—but he won the first Pulitzer Prize awarded to an AP staffer.

AP
The Story of News

The Associated Press was created in 1848 in New York City by six local publishers who wanted to save costs in a news-gathering war that was becoming expensive and, at times, violent. Today, AP is the world's largest and oldest continually operating news service.

In the United States, it serves more than 1,700 newspapers and 6,000 radio and television stations a daily diet of 4 million words. Its report is translated into dozens of languages for another 8,500 subscribers in 112 countries.

Worldwide, it is read and heard by more than a billion people.

When it was born, the telegraph linked barely a dozen cities, and month-old news from Europe arrived on American shores by ship. Today, AP dispatches circle the globe in seconds by satellite. The old teletype machines that clattered at 60 words a minute are gone. Today's nearly silent computers move almost 10,000 words a minute.

Domestically, The Associated Press operates some 140 bureaus, which not only cover the news but reap the stories of member newspapers and broadcast stations. Overseas, some 500 foreign correspondents and many more stringers or part-time correspondents work in 83 bureaus in 70 countries. These correspondents are constantly on the move to the various hotspots around the globe.

The AP translates its report into five languages: Spanish, French, German, Swedish and Dutch.

But other services and newspapers translate it into many more, among them Chinese, Malay, Hindi, Russian, Persian, Italian, Arabic and Afrikaans.

The Associated Press is not owned by or affiliated with any government, as news services in some countries are. It is a not-for-profit company owned solely by its members. It aims for objectivity without bias or viewpoint.

It always has. The AP's first Washington correspondent, Lawrence Gobright, covered the Civil War. It was a time when the nation and its newspapers were torn apart.

He wrote: *"My business is to communicate facts; my instructions do not allow me to make any comment upon the facts which I communicate. My dispatches are sent to papers of all manner of politics.... I therefore confine myself to what I consider legitimate news. I do not act as a politician belonging to any school, but try to be truthful and impartial. My dispatches are merely dry matters of fact and detail.... Although I try to write without regard to men or politics, I do not always escape censure."*

It was Gobright who, minutes after the assassination of Abraham Lincoln, held John Wilkes Booth's weapon in his hand. He put together the facts of the great crime from eyewitnesses at Ford's Theater.

His first dispatch said simply:

THE PRESIDENT WAS SHOT IN A THEATER TONIGHT AND PERHAPS MORTALLY WOUNDED.

The next morning, Secretary of War Edwin Stanton filed the last numbing news directly to The Associated Press in New York:

ABRAHAM LINCOLN DIED THIS MORNING AT TWENTY-TWO MINUTES AFTER SEVEN O'CLOCK.

All through American history, AP staffers were there. One reported Lincoln's emotional farewell to Springfield, Ill., another the Gettysburg Ad-

Left: This stainless steel plaque outside the AP headquarters in New York weighs 10 tons and was the first of its kind ever devised. Designer was Japanese artist Isamu Noguchi. The title of the work is simply "News." It depicts five men gathering news by camera, telephone, personal observation, pad and pencil and keyboard communication equipment. The plaque was dedicated in April 1940.

dress. There was an AP reporter with George Custer at the Battle of the Little Big Horn.

When the United States was not involved, AP staffers covered both sides of a war. When the Japanese and Russians fought at the turn of the century, an AP reporter on the Russian side was wounded. He was replaced by an AP man from the Japanese lines who had to detour hundreds of miles around the battle to get to his new assignment.

AP staffers sometimes got ahead of the front. When American troops entered Santiago, Cuba, in the Spanish-American War, an AP reporter was there to greet them.

In the early hours of New Year's Day 1935, The Associated Press added a new dimension to news coverage—pictures moved by wire over a 10,000-mile circuit to 25 cities. The first pictures were of an air transport plane that had crashed into the snow-filled Adirondacks.

Included in that first photo report were pictures of New York City's New Year's celebration and an answering picture from Los Angeles of Hollywood's welcome to 1935. The pioneering service was dubbed Wirephoto. By current standards it was painfully slow.

Today, AP's photo service transmits color photos via satellite in a matter of seconds after they are edited on TV-type monitors.

On May 6, 1937, an AP photographer captured on film the fiery explosion of the German dirigible *Hindenburg* at Lakehurst, N.J. AP photographers caught the body-strewn sands of Tarawa in the Pacific and the marching ranks of American GIs filling the Champs Elysees in Paris. AP's Joe Rosenthal shot the picture of American Marines raising their nation's flag above Mt. Suribachi, the most reprinted picture in history. And in Korea, a captured AP photographer snapped pictures of his fellow prisoners of war and smuggled them out, providing evidence to American families that their sons were still alive.

In June 1966, AP photographers caught the image of a shotgunned James Meredith alongside a Mississippi highway where moments before he had been marching for civil rights. They photographed the fiery protest deaths of Buddhist monks in Saigon, the summary execution of a Viet Cong suspect by a police chief's pistol, the naked Vietnamese girl fleeing a napalm attack.

And when Saigon fell to the North Vietnamese, a trio of AP correspondents elected to stay behind, after everyone else had fled, to report the story.

Associated Press reporters and photographers have won 39 Pulitzer Prizes; more than two dozen have lost their lives in the service of news.

Many have been imprisoned by governments and forces who sought to choke off or change their news reports. One of these was Beirut correspondent Terry Anderson, who spent more than six years in secret and dingy cells with other hostages during the Lebanese civil war.

The web of newsgathering reaches from Beijing, China, to Grants Pass, Ore., from Rangoon, Burma, to Cheyenne, Wyo., from Warsaw, Poland, and Harare, Zimbabwe, to Pikeville, Ky., and Peoria, Ill.

It is all stitched together at AP's headquarters, a 14-story Indiana limestone building in New York's Rockefeller Center.

It is here that any outgoing copy gets its last check for clarity and accuracy.

AP's management, virtually all of whom have come from the news ranks, has had to weather times of divisiveness, when the AP's coverage of the news was subject to criticism from all points on the political spectrum.

In the 1960s, one such time, the AP put out an administrative memo to its staff:

"The Associated Press' position on all these controversial areas must be that of a cool, clear voice amid a cacophony of dissident ones. We should take personal satisfaction in making sure that our own reporting and editing be divorced from partisanship of the social and political revolutions sweeping the world. This is in the tradition of The Associated Press built over a century by thousands of AP men and women."

TWENTIETH-CENTURY AMERICA

A Primary Source Collection from
The Associated Press

VOLUME 4

The Cold War at Home and Abroad 1945-1953

TIMELINE

President Harry S. Truman, 1945-1953.

January 12, 1946

A contingent of U.S. troops is welcomed home from Europe after the end of World War II.

April 16, 1945

Harry Truman addresses Congress for the first time as president.

October 23, 1945

Jackie Robinson signs the contract that would make him the first of his color to play in major league baseball.

1945   Jan.   Feb.   March   April   May   June   July   Aug.   Sept.   Oct.   Nov.   Dec.   **1946**   Jan.

May 24, 1946

A railroad strike hits
the nation.

June 23, 1947

The Taft-Hartley bill,
curbing labor unions,
becomes law.

June 5, 1947

Secretary of State
George Marshall
proposes a plan for
European recovery.

March 12, 1947

President Truman
asks Congress for aid
to Greece and Turkey.

March | April | May | June | July | Aug. | Sept. | Oct. | Nov. | Dec. | **1947** | Jan. | Feb. | March | April | May | June

February 25, 1948

A Communist-controlled government takes over in Czechoslovakia.

August 3, 1948

Alger Hiss is accused of spying.

May 11, 1948

The first cargo of postwar aid arrives in France.

June-July 1948

An airlift by Western Allies brings supplies to a blockaded West Berlin.

July Aug. Sept. Oct. Nov. Dec. **1948** Jan. Feb. March April May June July Aug.

November 3, 1948

To the surprise of many, Harry Truman defeats Thomas Dewey for the presidency.

September 23, 1949

President Truman reveals an atomic bomb test explosion by the Soviet Union.

April 4, 1949

Western Allies create the North Atlantic Treaty Organization.

October 1, 1949

Communist leader Mao Tse-tung proclaims the establishment of the People's Republic of China.

Sept. Oct. Nov. Dec. **1949** Jan. Feb. March April May June July Aug. Sept. Oct.

January 31, 1950

President Truman announces the U.S. decision to develop a hydrogen bomb.

February 9, 1950

Sen. Joseph McCarthy claims many in federal government are Communists.

July 1, 1950

U.S. troops are sent to support South Koreans.

Nov. | Dec. | **1950** | Jan. | Feb. | March | April | May | June | July | Aug. | Sept. | Oct. | Nov. | Dec.

September 15, 1950

Gen. Douglas MacArthur leads an invasion at Inchon, South Korea.

April 11, 1951

Gen. MacArthur is fired by President Truman.

February 1951

Gens. MacArthur and Ridgway direct the retaking of Seoul.

1951   Jan.   Feb.   March   April   May   June   July   Aug.   Sept.   Oct.   Nov.   Dec.   **1952**   Jan.   Feb.

July 27, 1953

Korean War truce is signed.

TWENTIETH-CENTURY AMERICA

VOLUME 4

The Cold War At Home and Abroad 1945-1953

When the second world war ended in August 1945, President Harry S. Truman and his fellow Americans beheld a world that was almost frighteningly new. The nation to which 13 million servicemen returned over the next year was far different from the one of December 1941, when the United States entered the war. Business was bigger, labor was bigger, government was bigger. Blacks had served notice they would no longer conspire in their own subjugation. Children were less obedient, and women more independent. Veterans, as Margaret Mead noted, found their wives, girlfriends and sisters "more interchangeable with men than they used to be, better able to fix a tire, or mend a faucet or fix an electric light connection, or preside at a meeting, or keep a treasurer's account, or organize a political campaign."

The war shattered the depression in agriculture—farm income had risen 250 percent since 1939—but the farm population declined by 17 percent in just three and a half years. The 3 million who left their farms tended to settle not inside the big cities but on their outskirts.

The suburbs also seemed like a promised land to veterans returning to crowded old cities, where few houses were for sale or apartments for rent. Two years after the war, 6 million families were doubling up with relatives; another half million were living in Quonset huts and other temporary quarters, including retired trolley cars, surplus grain bins, chicken coops and old iceboxes.

In New York, two newlyweds set up housekeeping in a department store window to publicize their need for an apartment. Squeezed onto in-laws' couches and huddled together in twin beds, veterans, who had crawled through the mud at Anzio or dodged bullets on Iwo Jima and their spouses dreamed of owning new suburban houses filled with appliances.

Thanks to the GI Bill, under which each veteran was eligible for a federally insured mortgage with little or no down payment, these dreams were realized. Single family housing starts surged from 114,000 in 1944 to 937,000 in 1946 and 1.9 million in 1948.

For the first time, houses were being mass-produced. Levitt and Sons, which had built war-worker homes, had learned how to lay dozens of concrete foundations in a single day, and how to preassemble uniform walls and roofs. The Levitts became experts at putting up relatively inexpensive homes even before they built the nation's biggest private housing development in 1947 on Long Island—Levittown.

But new social problems also developed. Los Angeles, which emerged from the war as both an agricultural and an industrial colossus, was having its first smog alerts. Back in New York, there were more and more reports of an old crime with a new name: mugging.

But America's new problems were nothing next to its new wealth. If Roosevelt's "Dr. New Deal" saved American capitalism, his "Dr. Win-the-War" promoted it. Private enterprise regained the prestige and self-confidence it had lost during the Depression. More new industrial plants were built during the war than in the 15 preceding years, and four-fifths of them were adaptable to peacetime production.

The age of postwar prosperity—even affluence—was about to begin.

Chapter 1

Harry Truman's smile during an April 25, 1945, broadcast seems to reflect his cautious approach to the job handed to him suddenly by the death of President Franklin Roosevelt.

A New President, A New World

At an informal press conference in October 1945, President Truman greeted members of the press at his new retreat at Reelfoot Lake, Tenn.

Nineteen-forty-five, with the end of World War II and Adolf Hitler's regime, and the beginning of the atomic age and the United Nations, was one of the most tumultuous years in American history. It was also the year Harry Truman took office as one of the worst-prepared presidents.

After their 1944 election, President Franklin Roosevelt rarely mentioned Truman to anyone and he never denied he had been a compromise candidate for the Democratic vice presidential nomination. The two had only three brief meetings following the inauguration. Most of the vice president's information about the war came from the newspapers and Senate gossip; he had never even been in the White House war room. Josef Stalin knew more about the

U.S. atomic bomb program than the vice president!

The nation that the new president led celebrated the most absolute triumph in human history. Its enemies had been laid low; its prosperity seemed assured.

Having escaped the devastation of invasion, the United States was the only prosperous nation left on Earth. In the early postwar years, the United States held two-thirds of the world's gold reserves and did more than half the manufacturing. Not since Imperial Rome had a nation known anything like the wealth and power the United States enjoyed immediately after the end of World War II.

The New President

Late on the afternoon of April 12, 1945, Harry Truman took the White House elevator to the second floor and walked toward Eleanor Roosevelt's study. As he entered the room, the first lady put her hand on his shoulder and said, "Harry, the president is dead."

Truman, who had been summoned from the Capitol, was stunned; he had heard Franklin Roosevelt was recuperating nicely in Warm Springs, Ga. Finally, he asked Mrs. Roosevelt, "Is there anything I can do for you?" She turned his question around. "Is there anything we can do for you? For you are the one in trouble now."

The next day, when the new president walked into the East Room of the White House for Roosevelt's funeral, no one thought to rise.

However, Truman was not completely without resources as he assumed his new role in the White House: He had common sense, courage, and the good will of the American people.

TRUMAN'S FIRST DAY

WASHINGTON, APRIL 13 (AP)—With a tearful plea—"pray for me!"—Harry S. Truman gathered up the presidential reins of a nation at war today as millions the world over mourned the passing of Franklin Delano Roosevelt.

The new president went quickly to work, conferring with the heads of the state and military departments of government.

But the emotional weight of his new responsibilities came down upon him at noon as he returned to his old haunts at the Capitol to confer with Congressional leaders.

Tears welled in his eyes when he saw the familiar faces of Capitol newsmen. He reverted to the language of his Missouri farm youth to describe the crushing weight of his new job.

"I don't know if any of you fellows ever had a load of hay or a bull fall on him," he said. "But last night the whole weight of the moon and stars fell on me. I feel a tremendous responsibility.

"Please pray for me! I mean that!"

Mr. Truman's first executive proclamation was a paper setting aside tomorrow as a day of national mourning for Mr. Roosevelt, stricken yesterday at "the little White House" in Warm Springs, Ga.

The proclamation called upon the nation "to pay out of full hearts their homage of love and reverence to the memory of the great and good man whose death they mourn."

Mr. Truman's first day at the White House followed the pattern he set for himself last night upon assuming the presidency: to follow the Roosevelt policies and press the war on all fronts.

Under dreary Washington skies, the new president motored to the White House from his Washington apartment at 9 a.m. today to start his career as chief executive. He wore a gray suit and blue bow tie.

He was accompanied only by two old friends— Lt. Col. A.E. Holland of the Office of Inter-American Affairs and Ernest B. Vaccaro, the Associated Press reporter who covered his vice presidential campaign.

"I just want the folks I love to know that if we can't get together in the old informal way it is not of my choosing," he told Vaccaro a bit wistfully. "Tell them that, will you?"

The car rolled up the White House drive and Mr. Truman turned immediately to the worry-laden tasks which fell to him so unexpectedly.

He went into immediate conference with white-haired Secretary of State Edward R. Stettinius Jr. Minutes later the secretary strode out of the White House Oval Room where the new president worked, and Mr. Truman closeted himself in a 48-minute conference with war leaders.
April 13, 1945

A sign writer takes the final step in refurbishing President Harry S. Truman's Kansas City office in the U.S. Courthouse—changing the designation on the door from "The Vice President" to "The President."

A RIDE WITH HARRY

By Ernest B. Vaccaro

WASHINGTON, APRIL 13 (AP)—Harry S. Truman asked me today to let his old friends know that his sudden elevation to the presidency hasn't changed his neighborly spirit.

If he can't get together informally with his pals—especially the boys of the old 129th with which he served during World War I—it's because of the duties of his new job and not because Truman wants it that way.

The president asked me to pass that word along as we rode to the White House this morning from his modest Connecticut Avenue apartment.

There were two of us with the president, the other being Lt. Col. A.E. Holland, of the Office of Inter-American Affairs, an old friend.

"You know if I could have my way," the new president said, and there was a plaintive note in his voice, "I'd have them all come in without knocking."

The door to Truman's vice presidential office at the Capitol was always wide open and people came in droves to shake his hand—reporters, old war "buddies" and countless others.

There were always school kids, privates, yeomen and folk of every description.

"I'm going to miss all of that," Mr. Truman said.

And he meant it, for President Truman likes people. He enjoys talking and joking with them.

Particularly, the president said, he will miss seeing the boys of the old 129th. They were always dropping by for little visits.

"You know how it will be," the president explained. "My schedule will be a busy one every day. It will be crowded with official appointments. I'll have all I can do to see everyone I must see in the course of these duties."
April 13, 1945

TRUMAN'S 21 POINTS SPEECH

WASHINGTON, SEPT. 6 (AP)—President Truman offered to Congress today a 21-point program designed to smooth the way for the greatest era of "high prosperity" in American history.

In a 16,000-word message which droning clerks read to the legislators, the president declared that if the government meets the problems of peace courageously, it will help usher in "the greatest peacetime industrial activity we have ever seen."

Among other things the president proposed:

Continued wartime controls until all fear of inflation is dispelled; limited tax relief; an increase in the 40-cent minimum wage; higher Social Security benefits; vast power, highway, flood control and reclamation projects; 3,000 new airports; a boom in housing; doubled salaries for senators and representatives; stockpiling of strategic war materials; and orderly disposal of surplus war materials.

Reaction in Congress ran all the way from hearty approval by the president's supporters to some Republican comment that "it's the same old New Deal dressed up in new clothing."

While some elements of the program seemed headed for easy sledding, others were already in trouble. There were demands for deeper tax cuts than the president proposed, and his plan for increasing unemployment compensation throughout the nation to a maximum of at least $25 a week had formidable opposition.

The message was so lengthy that Mr. Truman made no effort to deliver it himself. It was the bulkiest since President Theodore Roosevelt sent a 20,000-word document to Congress in 1901.

Mr. Truman took the occasion to praise the legislators' contribution to the war effort. He recounted what they already have done to speed reconversion and then he listed what he thought was yet to be done to fill in the gaps.

Moreover, Mr. Truman said, he'll have an addition to the program soon. It will urge a national health plan with "adequate" medical care for all, expanded education and Social Security phases.

"Let us now resolve," the president said, "to use all our efforts and energies to build a better life here at home and a better world for generations to come.

"The job, the full job, can and will be done."
Sept. 6, 1945

WASHINGTON, NOV. 19 (AP)—President Truman proposed to Congress today a compulsory "health insurance" system for "all persons who work for a living."

He suggested that the premiums be calculated on the first $3,600 of a person's yearly earnings. An amount equal to 4 percent of these earnings would be needed to carry out the program, he said.

This is one of five points in a health program the president outlined in a message urging "careful consideration now."

Sen. Wagner (D-N.Y.), with the co-sponsorship of Sen. Murray (D-Mont.), immediately introduced a Senate bill designed to carry out the program. The measure does not provide any particular method for financing the health insurance plan, however.

In suggesting $3,600 as the basis for the health insurance premium, Mr. Truman noted that the first $3,000 of yearly earnings is the basis on which Social Security premiums are calculated now. He proposed that Social Security also be figured on $3,600. The Social Security premium now is 2 percent, of which employer and employee each pays half.

Twice in his message Mr. Truman emphasized that his insurance is "not socialized medicine." Wagner made this same statement to the Senate.

Said the president:

"Socialized medicine means that all doctors work as employees of government. The American people want no such system. No such system is here proposed.

Senators, congressmen, Cabinet members and justices of the Supreme Court listen to President Truman (standing on rostrum) make his first address to Congress in the House of Representatives.

"Under the plan I suggest, our people would continue to get medical and hospital services just as they do now—on the basis of their own voluntary decisions and choices. Our doctors and hospitals would continue to deal with disease with the same professional freedom as now. There would, however, be this all-important difference: Whether or not patients get the services they need would not depend on how much they can afford to pay at the time."
Nov. 19, 1945

CHICAGO, NOV. 19 (AP)—The *Journal of the American Medical Association* today approved portions of President Truman's national health program but said compulsory sickness insurance provisions would submit physicians to "politically controlled medicine."

An editorial, to be published in the Nov. 24 issue, said President Truman's assertion that the insurance plan did not represent socialized medicine "will not be convincing to the physicians of the United States who would be compelled to submit to politically controlled medicine should such a measure ever become the law of the nation."

The editorial also contended Mr. Truman's proposal for extending medical education and research through federal grants "would place the federal government in control of medical education throughout the United States through its ability to allocate funds to medical educational institutions."

Nov. 19, 1945

Peace

Germany surrendered on May 7, 1945, but the celebration didn't really begin until the official announcement the following day.

Although most of the country erupted—a half-million people gathered in Times Square, and several tons of paper were thrown from the windows of Manhattan skyscrapers—in Washington it was not even a government holiday. As President Truman explained in his radio address to the nation, "We must work to finish the war. Our victory is only half won."

But what would it take to gain total victory? An invasion of Japan, it was estimated, could cost as many as 175,000 lives—more than half the number of soldiers already dead. Still, there was one optimistic sign: The great dome of the Capitol was lit for the first time since Dec. 9, 1941.

IKE COMES HOME

WASHINGTON, JUNE 18 (AP)—Gen. Dwight D. Eisenhower, returning triumphantly to his homeland from victory in Europe, declared today that his soldiers "passionately" believe "the problems of peace can and must be met."

Climaxing a spectacular homecoming that saw him ride over the capital's historic triumphal parade route—Pennsylvania Avenue—past wildly cheering men and women, the general of the Army told a joint session of Congress and the Supreme Court:

"The genius and power of America have, with her Allies, eliminated one menace to our country's freedom—even her very existence. Still another remains to be crushed in the Pacific before peace will be restored."

Saying that he spoke for the American men and women he commanded, the Allied supreme commander declared:

"Though we dream of return to our loved ones, we are ready, as we always have been, to do our duty to our country, no matter what it may be."

Hundreds of thousands of wildly shouting men, women and children, veterans of this war and the last, wounded veterans, the old and the young, raised their voices in a mighty tumult as the general of the Army rode through their midst.

It was one of the greatest ovations the nation's capital ever rendered. It started when the European commander left his giant plane at National Airport after a flight from Bermuda and continued through lines often 10 deep to the Pentagon Building, into the city past the Lincoln Memorial, down broad Constitution Avenue to historic Pennsylvania Avenue and thence to the seat of the lawmakers on Capitol Hill.

On arriving at the Capitol, the smiling Eisenhower strode down the center aisle of a House chamber reverberating with cheers and applause.

Members of Congress and packed galleries applauded, whistled and cheered for two full minutes as the tall, sunburned Kansan walked down the aisle to take up position behind a battery of 12 microphones. He nodded and grinned while the stirring welcome rolled in waves through the packed room. He chatted briefly with House Speaker Sam Rayburn and Senator McKellar (D-Tenn.), president pro tem of the Senate.

Every seat in the big House chamber was filled minutes before the general arrived.

President Truman presented Eisenhower with the Oak Leaf Cluster to the Distinguished Service Medal, the second such honor the general has received.

The huge ocean liner **Queen Mary** *heads for her pier in New York on July 11, 1945, with over 15,000 American and Canadian troops returning from Europe. The* **Queen Mary** *was one of eight transports that brought a record group of 35,000 troops from the European theater to the port of New York.*

When the president pinned the decoration on the general, Eisenhower remarked to him:

"I would rather have the distinction of receiving this from the president than any honor I know of."

"And I'd rather have this award than be president," Mr. Truman replied.

President Truman's own sleek C-54, one of four big transports bringing the general and his party home from the war, landed at Washington's National Airport at 11:11 a.m. Thousands of necks craned in a jammed Washington as the planes,

escorted by fighters, roared over the capital at 11:08 a.m., en route to the airport.

Cries of "Ike! Ike! Ike!"—a word now known in all languages, meaning a fighting general—rang from hundreds of throats as the modest, 54-year-old son of a Kansas farm family stepped from the huge flying ship. He flashed his famous grin in response.

Gen. George C. Marshall, chief of staff, and Eisenhower's petite and vivacious wife rushed to meet him as the door of his plane opened.

Mrs. Eisenhower ran to the general as he came

26

down the steps from the plane and embraced and kissed him.

Scores of photographers, who missed the first shot as the general ran down the steps, yelled "How about another kiss, general?"

"No posing, boys," the general said.

Eisenhower then snapped to a salute as an 86-piece Army band struck up with martial music.

Among the officers and men with Eisenhower was his son, 1st Lt. John Sheldon Eisenhower. It was a double reunion for Mrs. Eisenhower, who had not seen her husband or son for many months.

As the general embraced his wife, he said: "It's been a long time, darling."
June 18, 1945

TROOPS PROTEST ACCOMMODATIONS

WASHINGTON, JULY 6 (AP)—No more sleeping cars can be operated between cities 450 miles or less apart after July 15, the government ordered today, so that better accommodations can be provided to troops.

Announcement of this new control on civilian travel followed complaints of soldiers on transcontinental trips that they had been forced to make the long journey in day coaches when German and Italian prisoners of war were seen riding in Pullman cars.

The new order issued late today by the Office of Defense Transportation applies not only to those sleeping cars operated by the Pullman company, but also to those sleepers owned and operated by some individual railroads.

Col. J. Monroe Johnson of the Office of Defense Transportation said in a statement:

"I am mindful that this action will result in considerable inconvenience to civilians, but on the other hand I feel they will cheerfully accept the situation when they realize that it is one way in which they can make another important contribution to the war effort."

The War Department explained today that in one incident about which soldiers had complained, the Germans occupying Pullman accommodations were mental patients, plus their guards, who were being transferred from a camp in Oklahoma to a hospital in New York.

The department also said that the only Italians who got Pullman accommodations were sick and disabled men in process of being repatriated. In one movement of 103 Italians to the West Coast, they were put aboard Pullman tourist coaches but not sleepers.

Consultations between military and railroad officials preceded issuance of the new order by the ODT. The 450-mile distance was chosen, an ODT spokesman explained, as the one most likely to release sufficient cars to meet present needs. Should the demand for sleeper space for troops increase, he said, further action might be necessary.
July 6, 1945

CAMP SHANKS, N.Y., JULY 6 (AP)—Nine troop trains, composed of day coaches and including converted freight cars used as diners, left here today with 3,066 troops for various parts of the country. The men arrived here yesterday from Europe aboard the transport *Marine Dragon.*

Many protested to their officers over the accommodations. To emphasize their protests, some soldiers carried seats from the coaches and, placing the seats on the station platform, beat clouds of dust from them.

None of the coaches was air-conditioned. Three men were assigned to every two seats; it was understood that they would have to take turns lying down. Officers inspected the drinking water and sanitary facilities before the troops boarded the trains.
July 6, 1945

SALT LAKE CITY, JULY 6 (AP)—Two hundred veterans of ground and aerial warfare in Europe were transferred to well-equipped Pullman sleepers today after riding almost across the country in antiquated railroad coaches. For the rest of the way they'll ride in standard Pullmans on the Union Pacific Railroad en route to Fort MacArthur, Calif., and on the Western Pacific to Camp Beale, Calif.

The men were veterans of the 95th Division and of the Eighth Air Force. Sgt. Jack Frank of Los Angeles expressed the sentiment of most men when he observed: "We ride in chair cars for four

Allen J. Holzinger, one of more than 1,000 veterans who slept the night of Jan. 10, 1947, in Los Angeles' MacArthur Park in protest against the postwar housing shortage, settles down for a smoke before securing his gear for the night. The demonstration was sponsored by the American Veterans Committee.

days and four nights and one day from home they give us Pullmans."

To add to their discomfiture, the men said that at Kansas City they observed members of Italian service units transferring from chair cars, in which they had ridden from the East Coast, to tourist Pullmans to complete the trip to Sacramento, Calif. The railroad authorities said that the situation developed because of the rapid movement of troops from east to west. As a result, railroads have been unable to get the Pullmans moved east

again quickly enough to accommodate all troops.
July 6, 1945

WASHINGTON, JULY 6 (AP)—With redevelopment running ahead of schedule, civilian Pullman space will be reduced at least 50 percent in the near future when half of the 3,000 Pullmans now in civilian service will be transferred to troop trains.
July 6, 1945

GI ADOPTION

BOSTON, JULY 27 (AP)—Immigration officials are prescribing a "normal child's life with plenty of school and fun" for the duffel bag stowaway, "Chris" Piavello.

Chris had a happy reunion today with his would-be adopter, Pvt. David E. Hughes of Franklin, N.J. That is, it was happy so long as Chris didn't remember that Hughes was leaving again tonight to prepare for a date in the Pacific.

U.S. immigration officials have been chaperoning the 9-year-old Italian boy since he landed here on a troop transport.

And at the reunion today, Henry Nichols, district director of the U.S. Immigration Service, said that he believed Hughes was in earnest about wanting to adopt Chris, and he felt that he had a "priority" on the boy.

So, if they have their way, they'd like to keep Chris on ice for his favorite private.

But final disposition of the case is up to the Washington Board of Immigration Appeals, and it may take months. In the meantime, Chris will live with an unidentified family.

Hughes, who wears the Purple Heart with cluster and four battle stars, said he would take the boy now but his mother was unable to take care of him.

The soldier took the kid out for a fling and bought him a much longed-for "feetball" and they had a whale of a day together.

He promised Chris that he would legally adopt him "when I get back."

Chris listened closely, and then asked the question that couldn't be answered:

"How many men come back?"

July 27, 1945

Editor's Note

When President Truman announced at 7 p.m. on Aug. 14 that Japan had surrendered, the nation embarked on a celebration that lasted all night, all the next day (V-J Day) and well into the following night.

New York made its V-E celebration look like a pep rally. This time 5,000 tons of litter— not only paper, but hats, bottles, wastepaper baskets and underwear—were dumped out windows, and an estimated 2 million people jammed into Times Square to cheer each bit of V-J news on **The New York Times'** *electric sign.*

In Los Angeles, revelers commandeered trolley cars and played leapfrog in the middle of Hollywood Boulevard. Thousands of people in Salt Lake City snake-danced through the rain, and a crowd in St. Louis persuaded a minister to hold services at 2 a.m. On Main Streets and in town squares across the nation, Americans kissed and hugged, laughed and cried, sang and danced. Car horns honked, church bells peeled, firecrackers exploded. Yes, the shortages and controls would soon be gone, but the whole party was truly fueled by just one prospect: The men were coming home.

NY READIES FOR V-J DAY

NEW YORK, AUG. 10 (AP)—Millions of New Yorkers, hopeful that final victory over Japan was very near, settled down to a period of watchful waiting tonight after the city had experienced a few premonitory examples of what to expect when V-J Day becomes a fact.

The Domei news report of a Japanese surrender offer was sufficient to start paper showers from the Empire State Building, Rockefeller Center and in the garment district. GIs returning from Europe on troopships cheered the news as they disembarked in the harbor, and thousands on street corners, buses and subways were divided about evenly on this question:

Should Hirohito go or should he be permitted to stay?

The police department was ready with its V-J Day plan. Earlier today Chief Inspector John J. O'Connell had ordered 5,000 patrolmen and detectives, whose tours of duty ended at 4 p.m., to remain in their precincts. This order later was rescinded.

The Regional War Labor Board said industrial plants would be permitted an official holiday on V-J Day. Guy W. Vaughan, president of the Curtiss-Wright Corporation, said 150,000 workers in 16 Curtiss-Wright and Wright Aeronautical Corporation plants in Ohio, Pennsylvania, New Jer-

Thirty-eight-year-old Maj. Gen. James M. Gavin (left foreground), commander of the 82nd Airborne Division and the youngest division commander in the Army, strides smartly in front of his staff of officers as he leads his troops past Washington Square in New York City's victory parade, Jan. 12, 1946. In the background is the Washington Arch.

sey and New York would be given a 48-hour holiday when V-J Day was announced officially.

More than twice the usual number of worshippers attended Mass at St. Patrick's Cathedral, which said it would hold a special Mass and prayers on V-J Day. The Protestant Council of the City of New York also announced plans for special services in New York City churches when the war's end was announced.

Aug. 10, 1945

TICKER TAPE PARADE IN NYC

NEW YORK, AUG. 10 (AP)—Cheers and shouts of joy echoed over Staten Island's waterfront area today when 1,454 returning GI's on four troop transports learned of the Domei news agency broadcast that Japan was ready to surrender.

Many of the troops, including men of the 9th Air Force, were scheduled for redeployment to the Pacific. They marched jubilantly down the gangplanks, singing.

Col. Walter I. Black, of Glendale, Calif., a troop commander on one of the ships, was telling a reporter that his troops were to be redeployed, when the ship's loudspeaker system blared out the news of the surrender offer.

"Scratch that line out about redeployment. Make it read: 'We have been reprieved,'" Black exclaimed.

The enthusiasm of the troops was communicated to stevedores, civilian guards and customs and immigration officers on the docks who grinned and slapped one another on the back.

In Times Square, crowds emerging from the subway entrances wore wide smiles. Most commuters pouring into Grand Central Station had heard the news on their radios before leaving home. Those who hadn't were soon brought up to date.

A beribboned naval captain at Pennsylvania Station murmured, "I hope to God it's true." A Chinese naval lieutenant remarked: "I'm now awaiting orders which may not come."

A frequently heard phrase was: "Let's see whether they accept it before we celebrate."

Meanwhile the police department announced that it was standing by with its plan to keep a V-J Day celebration within bounds.

The Associated Press received an excited call from a woman who asked: "Is there anything to it?"

"It's merely a report by Domei," she was told.

"Oh," she said, and after a moment's silence, added:

"Can I have Domei's telephone number?"
Aug. 10, 1945

NEW YORK, JAN. 12 (AP)—Millions of New Yorkers, packed for four miles along Fifth Avenue, roared tribute today to the nation's foot soldier as 13,000 men paraded through a blinding paper blizzard celebrating America's World War II victory.

Tall, slender, 38-year-old Maj. Gen. James M. Gavin, youngest division commander in the Army, led the march in which his famed 82nd Airborne Division had the place of honor.

Many New York policemen—there were 8,000 on duty along the avenue—said they could not recall an ovation to equal the one an estimated 4,000,000 persons gave the veterans. The parade was dedicated, in Gavin's words, "to all the guys who walked through the mud—the slogging GI."

On display in the greatest parade since 1919, when Gen. John J. Pershing led the First Division up the same avenue, were the tanks, the artillery, the vehicles and most of the combat equipment with which the Axis nations were crushed. And in the air were fighter planes and transport-towed gliders with which the Allies spearheaded their invasion of Hitler's European fortress.

Behind Gavin, who said he had "walked all over the damned earth," were the colors of the United States, Great Britain, Soviet Russia and France. Gavin strode briskly up the avenue with eyes front except when he saluted Gov. Thomas E. Dewey and other officials in the main reviewing stand and Cardinal-designate Francis J. Spellman on the steps of St. Patrick's Cathedral.

In the stand with Gov. Dewey were Mayor William O'Dwyer; Gov. Walter E. Edge of New Jersey; acting Secretary of War Kenneth C. Royall; Admiral H. F. Leary, commander of the Eastern Sea frontier; and Gen. Jonathan M. Wainwright, Corregidor hero and new Fourth Army commander.

At 42nd Street and Fifth Avenue the storm of torn paper was so heavy it was difficult to see marchers half a block away. Near the corner a special reviewing stand held several hundred wounded veterans, some of them in wheelchairs.

Banners of the 82nd carried battle streamers of two wars and the men wore, in addition to their individual ribbons, the division-awarded Belgian fourragère and the Dutch lanyard. Marching with the 82nd were elements of the 13th, 17th and 101st Airborne divisions.
Jan. 12, 1946

Postwar Society

Soldiers and sailors kept on returning, and the nation kept on changing. Truman replaced a model gun on his desk with a shiny model plow, which he proudly pointed out to visitors. "It's the simple things that count," he would say. "I like the feeling of having the new little fellow there."

The little fellow may have been a symbol of the new peace, but for most Americans there was no returning to anything as simple as plowing.

NEW CARS

DETROIT, AUG. 30 (AP)—If you are expecting a lot of sharply changed new model passenger automobiles soon after the turn of the new year, you are likely to be disappointed.

And that probably is just as well for the average individual who wants a new car and has had an order on file for many months. Many retailers currently are filling orders placed more than a year ago; if there is to be an assembly-line shutdown for radically altered new models there will be an even greater gap between the order and the delivery date.

Some of the so-called "independents," like Hudson, Nash and Packard, may have new models in readiness on or before January 1, but the manufacturers whose cars represent the bulk of passenger automobile production are not likely to have their redesigned and re-engineered cars ready until well into next year.

Insofar as such producers as Chevrolet, Ford and Plymouth are concerned, there is more than a likelihood that the vehicles to be built in the early months of next year will be face-lifted versions of present models with the contemplated radical changes deferred perhaps until well into the spring.

The activity that goes with projected early industry-wide model changes is wholly lacking at present in the tool and die shops. This has led several authoritative industry observers to predict that Ford's much-talked about "completely new" model will not be ready until next June or July.

If that assumption be correct, it is more than likely that Chevrolet and Plymouth cars of next January will be only moderately different from those currently in production and that more fully redesigned models will be brought out later.

That procedure, some industry experts say, would permit Chevrolet, Ford and Plymouth to bring out 1949 models around mid-1948 as they did for most of the decade immediately preceding the war.

Another advantage the industry analysts attach to such a program is that it might permit a side-stepping of further price increases, for a time at least, in the model group that accounts for more than 50 percent of all the cars currently being made.

Most of the industry analysts are agreed that unless a lot of sizable manufacturing economies can be developed, the expense of retooling for sharply changed models will force another horizontal increase in retail listings similar to the one the industry has just completed.

When the car factories completed their August operations last night, they had turned out in the first eight months of this year approximately 2,270,000 passenger vehicles and 815,000 commercial units. That is only a little more than the volume they hoped to attain by the end of June.

It indicates a total for the year of 3,500,000 cars, and 1,000,000 passenger vehicles will be difficult to attain unless sheet steel in large quantities suddenly becomes available. Even the most optimistic among the automakers do not expect a major easing of the steel shortages next month and they are only hopeful regarding October.
Aug. 30, 1946

WASHINGTON, SEPT. 1 (AP)—Here are the major ways in which Americans planned early this spring to use their savings and income:

1. Some 5 million wanted cars this year. Two out of five had less than $500 savings, and yet only one out of five would settle for a used car. The great majority (62 percent) wanted to pay from $1,000 to $1,350.

2. Some 9.9 million definitely planned to buy refrigerators, furniture, radios, washing machines.

3. Some 3.1 million wanted homes.

These figures come from a study just made available by the Bureau of Agricultural Economics for the Federal Reserve Board, which has to worry about the channels American money is taking—and before the dollar hits the road.

The survey recognizes that shortages may stymie some intentions this year but that they likely will slop over into next. No later study has been completed.

A definite "let tomorrow take care of itself" philosophy was found; only one out of five people questioned thought this year (1946) was a good year in which to buy.

There appeared to be a wide discrepancy between the amounts the average American planned to spend on house and car. While 62 percent were figuring on a top of $1,350 for the car, 66 percent planned on a top of $300 for things for the house—such as refrigerators.

When it came to house buying, "the little home builder," if he's still around, had the popular vote. The average person wanted to pay $5,000 for his home. Federal Reserve remarks, cryptically, that he would "probably pay more," with no conjectures on what would then happen to the family's savings or indebtedness.

Only a third of the new home buyers would go above $6,000, and a third definitely wanted four walls for less than $4,000. Sixty percent of the people expecting to buy a house had less than $3,000 a year income. Only a sixth figured on paying cash.

The surveyors found that during the war big blocs of earners moved into higher wage groups. In 1935-36 half the American spending units (families pooling their take) got less than $1,000 a year. In 1945 only a fifth got that pittance. By 1945 half the American "spending units" took in more than $3,000.

Sept. 1, 1946

NEW FORDS

DETROIT, MAY 22 (AP)—Carefully shrouded in canvas, new Ford passenger automobiles are now being hauled from assembly plants across the country.

These are the 1949 models which the Ford company described as "new and revolutionary." They are going to dealers and certain strategic points for one of the biggest new-model auto presentations in the industry's history.

In effect, Ford is planning a nationwide automobile "show" all its own in the showrooms of some 6,500 dealers. These public showings are set for June 18.

Before that date, however, there are to be numerous "previews" and what Ford says will be a "world premiere" public showing.

The "world premiere" is scheduled for June 10-15 in New York's Waldorf-Astoria Hotel.

Styling of the new cars has not yet been disclosed by the Ford company. Not so secret are some other details. These include wider and deeper windshields and broader rear windows; lower overall silhouette; wider front and rear seats, the latter 60 inches; new "hydracoil" front springs; more luggage space and, at the same time, roomier interiors.

The cars are powered with new 100-horsepower V-8 or 95-horsepower six-cylinder engines. An "overdrive" said to achieve up to 25 percent fuel economy is available at extra cost. A new instrument and radio panel utilizes "black lighting," and a new thermostatic device controls interior temperature.

The changeover is the most drastic Ford has made since the Model "T," with its many early-day features, was discarded in 1927. That change closed the big Ford plants for more than six months. The present switch-over has been accomplished in six weeks.

So well was it planned that at no time during the six-week period were more than 14,000 of the company's approximately 132,000 workers throughout the country made idle. Actually, first work on the new models was done 30 months ago; it was carried on without interruption to current production until new tools and assembly facilities had to be installed.

Ahead of the new Ford models, the company introduced a completely new line of trucks and 1949 Lincoln Olds Mercury passenger cars. It has been estimated the changeover cost Ford around $100,000,000 in outlay for retooling and equipment alone. To this must be added the production

Mrs. David Ruby, wife of a 28-year-old war veteran, prepares a bottle for her infant daughter, Gloria Lynn, in the kitchen of their Quonset hut in the Jamaica Bay section of Brooklyn, N.Y. The hut is one of a large group of Quonsets and "prefabs" which were readied by New York City for occupancy by 2,000 war veterans and their families.

lost during the assembly-line shutdowns. This probably runs between 70,000 and 80,000 units.

More than 1,000 Ford dealers from the northeastern region attended a preview of the 1949 Fords at a private showing yesterday at the Waldorf-Astoria.

Henry Ford 2nd, president of the company, and Ernest R. Breech, executive vice president, described the new models and country-wide sales plans, through a specially prepared sound film sent from Detroit.

"We are going to regain leadership in the new low-price field and improve our position in other price fields," Mr. Ford said. "When the buyers' market comes it's going to come fast, but compe-

tition is a good thing for all of us. The spirit of American competition is perhaps the greatest single factor in bringing to us the world's highest standard of living. Competition always means a constant improvement in products."
May 22, 1948

NEW YORK, SEPT. 15 (AP)—The Automobile Club of New York said today complaints have been received from many of its members about their new cars.

Harry Marienhoff, manager of the club's service department, said reports from members showed considerable dissatisfaction over body designs of new models making them difficult and expensive to repair, and requiring garage alterations to house them. The reports, he said, came from new-car owners among the club's 169,000 members in a 14-county area that includes New York City.

"Many drivers," he said, "have found the hoods too long and the seats too low.

"This involves a safety factor, as oftentimes it is impossible to see enough of the road directly in front of the car for the operator's protection."

Restricted vision of some of the new models, Marienhoff continued, had been found to make them difficult to park and had resulted in dented and scratched fenders.

The increased width and length of some of the new models likewise has been the subject of complaints, he said, with some club members reporting they had been forced to alter their garages to get cars inside.
Sept. 15, 1948

POSTWAR POPULATION CHANGES

WASHINGTON, FEB. 13 (AP)—The Public Health Service reported today that the 3,260,000 births in the United States during 1946 set an all-time record.

Deaths last year were estimated at 1,400,000, compared with 1,401,719 in 1945.

The agency said the previous birth record was 2,934,860 in 1943, while the 1945 total was 2,735,466. Although total births in 1946 set a new high mark, the ratio of birth to population—23.3

to 1,000 last year—is considerably below the ratio for 1921 and prior years, the service said.

The death rate was 10.1 to 1,000 population last year, compared with 10.6 in 1945.
Feb. 13, 1947

THE BABY BOOM

WASHINGTON, FEB. 24 (AP)—The nation's baby crop was the largest in history last year. And the death rate was near the record low.

The Social Security Agency reported tonight that 3,720,000 live births were registered in 1947. This is an increase of 431,000 over 1946, the previous high, and 785,000 over 1943, the wartime peak. Unregistered births increased the total to an estimated 3,910,000. This compares with the 1946 estimate of 3,470,000.

The mortality rate for infants under 1 year old dropped to a record low. The 1947 rate was 32.6 deaths for each 1,000 live births. The 1946 rate was 35.1 deaths for each 1,000 births.
Feb. 24, 1947

THE VETERANS

WASHINGTON, JUNE 1 (AP)—War veterans and their families now make up one-third of the population and within five years they will account for 43 percent, the Veterans Administration estimated today.

Thereafter, unless new wars change the rate, the veteran-family population will level off and then gradually decline.

The Veterans Administration computed the Jan. 1, 1947, veteran-family population at 46,000,000, 32 percent of the nation's total. It forecast for Jan. 1, 1952, 32,300,000, or 43 percent, and for Jan. 1, 1957, 62,500,000, or 41 percent.

It defined a veteran's family as a family unit living together and headed by a veteran, which might include a wife, children, parents and relatives by blood, marriage or adoption.
June 1, 1947

MARRIAGE...

WASHINGTON, JULY 25 (AP)—The postwar boom in romance has reached its peak; marriages are on the decline.

The national Office of Vital Statistics reported today that 427,319 couples bought marriage licenses during the first quarter of 1947. That is 20 percent fewer than the number issued during the same quarter of 1946.

The report attributed the postwar increase in weddings to GI romances.

It said marriages started climbing "unusually high" as early as 1945, when veterans were returning, and lasted through most of 1946.

Last year set a new record in American marriages, a total of 2,313,795, or about 41.8 percent more than in 1945. In the war year of 1944 only 1,452,394 licenses were issued.
July 25, 1947

...AND DIVORCE

WASHINGTON, SEPT. 15 (AP)—One American family broke up for every three—approximately—that were formed last year, the Federal Security Agency reported tonight.

More than 82,000 marriages ended in divorce courts in 1945, an all-time record representing a 25.5 percent rise over the previous peak divorce year, 1944.

The divorces were 31 percent of the marriages, which totalled 1,618,331 last year or about 8.7 percent below Cupid's biggest year, 1942.

FSA's study, the first federal reporting of divorce statistics, generally steers clear of interpretation save to show that both marriage and divorce rates rise with prosperity, wartime or otherwise, and fall with depression.

"The marriage rate is the more sensitive of the two, since a marriage contract can be entered into more readily than it can be dissolved," FSA observes.

For lonely hearts there are few clues except this: The marriage rate is consistently higher in the West and South than in the rest of the country.

The divorce rate has nearly doubled in nine years, FSA reported. Fairly steady at 1.9 divorces per 1,000 population in 1937-39, it climbed to 3.6 in 1945. The ratio of divorces to marriage also soared from 17.8 divorces per 100 marriages to the 1945 total of 31 divorces per 100 marriages.

Two thousand war veterans and their families moved into long rows of Quonset huts and prefabricated houses set up by New York City in the Jamaica Bay area of Brooklyn. They were fitted with small dormer windows, furnished with a combination kitchen-parlor, two small bedrooms and a bath. Mrs. David Ruby, wife of a war veteran, is shown with her baby outside the Rubys' hut.

In the Depression the marriage rate fell to an unprecedented low of 7.9 per 1,000 in 1932. As business bettered, the rate rose until in 1937, it was 11.3. Then the brief recession of 1938 dropped it one point from where it began to rise again. With the start of the draft and of defense manufacturing in 1940, the wartime spurt was on.

The wartime marriage peak came in 1942, when 1,772,132 couples went to the altar. Weddings then declined for two years as eligible bridegrooms went overseas. Mid-1945 brought a new marriage rush as soldiers came home for redeployment, and V-J Day sent the marriage totals up again as veterans slipped into civilian life and marital harness.

No such wartime fluctuation occurred in divorce. The rate has gone steadily up since 1938, when 244,000 decrees were granted. Except for the Depression years, the divorce curve in the United States has gone up virtually without interruption since the first estimate—72,062—was made in 1906.

Sept. 15, 1947

WASHINGTON, JUNE 9 (AP)—A continuation in the upward divorce trend is indicated by statistics for 1946 assembled by the national Office of Vital Statistics. Officials of this branch of the Public Health Service added today, however, that the sharp increase in marriages that marked the first year of peace has ceased.

They added that the 1946 marriage and divorce report, which they hope to complete soon, will shed little or no light on comparative success or failure of wartime and prewar marriages. There is no way of determining from available data, they explained, whether the divorces reported mark the end of marriages made during or before the war.

In the half a century for which information has been compiled, the number of marriages and divorces for each 1,000 persons of the population has climbed. But the divorce increase has been greater.

For the recorded years since Pearl Harbor the figures for marriage—called the marriage rate—have been: 1942—13.2 marriages per 1,000 persons in the population; 1943—11.8; 1944—11; 1945—12.3. (The 1887 figure, the earliest, was 8.7.)

The corresponding divorce figures have been: 1942—2.4 per 1,000 population; 1943—2.6; 1944—2.9; 1945—3.6. (The 1887 figure was 0.5.)

The ratio of divorces to marriages—that is, the number of divorces per 100 marriages in specified years—has been as follows: 1942—18.1 divorces for each 100 marriages; 1943—22.8; 1944—27.5; 1945—31.

But analysis of the Vital Statistics Office cautioned against taking the figures to mean that any given number of marriages contracted in the stated years ended in divorce during those years.
June 9, 1947

RENO: THE DIVORCE CAPITAL
By Edward A. Olsen

RENO, NEV., DEC. 31 (AP)—Postwar nerves and an inflated economy combined during 1946 to give Reno its biggest divorce and marriage boom in history.

Almost 11,000 persons stopped at the divorce counter in the cramped office of County Clerk E.H. Bremer to pick up their decrees, while another 58,000 lined up at an adjacent counter to obtain marriage licenses.

In 1945—the previous record divorce year in Reno—8,500 decrees were granted. The previous big marriage year was 1942, when 25,539 couples obtained licenses.

Reno's permanent population, according to Chamber of Commerce surveys, is only 30,000.

In terms of money, the year's divorce and marriage business was worth something like $10,000,000 to the city's attorneys and businessmen. Not all of the money was fresh, however, for an increasing proportion of the lower income men and women seeking divorces found jobs in gambling clubs, stores and offices to pay their expenses.

Attorneys and jurists attribute the boom primarily to inflation and the war.

"Divorce, like jewelry, is a luxury," one high-priced attorney said. "People have been willing to pay tremendous prices for everything."

Another lawyer, Joseph P. Haller, who represented Lucy Malcolmson before she was jilted by Marine ace Gregory (Pappy) Boyington for a blonde actress, said he believed the notable increase in the number of middle-aged and older persons obtaining divorces was caused by the sudden removal of marital obligations as a result of the war.

"Many parents with teenaged youngsters expected to support them through college, but suddenly the children left home to become independent in military service," he said. "The parents drifted apart.

"Similarly, with an improvement in business, indebtedness was removed from several businesses and homes quicker than anticipated, and another marital obligation ended."

District Judge A.J. Maestretti, who presides over one of the two busy divorce courts, predicts a booming divorce rate for at least another 10 years.

"A large proportion of the men who saw service have had a shock that has affected seriously their social equilibrium," Judge Maestretti says. "Many will develop nervous troubles as they grow older and will be more likely to give way to erratic impulses."

The judge believes young women, properly

informed to understand what lies ahead of them, will have a big influence in maintaining stable homes in the future.

In the other court, Judge William McKnight also foresees a continued high divorce rate. He blames wartime separation and unfaithfulness.

Attorney Samuel Platt says the war and inflation have brought about a "reckless disregard for the seriousness of the marital relations." This, he says, will continue "until a different pattern toward marriage develops."

The housing shortage, listed by several attorneys as a strong contributing factor to divorces last year, was named by attorney Rob Clarke as the thing that kept even more people from using Reno's jammed facilities.

"I've had to advise several women with children to stay home because we simply didn't have a place for them to spend their six weeks here," the attorney said.
Dec. 31, 1946

STUDENT STRIKE

GARY, IND., NOV. 1 (AP)—More than 5,000 enraptured students joined Frank Sinatra, singer and actor, today in a pledge to the "American way," as "The Voice" sought to persuade striking white high school students to return to class rooms.

Bobby soxers screamed, shouted, whistled, stamped their feet and a few even sobbed as "The Voice" stepped to the stage of the overflowing auditorium to appeal for an end of the strike at Froebel High School which started Monday, the second this semester.

The auditorium's seating facilities of 4,800 were filled. Several hundred other students, both white and Negro, crowded aisles and a crowd estimated by fireguard Nick Odinsoff at 1,000 stood in the street to hear the proceedings over amplifiers.

Repeating after Sinatra, the students pledged "allegiance to the democratic ideals in our home, schools, in our independent youth organizations. We strive to work together to prove that the American way is the fair and only way."

"The eyes of the nation are watching Gary," The Voice asserted. "Maybe you think you have a right to pull a strike. Maybe you have. I am not going

to argue with you, but I have found out there are a few people from Gary who have nothing to do with schools who are not parents, and yet who have had a word in your strike.

"People who have absolutely nothing to do with your strike have taken charge of it. And now you have nothing more to say about what is going on at your school. What are you going to do about it? Are you going to get the situation back in your hands?"

There were some faltering shouts of "yes."

Sinatra urged the students to "practice patience with your fellow men."

The students struck originally in protest against what they described as biracial policies of their principal, R.A. Nuzum, whom they accused of showing favoritism to Negro students. Students returned to classrooms after several days, but struck for the second time Monday, after an investigating committee did not blame Principal Nuzum.

Sinatra came to Gary at the invitation of the Anselm Youth Organization. He was met at the Chicago airport by Mayor Joseph Finerty, of Gary, and five youths representing various Gary youth organizations.
Nov. 1, 1947

GARY, IND., NOV. 2 (AP)—Evidence that Frank Sinatra, radio singer and actor, had failed in his attempt to induce striking Froebel High School students to return to their classrooms was presented at the school today. Nearly all white students remained away from classes.

Sinatra spoke and sang before a teenage audience of 5,800 at municipal auditorium yesterday. He led the audience in repeating a pledge of allegiance to the "democratic ideals of our home, schools, in our independent youth organizations."

But Leonard Levenda, 17-year-old spokesman for the strikers, said Sinatra had "made the situation worse instead of better."

Levenda said the strikers had taken exception to some of the crooner's references to two Gary citizens. He said the students were angered by Sinatra's reference to one of the men as "a two-bit politician."

Mayor Joseph Finerty, who was instrumental in arranging Sinatra's visit here, said he was "amazed" at the singer's remarks and that he had told Sinatra after the meeting:

"Your remarks were most unfortunate. You were ill advised in your statements and what you said in your personal remarks was a disservice to the cause and to the community."

Finerty said he had apologized personally to the two men.

The strike was called several days ago. The students said they were not attending classes because the school board had not disciplined Principal R.A. Nuzum for what they termed his favoritism to Negro students. An earlier strike had been called in September in protest to Nuzum's so-called favoritism. The school board exonerated Nuzum of the charge.
Nov. 2, 1947

Jackie Robinson

When he joined the Brooklyn Dodgers in 1942 as president and general manager, Branch Rickey was already the most famed judge of talent in major league baseball. He was known as the man who perfected the farm system during his tenure with the St. Louis Cardinals.

Now he wanted to broaden his talent hunt to include black and Latin American players, and he decided to breach the unwritten all-white color barrier in pro baseball.

The Negro leagues were filled with great players; Rickey selected a player who had been a battler for black civil rights as a college athlete at the University of California at Los Angeles and as a soldier during the war.

Rickey wanted a man courageous enough to challenge the race barrier, but disciplined enough not to respond to the abuse he was sure to face. He wanted, as it turned out, a man named Jackie Robinson.

SIGNING

MONTREAL, OCT. 23 (AP)—The first Negro player ever to be admitted to organized baseball was signed tonight by the Brooklyn Dodgers for their International League farm club, the Montreal Royals.

Jackie Robinson, one-time UCLA halfback ace and recent shortstop of the Kansas City Negro Monarchs, put his signature on a contract calling not only for a regular player's salary, but also for a bonus for signing.

Product of a three-year search and $25,000 hunt for Negro diamond talent by Dodger President Branch Rickey, Robinson signed up in a history-making huddle with Hector Racine and Lt. Col. Romeo Gauvreau, Royals' president and vice president, respectively, and Branch Rickey Jr., who heads the Brooklyn farm system.

"Mr. Racine and my father," said young Rickey in making the surprise announcement, "undoubtedly will be severely criticized in some sections of the United States where racial prejudice is rampant. They are not inviting trouble, but they won't avoid it if it comes. Jack Robinson is a fine type of young man, intelligent and college bred, and I think he can take it too."

Robinson, himself, had little to say about his part in the unprecedented event.

"Of course, I can't begin to tell you how happy I am that I am the first member of my race in organized ball," declared the lean, quiet, 6-foot, 190-pounder. "I realize how much it means to me, to my race and to baseball. I can only say I'll do my very best to come through in every manner."

On making the announcement, young Rickey said: "It may cost the Brooklyn organization a number of ball players," he said. "Some of them, particularly if they come from certain sections of the South, will steer away from a club with colored players on its roster. Some players now with us may even quit. But they'll be back in baseball after they work a year or two in a cotton mill."

In addition to Robinson, it was learned Rickey

Jackie Robinson, first black baseball player to be signed by a major league team, goes through infield practice after reporting for spring training with the Montreal Royals club in Sanford, Fla.

Sr.'s hunt for Negro talent has produced some 25 others he expects to sign to contracts for double-A ball, with the intention of developing them into big leaguers.

Early last season, two of Rickey's scouts reported that the shortstop of the Kansas City Monarchs—Robinson—was ready for virtually any competition. In August, Rickey Sr. sent a third ivory-hunter to Chicago. Within a fortnight, this talent-searcher telephoned him to "grab the shortstop of the Monarchs—he's your man."

On Aug. 29, Robinson was quietly brought to Brooklyn. Rickey Sr. told him what he had in mind, and the broad-shouldered Pasadena, Calif.,

Negro came to terms, agreeing to sign a contract by Nov. 1. Today was the day.
Oct. 23, 1945

SPRING TRAINING

SANFORD, FLA., MARCH 4 (AP)—Baseball broke a precedent of long standing today when shortstop Jackie Robinson and pitcher John Wright, two Negro athletes, reported for spring training with the Montreal Royals, Brooklyn's farm club in the International League.

Before an uninterested gathering of seven spectators, Robinson and Wright went through the

Jackie Robinson (seated, second from right) signs with the Montreal Royals as (left to right) Hector Racine, president of the Royals; Branch Rickey Jr.; and Romeo Gauvreau, VP of the Royals watch.

routine practice motions in a drill that failed to create much excitement.

The two athletes reported to Bob Finch, assistant to President Branch Rickey. Robinson greeting Finch with a smile as he said, "Well, this is it."

Finch directed Robinson to take his turn with the other hitters facing the mechanical pitcher. He met some pitches squarely but was so busy answering reporters and posing for photographers that he had little time for a real workout. Wright threw to the hitters for a short time, cutting loose with a good curve ball.

Robinson is determined to make the Montreal club if he possibly can, although he realizes he will have tough competition for the shortstop job with Stan Breard, last year's regular, returning and the parent Brooklyn club so deep in rookie infielders.

"I don't know how our league (the Negro American League in which he played last year) compares with this league," said the former foot-

ball, basketball and baseball star at UCLA. He is personable, 27, married only three weeks ago and realizes full well the problems he may have to face.

"I never saw these fellows play so I can't say just how much chance I think I have," he told questioners. "Whatever they do is okay by me. Certainly, I would be willing to go to a lower-class league but I want to make this club."
March 4, 1946

WITH THE ROYALS

JERSEY CITY, N.J. APRIL 18 (AP)—Jackie Robinson, a 27-year-old Negro, broke through baseball's unwritten color line today with a dazzling .800 batting performance for Brooklyn's Montreal farm club in the International League.

The first man of his race to play in modern organized ball smashed a three-run homer that carried 335 feet and added three singles to the Royals' winning 14-1 margin over Jersey City. Just to make it a full day's work, Robinson stole two bases, scored four times and batted in four runs. He also was charged with an error.

Remnants of a crowd of over 25,000 almost pulled the shirt off Robinson's back as the game ended and the young second baseman was kept busy for several minutes shaking hands and autographing scorecards.

Aside from a slight round of applause when Robinson first went to bat, the crowd took little notice of the fact that diamond history was in the making. Back in the 1890's several Negroes had played pro ball in the so-called "white" leagues but none had tried in modern days.

The former UCLA football ace grounded out the first time up against lefty Warren Sandell, just sent back to Jersey from the parent New York Giants. In the third frame he made up for that by slamming Sandell's first pitch over the left-field barrier with two mates aboard.

Perhaps his fanciest exhibition of speed and quick thinking came in the fifth when he dragged a bunt down the third-base line and beat it out for a single. Robinson stole second base with feet to spare, moved to third on an infield roller and maneuvered relief hurler Phil Oates into a balk to score a run.

The fleet Negro ace dashed toward home and halted halfway, upsetting Oates in his motion. The young right-hander halted his delivery momentarily and Art Gore, plate umpire, waved Robinson home.

Robinson's seventh-inning single was a clean smash to right field. Once again he stole second and scored on John Jorgenson's triple.

The Royals' clubhouse was a mad scene after the final out with well-wishers fighting to get in to congratulate Robinson.

Robinson was so excited he had to tie his necktie three or four times but he was as happy as a kid on Christmas morning.

"The one thing that I cared about was the way my teammates backed me up all the way," he grinned. "There wasn't any riding out there but if there was I wouldn't have minded as long as my team was behind me. They have been swell."
April 18, 1946

WITH THE DODGERS

BROOKLYN, APRIL 10 (AP)—Jackie Robinson, brilliant Negro infielder, today became the first of his race to break into modern major league baseball when President Branch Rickey of the Brooklyn Dodgers announced the purchase of his contract from the Montreal Royals of the International League.

"The Brooklyn Dodgers today purchased the contract of Jackie Roosevelt Robinson from the Montreal Royals."

No other information was given. The purchase price was undisclosed. It was a straight cash transaction with no clauses involved. Robinson, who appeared at first base for Montreal against the Dodgers in today's game, will join his new club tomorrow. Montreal is owned by the Dodgers and won today's game, 4 to 3, with Jackie playing first base and collecting one single in three times at bat.

While Dodger officials declined to comment, it is believed the former University of California at Los Angeles athlete will appear at first base for the Dodgers in tomorrow's exhibition game at Ebbets Field against the New York Yankees.

The news of Robinson's purchase by the Dodgers came with startling suddenness, although in recent days it had been generally believed he would be brought up on or before the opening day of the season. Up to the last minute prior to the official announcement, Brooklyn officials were silent on the Negro's status.

Watching today's game with Rickey were Ford Frick, president of the National League, and Frank J. Shaughnessy, International League head. Frick declined to comment but Shaughnessy declared: "I am happy for Jackie. He is a great boy and deserves the chance. I feel certain he will make good. He was the best player in our league last year."

After the game, Rickey said that he reached a definite decision regarding Robinson just five minutes before making the announcement.

The Brooklyn president said he talked to Robinson before the game and told the athlete he might be brought up.

Reached after the contest, Robinson said that "I am happy to be with the Dodgers. I am glad that Mr. Rickey and the others on the Brooklyn club have the confidence in me and I certainly shall give them the best in me."

Jackie Robinson, at first base at Ebbets Field, Brooklyn, was the first black to ever be admitted into the major leagues.

Rickey declared that Leo Durocher, manager of the Dodgers until suspended yesterday by Commissioner A.B. Chandler, had recommended during the spring training season that the Negro be brought up and that the three Dodger coaches and manager Clay Hopper of the Royals voted unanimously last night to promote Robinson.

Asked if Jack would play against the Yankees, Rickey said that "is up to Clyde Sukeforth, who will manage the club again tomorrow."

Sukeforth tonight said that Robinson will play first base against the Yankees.

The club president added that "it still is difficult for me to believe that Mr. Chandler will insist on the penalty against Durocher."

He would not amplify his statement except to say he had not asked for reconsideration of the manager's case.

"Any of the three coaches or even someone outside the organization, could be named manager of the club," Rickey said.

"I have only one thing to say regarding the new manager," he added. "It definitely will not be one of the present players on the club."
April 10, 1947

ROBINSON'S FIRST MAJOR LEAGUE GAME

BROOKLYN, APRIL 15 (AP)—Pete Reiser, key to Brooklyn's flag chances, blazed a seventh-inning double off the screen a foot inside the right-field foul line at Ebbets Field today to drive across the tying and winning runs as the pilotless Dodgers opened their 1947 campaign with a 5 to 3 victory over the Boston Braves.

Although he did not get a hit in three official times at bat, Jackie Robinson, first Negro to play in modern big league ball, signalized his official debut as a Dodger by sprinting home with the deciding run on Reiser's smash and playing perfect ball at first base.

Reiser's hit, his second off Johnny Sain, was only the sixth produced by the Dodgers, and it was their last as Mort Cooper and Walter Lancanfroni combined the rest of the way to hold them in check. Boston made eight blows off lefty Joe Hatten and Hal Gregg, who relieved after Hatten had been lifted for a pinch hitter in the sixth.

With Brooklyn trailing, 3-2, to open the seventh, Eddie Stanky led off with a walk, bringing up Robinson. The Negro in three previous attempts had done no better than hit into a double play, roll to shortstop and loft an easy fly to left.

This time he laid down a perfect bunt midway to the pitcher's box and tore for first. Earl Torgeson grabbed the sphere and made a hard, hurried peg to first that hit Robinson on the leg and rocketed on into right field.

Robinson had no difficulty reaching second and Stanky pulled up at third. Reiser then weighed in with his double, a terrific clout, and soon scooted home with the fifth and unneeded run on Gene Hermanski's fly to deep center.

A disappointing crowd of only 25,623 paid to see the Dodgers get away in front of one of their main rivals for the National League flag.

After being held hitless by Sain's sharp curves for three innings, the Flock picked up a run in the fourth on a walk to Reiser, Hermanski's single and an infield out. The Braves tied it up in the fifth on hits by Connie Ryan and Johnny Hopp and a pair of sacrifices, and went ahead 3-1 in the sixth when Ryan socked across two scores after a hit batsman and an error by Bruce Edwards had opened the gates.

Reiser scored his second run in the sixth on clean hits by himself and Dixie Walker, a hit batsman and an infield out.
April 15, 1947

THREATS

PHILADELPHIA, MAY 9 (AP)—Branch Rickey, here for a conference with Herb Pennock, Philadelphia Phillies general manager, said tonight that the Brooklyn Dodgers Negro first baseman, Jackie Robinson, had received several threatening letters.

"Robinson turned them over to me," said the president of the Dodgers.

"He did not and would not show them to police headquarters. However, two of them were so vicious that I felt they should be investigated."

Investigation, Rickey added, revealed these letters to be of anonymous nature.

"I hope," Rickey said, "this ends the matter."
May 9, 1947

JACKIE ROBINSON DAY

BROOKLYN, SEPT. 23 (AP)—Brooklyn celebrated its newly clinched National League championship before the home folks today, clubbing the New York Giants, 6-1, on Jackie Robinson Day. St. Louis had eliminated itself from any mathematical chance last night by bowing to Chicago.

With the pressure off, the Dodgers had little trouble snapping their three-game losing streak.

Robinson, who was given a new automobile, a television set, a $500 watch, an interracial good will plaque and cash gifts before the game, went hitless in two trips before he was replaced by Ed Stevens, a rookie from Montreal. In fact, manager Burt Shotton tossed his reserves into action midway in the game and gave catcher Bruce Edwards and Dixie Walker a complete rest.
Sept. 23, 1947

Chapter 2

A Conservative Tide

President Harry Truman addresses the nation from the White House in Washington the night of May 24, 1946. The chief executive said if the railroad workers were not back on the job by 4 p.m., May 25, he would call upon the armed forces to help run the railroads and furnish protection for those willing to work.

- **Labor Trouble**

  Truman on Labor Crisis ... Government Seizes Railroads

- **A Republican Congress**

  Taft Denounces "Closed Shop" ... Taft-Hartley Law

On their way home for furloughs before being shipped overseas, GI's sit dejectedly alongside the tracks at the terminal station in Atlanta, Ga., May 23, 1946. Since all trains out of Atlanta stopped running several hours before the 4 o'clock strike deadline they may have waited a long time.

Labor Trouble

A Republican Congress

Harry Truman took office hoping to extend his predecessor's New Deal into the postwar period, with full employment and national health insurance. But he ran into a number of political roadblocks, effectively confirming skeptics' criticism that the New Deal was a casualty of the war. Now the question was whether it could be preserved and revived.

Truman contended with an electorate more prosperous and more conservative than the voters FDR charmed during the Great Depression, and a far more divided Democratic Party. Whatever their feelings about his eco-

nomic proposals, Southern Democrats vehemently opposed Truman's civil rights program. Roosevelt had been able to avoid an open rift in time of war and depression, but Truman had no such emergencies with which to rally his political forces.

Meanwhile, conservatives were ready to seize the initiative. They were particularly eager to curb the power of labor unions, which had grown dramatically over the preceding 10 years. By war's end, more than 12 million Americans were union members.

Labor Trouble

Under the New Deal's National Labor Relations Act, employers were legally obligated to bargain with unions that could demonstrate majority worker support, and strikers were given legal protection. The urgency of war production had created employment for almost anyone who wanted it, often in a union-organized factory.

Not even the war had been able to suppress growing differences between labor and management. Despite unions' no-strike pledges and government sanctions, walkouts were frequent. They usually were short, but they illustrated underlying tensions that would rekindle after V-J Day, when big business and increasingly big labor resumed their power struggles.

Each side sought to maximize its clout in collective bargaining, and more workers went out on strike in 1946, and more workdays were lost, than in any previous year. Some strikes were long, but—in contrast to the prewar years—most were peaceful.

By the early 1950s, about a third of American workers were organized union members, compared to about 10 percent of the labor force in the years before the Depression.

The power of organized labor was just one of many issues polarizing the nation as Truman attempted to push the nation further in the direction Roosevelt had pointed it.

TRUMAN SPEAKS ON LABOR CRISIS

WASHINGTON, JAN. 1 (AP)—President Truman tonight appealed directly to "the most powerful pressure group in the world"—the American people—to put the heat on Congress for strike-control legislation and other measures which he said are designed to avert economic "disaster."

He emphasized that he wanted no quarrel with Congress, but said that if Congress doesn't like his program, it should formulate one of its own.

"What the American people want is action," he declared.

He led off with a demand for legislation setting up fact-finding boards for major industrial disputes. Strikes would be barred for 30 days while the boards, equipped with power to examine employers' books, made their inquiry.

He also urged anew the so-called "full employment" bill, greater unemployment compensation, extended authority to impose price controls, a permanent fair employment practices commission and higher minimum wages.

Mr. Truman spoke up once more for comprehensive scientific research legislation, universal training, a health and medical care program, an "adequate salary scale" for government employees, development of river valleys and the establishment of a line of presidential succession.

The president said he was asking only that congressional committees give the representatives of the people a chance to vote soon, "yes" or "no," on vital issues.

"We cannot face 1946 in a spirit of drift or irresolution," he declared.

Mr. Truman took occasion to praise Congress for doing its "full share" to carry out its responsibility in foreign affairs. But he said there was no similar record of achievement and progress on domestic problems.

"These are as serious as international issues," he said.

"1946 is our year of decision. This year we lay the foundation of our economic structure which will have to serve for generations. This year we must decide whether or not we shall devote our strength to reaching a goal of full production and full employment.

"This year we shall have to make the decisions which will determine whether or not we gain that great future at home and abroad which we fought so valiantly to achieve."

Of equal importance to handling strikes, Mr. Truman listed "keeping prices on an even keel." If prices get out of hand, he said, purchasing power cannot stay high and business cannot remain prosperous.

Price and rent controls will have to be retained for many months, the chief executive declared, if we hope to maintain a steady and stable economy. So he said he would urge Congress when it meets again Jan. 14 to renew the price control act as soon as possible. It expires next June 30.

Furthermore, he said, the second War Powers Act should be extended again beyond June 30. That is necessary, he said, because warborn shortages of certain materials "will surely plague us" after that date.

Congress recently enacted a bill to extend this law for six months, carrying it up to June 30. The president had asked originally for a year's extension. The bill, among other things, confers authority to impose priorities.

Mr. Truman emphasized at one point the need for action in the field of housing—a field in which he said Congress is cooperating. Some 5,000,000 more homes are urgently needed, he said. He called this an emergency problem which demands an emergency method of solution.

Primarily, he said, it is a job for private industry

but it becomes a responsibility of government to provide the necessary housing where private enterprise is unable to do so. To help break bottlenecks and produce housing materials, Mr. Truman noted that he had appointed an emergency housing expediter.

Of the more than two dozen major measures which he has asked from Congress, the president spoke most strongly for fact-finding in labor disputes, "full employment" legislation, higher payments to the unemployed, higher minimum wages and a permanent Fair Employment Practices Code.

He contended that neither labor nor management had anything to fear from fact-finding proceedings. At the same time he struck at bills pending in Congress which he said seek to take from labor the right to bargain collectively or from a union its ultimate right to strike.

He said he was anxious for an effective statute with none of the "evil effect" of some of the measures.

The fact-finding plan, he said, keeps inviolate labor's right to strike. But he said there is no reason why a strike cannot be postponed for 30 days.

Labor has assailed this fact-finding plan bitterly.

He backed strongly the idea of giving a fact-finding board the power of subpoena so it could obtain all the facts. But he said no detailed information from books of any company would be revealed.

Without legislation, the president said, fact-finding boards cannot function as efficiently. Citing a specific example, he said the General Motors Corporation "has refused to cooperate" with the fact-finding board which he set up on a voluntary basis to look into the company's dispute with the CIO-United Automobile Workers.

"I thought the matter too urgent," he said, "to wait upon the passage of legislation. You have seen how the General Motors Corporation has refused to cooperate with this fact-finding board.

"There is no way that it can be compelled to cooperate unless a statute is passed giving the board the power of subpoena. That is what is now up to the Congress."

The president described full employment legislation as an essential part of the program to tide

over the reconversion period and move on toward the goal of full production and a higher standard of living.
Jan. 3, 1946

GOVERNMENT SEIZES RAILWAYS

WASHINGTON, MAY 17 (AP)—President Truman seized the nation's $27,000,000,000 railroad system today in an effort to head off a paralyzing strike set for 4 p.m. tomorrow, but union leaders declared the walkout would take place as scheduled.

The president appealed over the heads of the labor chiefs to the workers, addressing them directly in a statement:

"I call upon every employee of the railroads to cooperate with the government by remaining on duty."

He said the seizure and continued operation of the carriers were necessary in the interest of the "war effort." Legally the country is still at war.

The seizure order, which placed the Office of Defense Transportation in command of the carriers, empowered ODT to ask the secretary of war to furnish protection for railroad employees and to supply any equipment and manpower deemed necessary.

The ODT said both executives and employees of the rail lines had been "reminded that rail operations now are a governmental undertaking and are requested to fully and faithfully discharge their duties."

The strike, if it materializes, raises the prospect of a complete tie up of the nation's biggest transportation agencies, on the heels of a soft coal walkout that already has thrown the reconversion effort out of gear.

The seizure order was signed by Mr. Truman at 2:50 p.m. in the presence of A.F. Whitney, president of the Brotherhood of Trainmen, and Alvanley Johnston, chief of the Engineers Brotherhood, the two unions directly involved in the strike threat.

Then as they left the White House after a visit of only three or four minutes, the two union leaders told reporters the strike would go on. The time for it is 4 p.m. local standard time in all zones.

"Yes, sir," Johnston replied to a reporter who asked him whether the strike would go on as scheduled.
May 17, 1946

WASHINGTON, MAY 18 (AP)—A tie up of the nation's vast railroad system was postponed for at least five days yesterday following a request by President Truman to brotherhood leaders, but delay in getting the word to rank and file union men who run the trains disrupted service generally for several hours.

Widespread confusion was reported in practically all major rail centers because the walkout of 250,000 railroad trainmen and engineers—called for 4 p.m. local time yesterday—was cancelled only a few minutes before the deadline in the Eastern time zone.

The widespread disruption in normal traffic occurred after the federal government Friday seized the $27,000,000,000 rail system and prepared to operate it under the Office of Defense Transportation.

A.F. Whitney, president of the Brotherhood of Railroad Trainmen, and Alvanley Johnston, head of the Brotherhood of Locomotive Engineers, agreed to reset the strike call for 4 p.m. (local standard time) Thursday, after a telephone conversation with President Truman.
May 18, 1946

WASHINGTON, MAY 24 (AP)—John R. Steelman, presidential mediator in the railroad strike, said at 6:55 p.m. (EST), "I see no hope of a settlement tonight."
May 24, 1946

WASHINGTON, MAY 24 (AP)—President Truman called for a joint session of Congress tomorrow, with prospects dark for settlement of the railroad strike by negotiation and emergencies crowding fast.

The president also will broadcast to the nation at 10 o'clock tonight, at the close of the first full day of the critical tie up. These events came thick and fast:

1. Dr. John R. Steelman, key government conciliator trying to end the strike of engineers and trainmen, emerged from long hours of conferences to announce that "the situation is dark."

2. Secretary of War Patterson told reporters it is

An unidentified woman climbs through the window of one of the last trains to leave New York's Pennsylvania Station, May 23, 1946, just before the start of the threatened nationwide railroad strike. Trains leaving shortly before the strike was scheduled to begin closed their doors to prevent overcrowding.

"possible" that some discharged veterans who ran Army trains abroad during the war may be called back to service.

3. A War Department spokesman announced that troops are being moved to "strategic locations" in anticipation of requests for protection of the railroads and any workers willing to man the trains.

4. The White House disclosed that Mr. Truman was drafting a broadcast for tonight. All networks were cleared for it.

Attorney General Clark abruptly ended a three-day strike prevention conference here which 93 United States attorneys were attending and ordered them to speed back to their districts immediately by whatever means they could find. The purpose, an official said, is to prosecute "any violations of federal laws during the emergency."

The strike continued virtually 100 percent effective as it ran through its first day, the Association of American Railroads said. It reported only 50 passenger trains running in the entire country, out of some 17,500 for a normal day. Freight and mail traffic on the railways also was paralyzed, but milk cars moved.

Already hundreds of carloads of livestock were held up and prospective food shortages drew nearer for many cities. Some mines and factories closed, and many more were threatened with each hour the strike continued.

Mails were limited to first class and to airmail under 16 pounds. Postmaster General Hannegan issued an appeal to the public: "Please mail nothing that is not essential."

The Marines opened the way for all the men they have discharged and for men on inactive reserve to volunteer for temporary active duty "during this crisis" at the nearest recruiting station.
May 24, 1946

NEW YORK, MAY 24 (AP)—The full impact of the rail strike staggered New York City today, slowing its high-geared business life to a horse-and-buggy pace and threatening seriously to affect the welfare of every resident.

The nation's gravest transportation crisis left the city virtually isolated. Only a handful of the hundreds of trains normally entering and leaving the city were operating.

Hundreds of thousands of workers who live in suburban areas had to turn to makeshift transportation—buses, streetcars, private automobiles and taxicabs—to get to their jobs.

Many were hours late in reaching their offices and plants. Others were unable to get into town at all.

Highways leading into Manhattan from Long Island, New Jersey and Westchester were jammed with automobiles, many carrying up to eight passengers. Bankers as well as clerks thumbed rides.

Parking lots and garages in the business districts overflowed with cars.

Bus lines bore the brunt of the traffic and every available vehicle was put into service.

The city's two main railroad terminals—Grand Central and Pennsylvania Station—which at 5 p.m. (EDT) yesterday were jammed with shouting, pushing crowds, today were practically deserted.

A large question mark was written on the Pennsylvania Railroad bulletin board listing train times.

The line, however, said it would operate 19 passenger trains.

The Long Island Railroad operated shuttle service between certain points, bringing passengers close to subways.

The New York Central said it would operate no passenger trains today. Only milk trains will run.

Department stores and retail shops—many operating with reduced staffs—were without the usual crowds of shoppers.

Hotels took emergency measures to meet unprecedented demands for rooms, setting up cots in bedrooms and ballrooms, and turning lounges into dormitories to accommodate those who were stranded and others who refused to be stopped by the strike and had arrived by bus, car and plane in time to pick up reservations.

Mail, food and coal deliveries were interrupted. Post offices in the five boroughs reported that they had 725 trucks to keep mail flowing to points as far as Albany.
May 24, 1946

CHICAGO, MAY 24 (AP)—Actress Katharine Cornell announced today she had chartered an airplane to assure the Chicago opening of "Antigone" Monday night. The troupe has been playing in Washington. Scenery for the production will be trucked in from Canada.

Miss Cornell said she believed this would be the first time in theatrical history that an entire company trouped by air.
May 24, 1946

WASHINGTON, MAY 25 (AP)—President Truman counted today upon aroused public opinion to support his decision to end the railroad strike with troops if necessary.

Presidential advisers said Mr. Truman reached his decision to "get tough" with the heads of the railroad trainmen and engineers brotherhoods only after long consultations and study.

It was 3 p.m. yesterday when he decided finally to go on the air seven hours later.

But it was scarcely three minutes before he

President Truman (on rostrum) requests members of the Senate and House during a May 25, 1946 joint session, in the House chamber to enact drastic curbs on strikes against the government. These curbs would provide for the drafting of men who refuse to work and impose criminal penalties on employers and union leaders.

began to speak that the last phrase was added and the final change made in the address which made labor history from the White House standpoint.

"It was no easy decision to make," one adviser declared. "It was a decision that some people will interpret as a strike-breaking decision. The president weighed it, however, against the decision of 18 other railroad brotherhoods to support a presidential compromise which only two brotherhoods rejected."

Once the president had decided, this adviser said, he began a rough draft. Then, feeling the need for relaxation, he took a quick dip in the White House pool before going to his study to resume his work.

Still later, Mr. Truman called in Samuel I. Rosenman, former presidential special counsel, and others for their advice.

The final two paragraphs—in which the president appealed to the strikers to return to their jobs and expressed the determination to use troops if they did not—were polished into final form only minutes before the public heard them.

The speech off his chest, the president talked it

over later with staff aides and some Cabinet members.

They said that with the die cast, the chief executive seemed "immensely relieved." And he was encouraged, they added, when told that the White House switchboard and wire room were flooded with congratulatory messages.

Shortly after 11 p.m. Mr. Truman retired for the night.
May 25, 1946

WASHINGTON, MAY 2 (AP)—Within an hour after the railroad strike collapsed late yesterday, trains began leaving the nation's terminals, and the government moved to forestall any future paralysis of the nation's economy by labor disputes.

Most railroads expected resumption of normal passenger and freight schedules by today, and the government cancelled emergency orders and preparations.

John R. Steelman, labor consultant to President Truman, said the strike settlement was on the basis of the president's proposal for an 18½ cents an hour pay boost, with changes in working rules deferred for one year. Union leaders of the 250,000 striking engineers and trainmen—who previously had turned down this offer—reversed their stand just before Mr. Truman asked a joint session of Congress for emergency strike control legislation.

The railroad strike ended suddenly only minutes before President Truman asked, and got, action on legislation to permit drafting of men for industrial emergencies and penalizing strikes against government-seized properties.

Representatives of the carriers and two striking unions—engineers and trainmen—signed at a downtown hotel an agreement halting the strike. Then they went on a hand-shaking spree.

Mr. Truman announced to a wildly whooping Congress that the strike was over. Grim, unsmiling, he interrupted an address to a joint Senate-House session at the point where he said:

"I request the Congress immediately to authorize the president to draft into the armed forces of the United States all workers who are on strike against their government."

While legislators howled their approval for

that, Senate Secretary Leslie Biffle leaned over and whispered to the chief executive.

"Word has just been received," Mr. Truman said, "that the rail strike has been settled on terms proposed by the government."

That produced another tremendous outburst.
May 2, 1946

WASHINGTON, MAY 29 (AP)—Henry Morgenthau Jr., former Secretary of the Treasury, declared tonight that President Truman "has renounced the Roosevelt philosophy and the Roosevelt policy" and for that reason the nation is "in a state of crisis today."

Morgenthau suggested the voters "cleanse" the House of "many of the men who made such a disgraceful spectacle of themselves last Saturday." The House Saturday overwhelmingly passed the president's strike-control legislation, which Morgenthau called "vicious" and "undemocratic."

Morgenthau said in a broadcast talk that he listened to the president's speech before Congress that day and could only conclude that Mr. Truman "has decided to make an open and final rejection of the Roosevelt inheritance."

Morgenthau called it "an outright declaration that his methods, his policies and his purposes are totally different from those of the man to whom he actually owes the presidency."

Morgenthau said Mr. Truman's action "is only the logical outcome of a whole series of disastrous decisions extending over the past year. The inflationary conditions which are the underlying cause of strikes and economic dislocations today have their roots in the thoughtless haste with which Mr. Truman permitted many wartime controls to be scrapped."

He cited abolition of the War Labor Board, scrapping of the War Production Board's system of allocations and priorities, the ending of meat rationing, "mismanagement of America's treasury of food and scrapping of the nation's wartime tax structure."

"The history of foreign relations since Mr. Truman became president is one of deterioration and decline," he said, "and the destruction of everything we had achieved before."

At the Bretton Woods and Dumbarton Oaks

conferences, Morgenthau said, "the spirit which Franklin D. Roosevelt himself breathed" into them made a new concept of relationships between men and nations, something akin to a "new religion."

"All that is lost now," he continued. "It is hate that fills the international atmosphere today." He said United States delegates to international conferences attend them "with the atomic bomb bulging from their hip pockets—a symbol of what can happen to anybody who incurs our slightest displeasure."

Morgenthau said: "Threats have replaced persuasion and hatred has replaced brotherly love. Destiny, not the electorate, called him (Mr. Truman) to receive the torch of progress from President Roosevelt and he has failed his calling."
May 29, 1946

A Republican Congress

"Had Enough? Vote Republican" was the opposition rallying cry in the 1946 midterm elections. And the electorate responded that they had had enough, of strikes, shortages, rationing, the slow pace of demobilization— and Democrats. In November, for the first time in 18 years, the Republicans won control of both houses of Congress.

WASHINGTON, NOV. 2 (AP)—A revived GOP snatched control of Congress from the Democrats yesterday and suggestions arose immediately that President Truman resign to solidify the nation's leadership within a single party.

Back in Washington after voting in Missouri, Mr. Truman had nothing to say on that or on the damage the Democrats suffered.

Republicans elected at least 23 senators, 242 representatives and 20 governors. That gave them three more than a majority in the Senate, 24 beyond a majority in the House and a man in 25 of the 48 statehouses.

Sen. J. William Fulbright of Arkansas, a Democratic holdover, suggested that the chief executive appoint a Republican secretary of state and let him accede to the presidency. He said it would be "the wisest thing" for the president to do and "the best thing for the country," since "only one party should control the government."

The *Chicago Sun* urged editorially that Mr. Truman step down. It said this would be a "patriotic and courageous step." The *Sun*, which supported the Roosevelt-Truman ticket in 1944 and Democratic candidates generally in 1946, recently has criticized the Truman administration. It said that with Republicans running Congress and Mr. Truman in the White House, "our foreign policy will be vacillating and our part in the pacification of the world come to a stalemate."

Rep. Charles A. Halleck of Indiana, chairman of the Republican congressional committee, commented:

"The New Deal's long abuse of public power has been rebuked by an aroused and indignant electorate."

Republicans hit the political jackpot for the first time in 15 years.

With their winnings, they promised to cut individual income taxes 20 percent in 1947, lop perhaps $10,000,000,000 off government spending, balance the budget, revoke the presidential war powers and undertake a number of investigations.

Millions of people, obviously fed up with controls, strikes and shortages, gave them an irresistible "yes" to their "had enough?" campaign slogan—a landslide vote that toppled Democratic strong men from Massachusetts to California and even crunched into the edge of the still "solid South."

This is what it means:

The widest possible split between the White House and Congress. A Democratic president remains in office. But Republicans will be in undisputed command of the 80th Congress which meets Jan. 3.

Probably little change in United States foreign

policy. Leading Republicans endorsed its present lines and even helped mold it.

A wholesale housecleaning of congressional officeholders, from speaker of the House and president pro-tem of the Senate down to page boys and Capitol cops. Republicans seize chairmanships of all committees.

A brighter political luster for big names in the GOP, men like Dewey, Bricker, Vandenberg, Taft, Warren, Lodge and others. They have been discussed for presidential or vice presidential nominations in '48.

A trend that could carry into 1948 and beyond. The Republican torrent swept Democrats from power in such key states as New York, Pennsylvania, Massachusetts, Ohio, Illinois, California, and Mr. Truman's own Missouri.

Former Secretary of Commerce Henry A. Wallace, bounced out of the Cabinet during the campaign in a row over foreign policy, interpreted the election as signifying:

"The Democratic Party will either become more progressive or it will die."
Nov. 2, 1946

WASHINGTON, JAN. 3 (AP)—Republicans came whooping and shouting back to control of the House today after 15 lean years, electing Joseph W. Martin Jr. of Massachusetts speaker and introducing a 20 percent income tax cut as bill No. 1.

The president watched the House opening by television at the White House. The 80th Congress was the first in history to have its opening televised.

The House session lasted just two hours and 22 minutes and went like a clock.

Martin was elected speaker by a strict party-line vote of 244 to 182 over the retiring Democratic speaker, now plain Rep. Rayburn of Texas.

Martin delivered an address expressing hope for "a degree of cooperation... unsurpassed in the history of our nation" between the Republicans and Democrats in the House, and between the House and Senate.

Opening day bills dealt with labor measures.

Many more are planned in both chambers, and what ultimately emerges for floor consideration will depend in large part on the Senate and House

labor committees which will handle them. Rep. Hartley, R–N.J., who was opposed for re-election by the CIO, decided during the day to accept chairmanship of the House group. Sen. Taft, R–Ohio, heads the one in his chamber.
Jan. 3, 1947

Editor's Note

The foremost aim of the Republicans controlling Congress was to curb the power of organized labor.

TAFT DENOUNCES "CLOSED SHOP"

WASHINGTON, JAN. 28 (AP)—Chairman Robert A. Taft, R-Ohio, of the Senate Labor Committee said today that the closed shop gives unions "such tremendous power" over workers that Congress may have to outlaw it.

"I think we have this alternative: If we are going to have closed shops, we are going to have to insure more democracy in unions," he told the committee.

The closed shop arrangement, under which only union members can be hired, came up for discussion during testimony by Secretary of Labor Lewis Schwellenbach.

Schwellenbach opposed a ban on the closed shop. He also argued against any other sweeping labor law changes and predicted a drastic reduction in work stoppages.

Another important figure in the labor picture, President Philip Murray of the CIO, disclosed in an interview that he has asked CIO unions to go slow on new contract demands to reassure the public and "promote real collective bargaining."

Murray said he has urged unions in the CIO to follow his lead as president of the steel workers union and agree to contract extensions when more time is needed for discussion of issues.

Schwellenbach urged Congress to act on President Truman's proposal for a commission to study the causes and cures of strikes.

The trouble recently in the labor-management field, Schwellenbach said, is that "the art of collective bargaining has been forgotten.

"Despite the difficulties inherent for labor and management in relearning the free collective bargaining process, it may be asserted safely that the process is being relearned and that the number of stoppages in 1947 will be drastically reduced from the number that occurred in 1946.

"As we entered the new year 1947, work stoppages were at the lowest point since V-J Day. Not only was the number of strikes less than at any previous postwar period but workers involved and idleness were also well below the early months of 1946, when reconversion problems resulted in widespread labor-management controversies."

Schwellenbach found an ally in Sen. Pepper (D-Fla.) in arguing against the contention of Sen. Joseph Ball (R-Minn.) that the check-off system should be outlawed.

This is the arrangement by which union dues are deducted from paychecks by the company and delivered to the union.

"If a man belongs to a union," said Schwellenbach, "I see no objection to collection of his dues. There is nothing immoral about it."

Pepper said that collective bargaining contracts can provide for the checkoff and that union employees should be bound by the acts of "their chosen representatives."

Ball said a worker should have final control of the wage he receives and that deducting dues was no more proper than deducting grocery bills.

Schwellenbach told the committee, which is considering a raft of bills opposed by labor union leaders, that enactment of laws outlawing the closed shop and maintenance of union membership would destroy a substantial advance made over the years in union-management relations.

Schwellenbach read a long statement to the committee in which he opposed such suggestions as have been made in congress:

1. That a mediation board be set up either inside or outside the Labor Department.

2. That the department's Conciliation Service be abolished.

3. That supervisory employees such as foremen be denied the right to organize into unions.
Jan. 28, 1947

WASHINGTON, MARCH 7 (AP)—Chairman Fred Hartley (R-N.J.) of the House Labor Committee said tonight the committee is going to report

President Harry Truman goes over his script at the White House on June 20, 1947, just before addressing a radio message to the people on his veto of the Taft-Hartley labor control bill. Truman asserted the measure is "bad for labor, bad for management, bad for the country."

legislation which "will be called punitive" but that "labor's right to organize and to bargain collectively will in no way be impaired."

Hartley declared in a radio speech that "Congress must do something about labor monopolies" if another coal strike and walkouts in other industries are to be avoided.

He remarked that the Supreme Court decision in the John L. Lewis case, upholding an injunction, will be effective only until June 30 because it is based on the Smith-Connally Act, which expires then.

Ira Mosher, spokesman for the National Association of Manufacturers, told the Labor Committee during the day that the decision proves

Sen. Robert A. Taft (R-Ohio), center, smiles, June 23, 1947, after the Senate voted, 68 to 25, to override President Truman's veto of the Taft-Hartley bill, curbing the power of labor unions. The action made the bill law.

"you've got to have some legislation" to protect the public.

Hartley said in his speech that "no special interest, be it that of management or labor, rises above the general welfare of all our people." *March 7, 1947*

TAFT-HARTLEY LAW

WASHINGTON, JUNE 23 (AP)—The Taft-Hartley labor bill became the law of the land today.

The Senate overrode President Truman's veto and his all-out opposition, 68 to 25.

This was six votes more than the required two-thirds majority—more even than the bill's supporters had expected.

And the chamber spurned a final appeal which the president sent by Democratic Leader Alben Barkley (D-Ky.) two hours before the roll call.

The president insisted that "this dangerous legislation" will hurt "our national unity" and so "render a distinct disservice not only to this nation but to the world."

Sen. Robert Taft (R-Ohio) told the tense Senate just before it voted, however, that the GOP Congress would "be held delinquent" if it failed to

Cars comprising a motor caravan of CIO union members leave New York City, June 17, 1947, for a trip to Washington, D.C., to protest the Taft-Hartley labor bill. Signs on the cars ask for President Truman's veto of the bill and for free labor.

pass the bill. He shouted that "unions today are big business" and "should have the same responsibility as corporations."

The outcome was Mr. Truman's sharpest setback at the hands of the Republican-controlled Congress, elected last November.

It was a tremendous victory for Taft, widely mentioned as a possible GOP presidential candidate next year. Taft sponsored the bill with Rep. Fred Hartley (R-N.J.).

The Senate showdown found 20 Democrats going along with 48 Republicans to override. For upholding the president and his veto were 22

Democrats and three Republicans—Senators William Langer (N.D.), George Malone (Nev.) and Wayne Morse (Ore.).

Sen. Robert Wagner (D-N.Y.), ill in New York, sent a message from his sickbed which the clerk read just before the roll call. He called upon his colleagues to uphold the veto and concluded:

"The president would not lie at this critical moment in history."

This apparently was a reference to the arguments of Taft and Hartley. They had said that some of the president's statements were "not so" and "false."

Just as quickly, Gerhard P. Van Arkel, general counsel of the National Labor Relations Board, resigned. He expressed "grave doubts concerning both the workability and the fairness" of the act. The law creates a new post of general counsel with broader duties and $12,000 salary compared with the present $9,975 but Van Arkel said he does not want it.

The new law bans the closed shop, under which non-unionists may not be hired, but permits the union shop with certain restrictions. In a union shop, non-unionists may be hired but then must join up.

It also imposes a long string of restrictions on union activities which have sprung up under the Wagner Act.
June 23, 1947

ST. JOSEPH, MICH., JUNE 28 (AP)—As a group of CIO pickets stood across the street from the church, Lloyd Bowers Taft, third son of Sen. and Mrs. Robert Taft, of Ohio, was married today to Miss Virginia Stone.

Despite earlier threats of mass picketing, only 10 men and five women, members of a CIO electrical workers' union and some of them employed by the Tafts' host here, marched with placards from a union hall to the vicinity of the First Congregational Church shortly before the ceremony.

The pickets marched around a nearby square up and down an alley twice, then returned to their headquarters. The signs read: "Taft obstructed housing," "Congratulations to the bride and groom," and "Senator Taft is a bad boy."
June 28, 1947

NEW YORK, OCT. 2 (AP)—Federal Judge Stephen Brennan today signed an order under provisions of the Taft-Hartley Act temporarily restraining about 150 members of the AFL International Longshoremen's Association from continuing a strike in the port of Albany—the first such move since the new legislation went into effect.

The strike had blocked grain shipments to Europe, delivery of fuel oil to various New York State communities, and had threatened a curtailment of operations in paper mills, the government said.
Oct. 2, 1947

KNOXVILLE, TENN., MARCH 20 (AP)—A threatened strike in an atomic bomb laboratory at Oak Ridge, Tenn., was averted yesterday when the government obtained an injunction banning a walkout for 80 days.

The court order, issued here by federal Judge George C. Taylor, marked the first time national emergency provisions of the Taft-Hartley Law had been invoked.

About 900 members of the AFL Atomic Trades and Labor Council were restrained from leaving their jobs at Oak Ridge National Laboratory, and Carbide and Carbon Chemicals Corp., operator of the plant, was restrained from disturbing the "status quo" of an existing labor contract with the union.

In recent Washington negotiations, the union claimed the workers were threatened with a wage cut. Carbide took over the laboratory March 1 from Monsanto Chemical Co. Monsanto had been paying the AFL workers higher wages than those received by CIO workers at a nearby atomic production plant, also operated by Carbide.

Carbide sought in negotiations to establish wages and working conditions similar to those prevailing in a contract with the CIO Gas, Coke and Chemical workers at another atomic plant.

The AFL workers claimed their laboratory work is more dangerous and requires more skill. Their present rates range from 88 cents to $1.75 an hour.
March 20, 1948

WASHINGTON, MAY 2 (AP)—A National Labor Relations Board trial examiner ruled today that AFL carpenters in Kansas City were violating the Taft-Hartley Act by picketing a prefabricated housing project.

The picketing was to enforce a secondary boycott, examiner Charles W. Schneider said. By so doing, truck drivers who were members of AFL teamsters were persuaded not to deliver goods to Klassen and Hodgson, Inc., erector of prefabricated homes at Overland Park, Kan.

That, in turn, was intended to force the firm to

stop doing business with the Wadsworth Building Company, Inc., manufacturer of the prefabricated houses, Schneider said. Neither firm was employing union carpenters in making or assembling the ready-made dwellings.

It was the first time that an examiner has ruled on the application of the "free speech" provision of the Taft-Hartley Act to picketing in a secondary boycott.

Three days earlier, another examiner, Sidney Lindner, ruled against the carpenters in a secondary boycott at the Montgomery Fair Company, Montgomery, Ala. Lindner, also making a precedent ruling, ordered the carpenters to quit picketing the department store in an effort to make the Fair Company stop doing business with Bear Brothers, a building contractor who employed non-union help.

Schneider said the truck drivers' union and other building trade unions acted with the carpenters in establishing the picket in the Kansas case. The truck drivers were the only ones shown to have been turned back by the picket, however.

"It is found," he said, "that employees of suppliers of materials to Klassen, by means of threats of reprisal, were induced and encouraged by the respondents (carpenters and the agent) to engage in concerted refusal to deliver materials to Klassen."

This violated the Taft-Hartley Act's ban on secondary boycotts, he said.

Schneider ruled that it was a "foreseeable consequence" that employees affiliated with the building trades council members "would decline to cross the picket line because of a reasonable fear of reprisal from their own union."

The act's provision on free speech protected the picketing insofar as it was aimed at the non-union Klassen employees. It was not coercive of them, Schneider said, because there were no threats of reprisals or ways of carrying out such threats if they were made.
May 2, 1949

WASHINGTON, AUG. 20 (AP)—On Monday the Taft-Hartley Act will be in effect two years.

The National Labor Relations Board (NLRB) and the courts have been interpreting this staggeringly complex law and applying it to actual cases. Some provisions are still pretty much unexplored, but steady progress has been made.

The non-Communist provision is perhaps the most thoroughly interpreted part of the Taft-Hartley Act.

Union officers must sign non-Communist oaths or else a union can't charge an employer with an unfair labor practice. It can't even get on a ballot in a plant election.

The effect has been that most non-complying unions have been squeezed, raided, defeated and weakened to the point where lately even extreme left-wing unions have been falling into line. The only major unions which haven't complied are the United Mine Workers, the AFL International Typographical Union, and a handful of CIO leftist unions.
Aug. 20, 1949

Chapter 3

Gen. George C. Marshall, United States secretary of state, speaks a few words into the microphone on arrival at the Moscow airport for a 'Big Four' conference of foreign ministers. With him is M. Andrei Vishinsky, Russian vice minister of foreign affairs, who greeted him.

End of the Alliance

• Growing Tensions

Truman on Bomb Secrets ... Churchill Speaks in Missouri ... Truman Fires Wallace

• The Truman Doctrine

Aid to Greece, Turkey

• The Marshall Plan

Europe Recovery Program ... Soviets Denounce Marshall Plan ... Communists Control Czechoslovakia

Secretary of State James F. Byrnes (fourth from left at table) speaks to the United Nations Security Council in favor of the council hearing Iran's complaint that Soviet troops were stationed in Iran. Listening to Byrnes at the session, March 26, 1946, in New York, are, left to right, around table, Ambassador Andrei Gromyko, USSR; Sir Alexander Cadogan, United Kingdom; Edward R. Stettinius Jr., U.S.; Byrnes; Col. W.R. Hodgson, Australia; Dr. Pedro Velloso, Brazil; and Trygve Lie, United Nations Secretary-General.

When V-J Day finally arrived, people had been waiting outside the White House for two days. They kept chanting, "We want Harry!" So finally Truman and his wife Bess walked onto the lawn and shook hands through the fence. Later, speaking into a microphone placed under the portico, he told them, "This is the great day."

But then Truman's smile faded as he warned of "an emergency ahead—a crisis as great as Dec. 7, 1941." He was not alone in his reticence. One reporter wrote that it seemed "a peculiar peace…. And everyone talked of 'the end of the war,' not of 'victory.'"

It soon became obvious there was ample basis for the president's somber mood—among the wartime Allies.

The great question of the immediate postwar period involved the Soviet Union and its true intentions. Toward the end of his life, Franklin Roosevelt's view of Stalin had hardened; among the last things the president wrote was a note to Winston Churchill in which he insisted "We must be firm" with Moscow.

Roosevelt believed he had struck the best deal possible in 1945 at the Allies' Yalta Conference. However much Britain and America might want a democratic, capitalist Eastern Europe, in fact the region was securely under the control of the Red Army. After the war ended, it soon became clear Stalin intended to consolidate his position, and East and West increasingly viewed each other with suspicion.

Growing Tensions

The atomic bomb, which had ended the war, some hoped would secure the peace.

Although many Americans did not fully appreciate the theory behind, or the potential of, the bomb, they were inundated with predictions about the significance of atomic energy. Some analysts said it was the crowning achievement of science; others said it meant the end of civilization. That the future of nuclear power might be more complex and less dramatic was ingnored in the excitement. One matter that did not at all seem complex to President Truman was the issue of who would control the "secret" of nuclear power.

TRUMAN ON BOMB SECRETS

TIPTONVILLE, TENN. OCT. 8 (AP)—President Truman declared unequivocally tonight that the secrets of the atomic bomb will not be shared with additional nations. That secret, he told a wholly unheralded press conference, is the industrial knowhow, since other nations have access to the scientific knowledge that led to its development.

Great Britain and Canada, he asserted, share the industrial knowhow, and while he has not discussed his decision with them, the president said he was certain they will agree its secrets will not be shared.

His comment, made at Linda Cottage near Reelfoot Lake where he moved in today for a two-day rest, came when reporters appeared expecting an off-the-record gabfest.

He added that there was no clash of American interests with Russia and that Russia has been as badly misrepresented in this country as we have been in Russia.

Our interests, he said, do not clash. He added that understanding sometimes was made more difficult by differences in language and translations.

The president said flatly that none of our Allies have asked for the secret of the atomic bomb.

A reporter said it had been reported that one of the causes of a lack of ardor of Russia toward the United States grew out of the fact that we have the industrial knowhow and they have not.

That isn't true, the president replied, the difficulties are a matter of difference in language, principally because we don't have a common language and translations are not always exactly the same.

James F. Byrnes, the president asserted, will initiate a discussion with Great Britain and Canada, looking to international agreements which the president wants with a view to outlawing the use of the atomic bomb.

Speaking on the screened front porch of Mrs. T.O. Morris' summer cottage to more than three dozen reporters, the president plunged unhesitatingly into a discussion of the atomic energy problem.

He made it clear that the scientific knowledge utilized in the final perfection of the bomb was available to virtually any nation.

The secret, he said, was the engineering knowledge of putting all the different pieces together and the finding of resources and plant capacity to complete the work.
Oct. 8, 1945

STALIN ON PEACE

LONDON, FEB. 9 (AP)—Generalissimo Josef Stalin, declaring the last two wars resulted from the development of capitalistic world economy, tonight announced a new five-year plan for Soviet Russia and stupendous production goals "to guarantee our country against any aggressor."

He predicted, too, that Soviet scientists could "not only catch up with, but surpass those abroad." He did not mention atomic research specifically.

Stalin said the new five-year plan—Russia's fourth including the one interrupted by German invasion in 1941—would be inaugurated soon, and "for the further future" set goals for steel, pig iron, coal and oil production close to the output of the United States.

In a speech broadcast by the Moscow radio, the Soviet chieftain promised that "soon rationing will end," and that the Russian worker's standard of living would be raised.

Declaring that the war was "the inevitable result of the development of the world economic and political forces on the basis of monopoly capitalism," Stalin asserted:

"Perhaps the catastrophe of war could have

been avoided if the possibility of periodic redistribution of raw materials and markets between the countries existed in accordance with their economic needs, in the way of coordinated and peaceful decisions.

"But this is impossible under the present capitalistic development of world economy. Thus as a result of the first crisis in the development of the capitalistic world economy the first war arose. The second world war arose as a result of the second crisis."

"The point is that the Soviet social system has proved to be more capable of life and more stable than a non-Soviet social system, that the Soviet social system is a better form of organization of society than any other non-Soviet social system."
Feb. 9, 1946

BYRNES SAYS U.S. WILL USE FORCE IF NECESSARY

NEW YORK, FEB. 28 (AP)—Secretary of State James Byrnes served notice on the world tonight that the United States must stand ready to use force, if necessary, to prevent aggression.

Only an "inexcusable tragedy of errors could cause serious conflict between this country and Russia," he said at one point, and at another: "I am convinced that there is no reason for war between any of the great powers."

But, Byrnes asserted flatly that "we must make plain that the United States intends to defend" the United Nations charter, which outlaws aggression.

He called for a "stop to this maneuvering for strategic advantages all over the world and to the use of one adjustment as an entering wedge for further and undisclosed penetrations of power."

Byrnes' remarks came one day after Sen. Arthur H. Vandenberg (R-Mich.), a delegate to the United Nations, called on the United States to be as firm and frank as Russia in the interest of mutual understanding.

Openly acknowledging that "all around us is suspicion and distrust," he termed some of it unfounded and unreasonable but said "the basis of some suspicions persists and prompts me to make some comments as to our position."

Without specifically mentioning any individual power, he laid down this seven point list of "must nots" for great and small nations:

1. "We will not and we cannot stand aloof if force or the threat of force is used contrary to the purposes and principles of the charter.

2. "We have no right to hold our troops in the territories of other sovereign states without their approval and consent freely given.

3. "We must not unduly prolong the making of peace and continue to impose our troops upon small and impoverished nations.

4. "No power has a right to help itself to alleged enemy properties in liberated or ex-satellite countries before a reparations settlement has been agreed upon by the Allies. We have not and will not agree to any one power deciding for itself what it will take from these countries.

5. "We must not conduct a war of nerves to achieve strategic ends.

6. "We do not want to stumble and stagger into situations where no power intends war, but no power will be able to avert war.

7. "We must not regard the drawing of attention to situations which might endanger the peace as an affront to the nation or nations responsible for those situations."
Feb. 28, 1946

CHURCHILL SPEAKS IN MISSOURI

FULTON, MO., MARCH 5 (AP)—Winston Churchill today asked a virtual military alliance between the United States and Britain, and President Truman, speaking from the same platform, pleaded for "full support" of the United Nations charter to save mankind from "destruction."

The president spoke after the fiery wartime prime minister of Great Britain and bluntly accused Russia of seeking "indefinite expansion of its power and doctrines." Speaking in the Westminster College gymnasium where both Mr. Churchill and the nation's chief executive received honorary degrees, the former prime minister called for an end to the "quivering, precarious balance of power" which he asserted offered a temptation to "ambition or adventures."

"These are perilous times," Truman said gravely. "The world either is headed for destruction or the greatest age of progress in history."

The president, however, made no reference to the suggested Anglo-American alliance and strictly refrained from any criticism of Russia.

As vital support for the United Nations Organization and the best means of maintaining the peace, Churchill advocated:

1. Joint use of all naval and air bases of either the United States or the United Kingdom "all over the world."

2. "Intimate" relationships between Anglo-American military advisers, common study of "potential dangers," similar weapons and manuals of instruction, and interchange of officers and cadets at colleges."

Except in the British Commonwealth and in the United States, he said fearfully, "the Communist parties or fifth columns constitute a growing challenge and peril to Christian civilization."

"I do not believe that Soviet Russia desires war. What they desire is the fruits of war and the indefinite expansion of their power and doctrines."

The Russians, he said, admire nothing so much as strength "and there is nothing for which they have less respect than military weakness.

"We cannot afford to work on narrow margins, offering temptations to a trial of strength."

To prevent another "awful whirlpool," he said, there must be a "good understanding" with Russia this year on all points under UNO authorities with support of the world organization "by the whole strength of the English-speaking world and all its connections."

Asserting "a shadow has fallen upon the scenes so lately lighted by the Allied victory," Churchill added:

"Nobody knows what Soviet Russia and its Communist international organization intends to do in the immediate future, or what are the limits, if any, to their expansive and proselytizing tendencies."

He said it would be "wrong and imprudent" to entrust the secret of the atomic bomb to a UNO still in its infancy and it would be "criminal madness to cast it adrift in this agitated and ununited world."

There is, he said, an "anxious" outlook in Manchuria and alarm in Turkey and Persia over Soviet policies. He said Warsaw, Berlin, Prague, Vienna, Budapest, Belgrade, Bucharest and Sofia are subject in one form or another "not only to Soviet influence but to a very high and increasing measure of control from Moscow."

Adding to this, he said that the Russian-dominated Polish government was making "wrongful inroads upon Germany" and that Communist influences were at work in Italy and France. He added: "This is certainly not the liberated Europe we fought to build up."

American custodianship of the atomic bomb secret, he continued, has not caused sleepless nights anywhere.

"I do not believe we should all have slept so soundly had the positions been reversed and some Communist or neo-Fascist state monopolized, for the time being, these dread agencies."
March 5, 1946

LONDON, MARCH 5 (AP)—The lobby correspondent of the Press Association said tonight that former Prime Minister Churchill's speech in Fulton, Mo., today was criticized by some members of Parliament "on the ground that it was very unhelpful to the United Nations Organization."

He said the first report of the speech to reach members caused "a good deal of interest and some surprise" and added the speech probably would result in the questioning of Foreign Minister Ernest Bevin.

"For one thing, some members would like to know whether the speech was made with the prior knowledge of the British government," the correspondent said.
March 5, 1946

Editor's Note

The increasingly anti-Soviet policy of President Truman and Secretary of State Byrnes found its most outspoken critic within the administration itself: Secretary of Commerce Henry A. Wallace.

Wallace was more than a run-of-the-mill Cabinet secretary. A visionary, sometimes a mystic, Wallace had served as vice president

Secretary of Commerce Henry Wallace waves to Madison Square Garden crowd Sept. 12, 1946, just before delivering an address in which he advocated an independent American foreign policy. The speech was delivered at a meeting sponsored by the National Citizens Political Action Committee and the Independent Citizens Committee of the Arts, Sciences and Professions.

from 1941 until 1945, and many in the American left viewed him as the rightful heir of Franklin D. Roosevelt. A revolt of conservative and moderate Democrats had forced FDR to drop him as his running mate in 1944 and to replace him with Truman.

WALLACE ATTACKS "GET TOUGH WITH RUSSIA" POLICY

NEW YORK, SEPT. 12 (AP)—Henry A. Wallace, secretary of commerce, said tonight "British imperialistic policy" in the Near East, together with "Soviet retaliation," would lead the United States to war "unless this country formulates a clearly defined and realistic foreign policy of its own."

"To prevent war and insure our survival in a stable world, it is essential that we look abroad through our own American eyes and not through the eyes of either the British Foreign Office or a pro-British or anti-Russian press."

In dealing with the Soviet Union, Wallace said this nation was reckoning with a force which cannot be handled successfully by a "get tough with Russia" policy.

"The tougher we get, the tougher the Russians will get," he predicted.

Wallace asserted that the United States wants peace with Russia, but "we want to be met halfway."

On our part, he declared, we should recognize that we have no more business in the political affairs of Eastern Europe than Russia has in the political affairs of Latin America, Western Europe and the United States.

"We may not like what Russia does in Eastern Europe," the secretary said. "Her type of land reform, industrial expropriation, and suppression of basic liberties offends the great majority of the people of the United States.

"But whether we like it or not the Russians will try to socialize their sphere of influence just as we try to democratize our sphere of influence."
Sept. 12, 1946

WASHINGTON, SEPT. 12 (AP)—President Truman announced today his full approval of Secretary Henry A. Wallace's foreign-policy speech in New York and declared it involved no conflict with Secretary of State Byrnes, but diplomatic authorities persisted on speculation that the speech might have far-reaching effects.

Despite the president's statements, authorities at the State Department and elsewhere continued to study the speech for possible basic differences between Wallace and Byrnes over United States policy toward Russia.

The focal point of diplomatic interest was Wallace's call for frank recognition of the existence of Russian and American "spheres of influence" and the working out of an agreement with Russia on that basis.

While the Wallace speech contained no direct criticism of American foreign policy as developed by Secretary Byrnes and the State Department,

some of those familiar with the commerce secretary's purpose in writing the speech let it be known that any such implications seen in the speech would not be considered misleading.

When advance copies reached some high officials in the State Department today, initial reactions indicated astonishment, although there was no formal or public comment.

In the speech, Wallace disclosed that the president had read it. Mr. Truman was asked at his news conference whether he approved it in part or in whole and he said he approved the whole speech. As to whether the Wallace proposals involved any departure from policies of Secretary of State Byrnes, the president said emphatically the Wallace and Byrnes policies were exactly in line.

The main points on which diplomats professed to see a divergence between Wallace's words and Byrnes's recent course are these:

1. Wallace said Americans "should recognize that we have no more business in the political affairs of Eastern Europe than Russia has in the political affairs of Latin America, Western Europe and the United States."

He referred to "their sphere of influence" and "our sphere of influence," saying that Russia may eventually socialize about one-third of the world and the United States may democratize much of the remainder and what is most needed now is a peace agreement between the two.

On May 20, when he returned from one of the Paris foreign ministers' conferences, Byrnes declared in a speech that the United States is opposed "to the formation of exclusive political and economic blocs." He said that "if we fail to cooperate in a peace which is indivisible we may again find that we will have to cooperate in a war which is worldwide."

2. Wallace said what is needed now to get Russian cooperation is to make Russia understand "that our primary objective is neither saving the British Empire nor purchasing oil in the Near East with the lives of American soldiers." He referred to Britain's "imperialistic policy" in the Near East and "Russian retaliation" as certain to lead to war in the absence of any clearly defined and strictly American policy.

At the present Paris conference, while Byrnes

has consistently disavowed any Anglo-American bloc, United States and British policies have been parallel on one issue after another. In the Near East particularly, the United States and Britain stand shoulder to shoulder in backing Turkish opposition to Russian proposals for the Dardanelles.

3. Wallace denounced American use of any "get tough with Russia" policy, saying that "the tougher we get, the tougher the Russians will get."

Almost a year ago, after the failure of the London conference of foreign ministers to make progress on peace treaties, Byrnes began the development of what is known at the State Department as a policy of refusing to compromise on basic American principles or interests with the Russians. This has become widely known as a "tough policy," although American officials do not like that term. Whether it is this policy that Wallace had in mind, he did not say.
Sept. 12, 1946

TRUMAN FIRES WALLACE

WASHINGTON, SEPT. 20 (AP)—President Truman today dismissed Secretary of Commerce Wallace for criticizing administration foreign policy and Wallace quickly took to the air with a plea for a popular crusade for world peace.

Mr. Truman, in ousting Wallace, gave an all-out endorsement to Secretary of State Byrnes and forbade all officials in the executive branch of the federal government to take public issue with the established foreign policy.

Private citizen Wallace then went on the radio tonight with a warning that the policy is blind to "basic realities" which threaten "an atomic war." He served notice that he will "carry on the fight" and called on fellow citizens to support it "as a holy duty."

Mr. Truman determined upon his sensational ouster of his disagreeing Cabinet officer after plain indications from Paris, where Byrnes is battling in the peace conference, that a White House settlement of two days ago was not good enough. It provided for Wallace to stay in office but keep quiet temporarily.

After mulling on it overnight, the chief executive seized his telephone this morning less than half an hour before he was to receive reporters in a news conference and told the secretary of commerce he was out.

Then he announced his decision, and with it he wrote clear-cut assurances of "my full endorsement" for the embattled Byrnes. He wrote, too, that Wallace's views are not those of the administration, and that "no change in our foreign policy is contemplated."

Relieved of his gag, Wallace issued a statement to the Commerce Department employees explaining that he had resigned "in order that I may be free as a private citizen to continue to fight for world peace."

He followed this up with his nationwide broadcast tonight. He spoke only briefly, saying he would not wish to interfere with the Paris negotiations, but he declared that no policy can succeed unless the people "are given all the facts."

In addition to his fresh warning of war and criticism of present policy, he explained that his Madison Square Garden speech in New York last week, which touched off the uproar, had been misunderstood.

His statement then that the United States has no more business in the political affairs of Eastern Europe than Russia has in American affairs was widely interpreted as advocating two world spheres of influence.

It flashed to Paris, giving Byrnes and his delegation their reassurance. Later they got official confirmation through diplomatic channels. There was no comment there immediately.

It travelled on the brokers' tickers. The stock market rallied from yesterday's lows as traders rushed to buy instead of sell. Shares rose $1 to $8 a share after the announcement.

It was seized upon by politicians, eager to assay its meaning in terms of the November congressional elections and even the 1948 presidential outlook. Wallace commands loyal support from one wing of the Democratic Party. Some thought the party weakened by the open Truman-Wallace split, some thought it strengthened with Wallace removed from official status.

It reached Wallace in his office at the Commerce Department a block from the White House, going over mail in response to his Thursday speech, and caught his personal staff completely by surprise.

Henry A. Wallace strides away from the Department of Commerce Building in Washington, Sept. 20, 1946, following his forced resignation as secretary of the department. President Truman asked Wallace to quit the Cabinet because his views on foreign policy were at variance with those of the president and secretary of state.

They told reporters, as Wallace himself had done, that nothing was said about a resignation when the secretary met with Mr. Truman on Wednesday.

Undersecretary Alfred Schindler, now on the West Coast, will be in charge of the department temporarily.

Guessing over a possible new secretary centered on the names of Paul Porter, price administrator, and William L. Clayton, undersecretary of state in charge of international trade. Porter had a conference with Mr. Truman later and merely laughed, without replying, when asked whether he was offered the post.

Another name mentioned was that of Eric Johnston, former head of the U.S. Chamber of Commerce, now president of the Motion Picture Association of America.

At the White House, however, it was said that Mr. Truman has not had much time to consider a successor for Wallace and certainly no selection has been made.

The president's decision to remove Wallace was made "overnight," a White House authority related. Mr. Truman telephoned the secretary at 10:05 a.m. and broke the news to him. The presidential news conference, set for 10:30, was held up 20 minutes so the announcement could be mimeographed.
Sept. 20, 1946

AN INTERVIEW WITH STALIN
By Eddy Gilmore

MOSCOW, MARCH 22 (AP)—Premier Stalin expressed today his conviction that neither the nations of the world nor their armies were seeking another war, and affirmed his confidence in the United Nations Organization as "a serious instrument" for preserving peace.

He declared that the nations "desire peace and are endeavoring to secure peace," but that "certain political groups" had spread fear through the world by a propaganda campaign that was "sowing seeds of discord and uncertainty."

The Russian leader made his assertions in a written reply to three questions put to him by The Associated Press last Tuesday. His reply was dated today.

(Stalin's forthright statements immediately produced worldwide reaction, and were hailed generally with gratification and hope. U.S. congressmen quoted it as indicating greater success for the United Nations Organization, and as a renunciation of any militaristic ambitions by Russia. Observers in London said the interview had eased tension.)

As a solution to the "current fear of war," Stalin urged a worldwide counter-propaganda campaign "to expose the warmongers without loss of time and give them no opportunity of abusing the freedom of speech against the interests of peace."

(Stalin did not identify the "warmongers" in his letter, but on March 13 *Pravda* published an inter-

In March 1946, Soviet leader Josef Stalin expressed support for the new United Nations Organization, saying that it would play a "positive role in guaranteeing universal peace and security."

view quoting him as calling Winston Churchill a "warmonger" and accusing Churchill of trying to inflame a war against Russia.)

He said he attached "great importance" to the United Nations Organization, and added that "it will unquestionably play a great and positive role in guaranteeing universal peace and security" if it succeeds in preserving the principles of "equality of states."

March 22, 1946

Editor's Note

Ed ("Eddy") Gilmore, AP Moscow bureau chief, won the Pulitzer Prize in 1947 for his stories on Russia and especially the interview with Stalin.

BYRNES RESIGNS

WASHINGTON, JAN. 7 (AP)—James F. Byrnes resigned tonight as secretary of state and President Truman chose as his successor the man who guided America's military fortunes in the war— Gen. George C. Marshall.

Byrnes declared the doctors had warned him he must "slow down" and that he couldn't slow down in the job of secretary of state.

Marshall, Army chief of staff in the war, is presently ending a presidential mission to China.

The announcement of the selection to the Cabinet came at almost the exact hour, 7:05 p.m., Eastern Standard Time, that Marshall left for home by plane from Nanking.

The Pennsylvania-born, Virginia-educated Marshall takes over the job of helping make peace secure at a time when Republicans have taken over Congress. In the Army tradition, he has shown no political connections.

This was not believed to be the reason for the change, however. The Senate, which rules heavily on foreign relations, already had shown a disposition to follow Byrnes' policies.

Congressional leaders were swift to heap praise on both men when the news reached Capitol Hill. Republicans and Democrats alike joined in.

The change in the top diplomatic post was a surprise. It had been known that Byrnes had grown tired some months ago, but the 67-year-old South Carolinian looked to be in very good health lately.

For Byrnes, the secretaryship was the last in a string of distinguished posts. He had served as a senator, as a Supreme Court justice and as "assistant president" to Franklin D. Roosevelt in the role of war mobilizer.

With Senate confirmation of Marshall—and no one doubted that it was sure—the change means that Marshall instead of Byrnes stands next in line for the presidency in the next two years. There is no vice president now and the secretary of state heads the line of succession under law.

Marshall turned 66 last Dec. 31, having retired earlier as chief of staff. Hailed as one of America's military geniuses, the five-star general was President Truman's pick to try to unsnarl the affairs of unhappy China.

The nation's new secretary of state, Gen. George Marshall, steps from his plane at Hickam Field, Hawaii, where he stopped en route to Washington from China. He was met by Mrs. Marshall, who had been in the islands.

In a report today, Marshall said that China won't be saved until extremists of the right and left give way in the government to middle-of-the-roaders.

Now, he will transfer his talents to the world. Foremost among the jobs he faces is getting along with the Russians with anything like the success he did during the war.

Incidentally, a longtime military associate of Marshall, W. Bedell Smith, is now ambassador to Russia. In the early part of the war, Smith was secretary of the Army general staff under Marshall. In September 1942, he became chief of staff to Gen. Dwight D. Eisenhower.

The White House made public an exchange of telegrams in which the president accepted "with great reluctance and heartfelt regret" Byrnes' resignation, to become effective Jan. 10.

Marshall, who has been Mr. Truman's special envoy to China, is now en route to Washington from Nanking. He will stop several days in Hawaii en route to Washington.

The correspondence disclosed that Byrnes first sought to resign on April 16 in a letter in which he told the president that he was advised after a medical examination that he must "slow down." He wanted that resignation to become effective last July 1.

Again on Dec. 19, Byrnes wrote the president that he had intended to leave his post July 1, hoping that the peace conference would have concluded its deliberations at that time.

"When it became obvious that it was too optimistic as to the completion of the work upon the five treaties with the Axis satellite states, I told you I would continue until they were finally agreed upon," Byrnes wrote.

"Now that we have reached complete agreement and the treaties are scheduled to be signed February 10 I should like to be relieved." He ended by saying that "no man serving as secretary of state could ask or receive greater support and encouragement than you have given me."

Disclosure of the resignation and its acceptance by the president came a few hours after Byrnes paid an unscheduled call upon Mr. Truman.

The president, in accepting the resignation, wrote:

"I realize full well how arduous and complex have been the problems which have fallen to you since you took office in July 1945."

He complimented the South Carolinian, a former senator and Supreme Court justice, on his work, particularly his "rare tact and judgment and—when necessary—firmness and tenacity of purpose."

"Yours has been a steadying hand as you have met the difficult problems which have arisen in such unvarying succession," the president continued.

"For all that you did during the war, and in making of the peace, you have earned the thanks of the nation. So I say: Well done, in the hope that we can continue to call upon you for the counsel which you can give out of so rich and varied an experience."

The announcement of the resignation of the top member of the President's Cabinet, first in line of succession in the event of a presidential vacancy, came rather dramatically at the White House.

Reporters had been told that "the lid" was on shortly after 5 o'clock.

This meant no further news was expected from the White House.

Later such reporters as were still around were told to wait, that there might be something coming.

Only four newsmen were on hand when presidential press secretary Charles G. Ross summoned them to his office.

Slowly he began his announcement. In about three minutes all of the reporters were rushing for their telephones.

The letters explained that while Byrnes' resignation is scheduled for Jan. 10, Mr. Byrnes will remain on the job until Gen. Marshall has been nominated and confirmed by the Senate.

Marshall's first experience in diplomatic service was when the president sent him to China as a special envoy to help reconcile differences among the factions in that republic. That appointment came shortly after Marshall retired as War Department chief of staff.

He was sent to China to fill a gap created by the sudden resignation of Ambassador Patrick Hurley, who quit with a blast at some officials of the State Department.

In his original letter of April 16, Byrnes wrote the president that he thought when he retired as war mobilization director he had earned the right "to take a rest."

However, he said, shortly after the death of former President Roosevelt, "because of our intimate friendship I offered my services to you."

As secretary of state he said he had found it necessary to work long hours six and at times seven days a week.

Last April, he said, he was advised after a medical examination that he would have to slow down—and he could not slow down and hold his office. He therefore tendered his resignation to take effect July 1. He said he selected that date because of the then forthcoming Council of Foreign Ministers meeting in Paris and the subsequent peace conference there.

At that time Byrnes thought it would be possible to make the change last July.

In this April 16 letter, Byrnes asserted:

"Some weeks ago several newspapers published a story that I had resigned and you had selected my successor. You stated it was untrue. It certainly was untrue because we had never discussed the subject.

"I presume these newspapers now will state that their story was true, but I cannot be deterred from doing what I believe to be right simply because it may give the appearance of truth to that which is false."

He referred to "whole-hearted support" from the president and said "it is rather remarkable that we have never failed to agree as to foreign policies."

The Dec. 19 letter takes up the story. It follows in full:

"Dear Mr. President:

"On April 16 I submitted to you my resignation to take effect July first. I hoped by that date the peace conference would have concluded its deliberations and the work upon the five treaties with the satellite states would be completed.

"When it became obvious that was too optimistic as to the completion of the work upon the treaties, I told you I would continue until they were finally agreed upon.

"Now that we have reached complete agreement and the treaties are scheduled to be signed February 10 I should like to be relieved.

"I think it important that the change should be made at this time. We have scheduled for March 10 the meeting at Moscow when work will be started upon the German treaty and the Austrian peace settlement. That work will continue for many months and the secretary who undertakes the task should be in office sufficiently far in advance of the conference to familiarize himself with the problems.

Gen. George C. Marshall (left), the new secretary of state, chats with his predecessor, James Byrnes, at White House oath-taking ceremony, Jan. 21, 1947.

"Therefore, I ask that any resignation become effective January 10 or as soon thereafter as my successor is appointed and qualified. I fix that date because the Senate will then be in session and the nomination of my successor can be sent to the Senate simultaneously with the announcement of my resignation.

"I repeat what I said in my letter last April, that no man serving as secretary of state could ask or receive greater support and encouragement than you have given me.

"Sincerely yours,

"James F. Byrnes."

Administration sources said there had been an understanding for days between the president and his secretary of state that he would be permitted to retire in view of his health and the strenuous work he has undergone.

It was during their talk at the White House this afternoon that they decided to release the announcement of the resignation.

Jan. 7, 1947

The Truman Doctrine

As the atmosphere of wartime cooperation evaporated, Americans searched for a strategy to counter Soviet aggression and intransigence.

After the war ended, the British aided the Greek government in fending off Communist guerrillas widely believed to be receiving military support from Moscow. However, in February 1947, while facing financial problems tied to the disintegration of its empire, Great Britain announced plans to withdraw from Greece. U.S. officials feared that Greece and perhaps Turkey would fall under Soviet control or influence.

President Truman met with military and congressional leaders, and on March 12 announced what became known as the Truman Doctrine. It was to play a large role in the emerging Cold War between communism and capitalism, and to become a basis for the U.S. policy of containing communism around the world.

TRUMAN: HELP GREECE & TURKEY

By Alex H. Singleton

WASHINGTON, MARCH 12 (AP)—In a historic turning point of American foreign policy, President Truman called on the nation today to devote money, materials and military skill to halt the world march of communism.

Addressing a joint session of Congress, the president specifically requested $400 million to aid Greece and Turkey, hard-pressed Mediterranean bulwarks against the totalitarian tide.

A great, heart-searching debate began immediately on Capitol Hill. Some Congress members expressed fear of eventual war with Russia, others spoke sadly of the blow to attempts at domestic economy.

But from influential Sen. Vandenberg (R–Mich.), presiding officer of the Senate and chairman of its Foreign Relations Committee, came this statement:

"We cannot fail to back up the president at such an hour—even though many critical details remain to be settled in consultation with Congress."

Word that budget plans had been "knocked askew" by the president's program came from Sen. Bridges (R–N.H.), chairman of the Senate Appropriations Committee. He said the new $400 million request would have to be taken into consideration by legislators trying to cut Mr. Truman's $37.5 billion budget for the fiscal year beginning July 1.

The development threw a further hurdle in the path of the drive, being pushed by some Republicans, for a 20 percent cut in income taxes.

Mr. Truman, in his speech, served notice that he would not hesitate to ask for more than $400 million if necessary "to help free peoples to maintain their free institutions and their national integrity against aggressive movements that seek to impose upon them totalitarian regimes."

Before his taut-faced, tense and anxious audience, he laid a request for:

1. Permission to spend $400 million in Greece and Turkey for the period ending June 30, 1948.

2. The right to send civilian personnel and military men to the two countries to assist in reconstruction and to supervise use of the aid.

3. Legislation giving the administration scope in making the "speediest and most effective use" of the funds in terms of "needed commodities, supplies and equipment."

4. Authority to provide for the instruction and training of "selected" Greek and Turkish personnel. This could mean military training in the United States such as was provided during the war for British aviators.

March 12, 1947

WALLACE ATTACKS TRUMAN DOCTRINE

NEW YORK, MARCH 13 (AP)—Henry A. Wallace said tonight President Truman's proposed loans to Greece and Turkey "will bring the world nearer to war."

Insisting in a radio address that "it is not a Greek crisis that we face, it is an American crisis," the former vice president and Cabinet officer asserted:

"As one American citizen I say: No loan to

President Truman speaks before members of Congress in a joint session in Washington, March 12, 1947, urging provision of money, military advice and materials to Greece and Turkey, and backing on a global foreign policy to restrict Communist aggression.

undemocratic and well-fed Turkey. No loan to Greece until a representative Greek government is formed and can assure America that our funds will be used for the welfare of the Greek people."

Wallace said he believed the program outlined yesterday by the president would worsen seriously American relations with the Soviet Union, and he declared both the present Greek and Turkish governments were undemocratic.

"How can we wage a war of nerves against Russia and expect her to take in good faith our proposals to the United Nations on atomic energy?" he asked.

"When President Truman proclaims the worldwide conflict between East and West, he is telling the Soviet leaders that we are preparing for eventual war.

"They will reply by measures to strengthen their position in the event of war. Then the task of keeping the world at peace will pass beyond the power of the common people everywhere who want peace."
March 13, 1947

SENATE OKS DOCTRINE

WASHINGTON, APRIL 22 (AP)—The Senate stamped approval, 67 to 23, today on a momentous new departure in U.S. foreign policy by voting a $400,000,000 fund to stiffen Greece and Turkey against communism.

The bill, which provides financial and limited military assistance to these two strategic nations, now goes to the House, where the Foreign Affairs Committee has approved a similar measure.

Led by Sen. Arthur Vandenberg (R-Mich.), the GOP-controlled Senate bowled over vocal but numerically weak opposition to the new policy laid down by President Truman in a March 12 address to Congress.

Through five hours of torrid debate before voting began on amendments late in the afternoon, opponents assailed the Truman plan as one which would "destroy" the United Nations, invite retaliation by Russia and roll up tremendous expenditures which might bankrupt this nation.

Replying, Vandenberg told his colleagues that if Congress fails to act "aggression gets the green light and the rest of the world, including America, gets the red light."

April 22, 1947

WASHINGTON, APRIL 22 (AP)—Sen. Arthur Vandenberg (R–Mich.) described as "inflammable" today statements that President Truman's program to bulwark Greece and Turkey against communism is "a declaration of war on Russia."

The chairman of the Senate Foreign Relations Committee took the floor as the hour for a vote on the $400,000,000 Greek-Turkish assistance measure approached.

Vandenberg said he arose to "categorically repudiate" the statement he said had been repeated by Sen. Edwin C. Johnson (D–Colo.) that the president's policy will lead to war with the Soviets.

"That statement, which has been made repeatedly by the senator from Colorado, is an invitation to the precise disaster that this bill seeks to prevent," Vandenberg said, adding:

"That is an inflammable statement and it is a grave error. I deny there is any such purpose in the heart of any senator who today supports the president of the United States."

Johnson, who had asserted previously that the president's program involves American "aggression in the Middle East," sat silently nearby as Vandenberg continued. He had spoken at length earlier.

Great Britain and the United States appear to be "determined at any cost, including war, to keep Russia out of the Dardanelles," the Colorado senator said.

"Turkey now has consummated a military alliance with the greatest military power on earth— the United States of America," he added.

Johnson made it clear he had no hope of defeating President Truman's proposal to extend $400,000,000 of financial and limited military aid to the Greeks and Turks. He said:

"The Congress of the United States is about ready to underwrite this alliance. Today the Senate will take this fateful step."

Sen. Williams (R–Del.), another opponent, told the Senate the president's plan involves "a new American political doctrine for the world, the cost of which could reach untold billions and the deployment of American manhood in the front-line trenches of the global ramparts."

The Delaware senator said he can't see why the United States should be asked to assume Great Britain's "responsibility in the rehabilitation of the world and preserve her empire" at a time the British are balancing their budget for the first time in 10 years and reducing taxes.

"Why should the United States continue to send money, materials and food to aid Communist Russia and her satellites and at the same time send money, materials, food and men to fight communism in Greece and Turkey?" he demanded.

Sen. Kenneth McKellar (D. Tenn.) told his colleagues the United States can't afford financially "to enter upon a career of interfering in the affairs of other nations."

McKellar said he believes President Truman is "making a great mistake" in keeping Secretary of State George Marshall at the Moscow Conference to work under "the most humiliating and mortifying circumstances."

"I sincerely hope he will soon recall him and our

representatives with him," said McKellar. "I am sorry they were ever sent there."

The new venture in foreign policy approached its first congressional showdown amid indications that it would receive far less emphatic backing than the last major decision in that field—the Senate's 89-to-2 ratification of the United Nations Charter on July 28, 1945.

A score, more or less, of dissenters apparently stood ready to cast their votes against the first segment of the developing program of aiding "free peoples."

Nearly three times that number of senators have lined up to pass the bill and send it to the House. Favorable action there also seems assured later.

This would put into almost immediate effect, through a proposed $100,000,000 advance, a program Secretary of State Marshall called "indispensable" in a message from Moscow yesterday to Chairman Vandenberg (R–Mich.) of the Foreign Relations Committee.

As it went to a final Senate vote, the bill carried a provision inserted by Vandenberg and Sen. Tom Connally (D–Texas) under which the United Nations could order the American assistance program halted any time seven of the 11 Security Council members or two-thirds of those voting in the General Assembly find that the United Nations is acting to supplant it.
April 22, 1947

GREECE HOLDS ON

WASHINGTON, NOV. 28 (AP)—President Truman reported today that the Greek government, with American military help, has "substantially eliminated" the Communist guerrilla threat in Greece.

The president warned in a report for Congress, however, that "persistent vigilance and patience" will be required to prevent the Communist-led rebels from again threatening to overthrow the Greek government.

The report said most of the Communist revolutionaries have now fled into Albania, Bulgaria and Yugoslavia, abandoning most of their artillery and other weapons and equipment.

The report disclosed that in order to crush the Communist rebellion, the United States supplied a total of $472,461,000 in military and economic aid. Of this total $345,335,000 went for military supplies.
Nov. 28, 1947

The Marshall Plan

The Truman Doctrine focused on the military challenge of communism. But what of that movement's appeal to peoples whose economies had been shattered by World War II?

ACHESON PROPOSES AID FOR RECOVERY

CLEVELAND, MISS., MAY 8 (AP)—Germany and Japan were called the "great workshops" of Europe and Asia today by Undersecretary of State Dean Acheson, who urged that their reconstruction be speeded.

Acheson told the Delta Council that "the ultimate recovery of the two continents" largely depends upon such a policy and that:

"We are going to have to concentrate our emergency assistance in areas where it will be most effective in building world political and economic stability, in promoting human freedom and democratic institutions, in fostering liberal trading policies, and in strengthening the authority of the United Nations."

The undersecretary of state spoke at the annual meeting of the council, an organization of agricultural and business men, on "what the facts of international life mean for the United States" and its foreign policy.

He proposed that this country take a large volume of imports to promote trade and world recovery and that it undertake further emergency financing of foreign purchases.

Acting Secretary of State Dean Acheson (right) leans over table as he appears before Senate Foreign Relations Committee in Washington, D.C., March 24, 1947, to testify on details of proposed U.S. aid to foreign nations. He said that in addition to helping Greece and Turkey, the United States should aid Korea to block Russian influence there. Listening are, left to right: Senators Arthur Vandenberg (R-Mich); Tom Connally (D-Texas); Elbert Thomas (D-Utah); and Carl A. Hatch (D-N.M.).

He said a further extension by Congress of "certain executive powers" would be required to carry out the proposals.
March 8, 1947

MARSHALL OFFERS EUROPE A PLAN

CAMBRIDGE, MASS., JUNE 5 (AP)—Secretary of State Marshall called today upon the countries of Europe to take the "initiative" in drafting a reconstruction program to put that continent on its feet economically and promised American assistance "so far as it may be practical."

He coupled this pledge with a warning that the United States would oppose anyone seeking to profit by perpetuating "human misery"— whether they be governments or political parties.

Speaking before the Harvard alumni after that university awarded him an honorary doctorate of laws, Marshall mentioned no foreign country by name as he gave a broad outline of America's long-range foreign policy.

Asserting a "very serious situation is rapidly developing" in Europe which "bodes no good for the world," the secretary said:

"The rehabilitation of the economic structure of Europe quite evidently will require a much longer time and greater effort than had been foreseen."

Marshall said it was "logical that the United States should do whatever it is able to do to assist in the return of normal economic health in the world, without which there can be no political stability and no assured peace."

But, he declared, "it is already evident that, before the United States government can proceed much further in its efforts to alleviate the situation, there must be some agreement among the countries of Europe as to the requirements of the situations and the part those countries themselves will take."

The secretary did not specify just how much money the American government intends to make available, but he did say:

"The truth of the matter is that Europe's requirements for the next three or four years of foreign food and other essential products—principally from America—are so much greater than her present ability to pay that she must have substantial additional help, or face economic, social and political deterioration of a very grave nature."

Marshall said the remedy lies in "breaking the vicious circle and restoring the confidence of the European people in the economic future of their own countries and of Europe as a whole."

American assistance in the future, he said, "should provide a cure rather than a mere palliative."

June 5, 1947

SOVIETS REFUSE MARSHALL PLAN AID

PARIS, JULY 2 (AP)—The three-power foreign ministers' conference on the Marshall proposal ended in failure today when the Russians refused to agree to join in a cooperative international effort for European economic recovery.

The French government immediately announced that France and Great Britain would pursue a study of the Marshall aid-to-Europe program along with any countries which wish to join them.

Before the conference was terminated, Soviet Foreign Minister V.M. Molotov declared that British-French proposals relating to Secretary of State Marshall's suggestions would lead to a division of Europe. He also predicted that the proposals would "lead to no good results."

The British-French suggestions had dealt with organizing the Continent for mutual self-help with financial aid from the United States, as suggested by Secretary Marshall in a speech at Harvard University June 5.

An official British informant predicted earlier that Great Britain and France soon would invite other European countries to participate in a program of overall economic planning to help restore the continent's war-shattered economy.

A French informant said British Foreign Secretary Ernest Bevin declared in a heated outburst that Molotov's statement was "a travesty of facts." The informant quoted Bevin as continuing:

"I don't know if he (Molotov) is repeating intentionally a false interpretation of things in the hope that people will finish by believing this erroneous interpretation."

The French-British plan would have set up a steering committee for Europe. Molotov assailed the plan as invading the sovereignty of European states.

Molotov's statement, issued by a Soviet embassy official, said the plan called for a new organization "standing over and above the countries of Europe and interfering in their internal affairs down to determining the line of development to be followed by the main branches of industry in those countries."

Asserting that American control would call the tune, he continued: "It is now suggested that the possibility of American aid being received by this or that country involves an obedient attitude on its part vis-à-vis the above-mentioned organization and its steering committee.

"Where is this likely to lead?"

Molotov left the meeting about five minutes

before British Foreign Secretary Bevin. French Foreign Minister Bidault accompanied him to the door of the Foreign Ministry, shook hands, and went back upstairs to confer with Bevin.
July 2, 1947

EUROPE SUBMITS A REQUEST

PARIS, SEPT. 22 (AP)—Sixteen nations of Western Europe, warning of possible economic "catastrophe" and revolution, asked America today for $19,300,000,000 to carry them through the next four years.

Representatives of the 16 countries, which are looped like a giant sickle geographically around western Russia and her associates, formally signed a report of their needs in accord with a request made by Gen. George C. Marshall, Secretary of State, in a speech at Harvard University on June 5.

Ernest Bevin, British foreign secretary, who flew from London for the signing of the report in the clock tower of the Grand Palais overlooking the Seine, said:

"Well, here is our report. It is now for the American people and the American Congress to decide whether this program, undertaken at Mr. Marshall's initiation, should be fulfilled and whether Europe can by this means contribute to the peace and prosperity of the world."

Bevin declared that immediate aid was necessary in order to remove the threat of a crisis for which "there is no precedent in history for judging what shape it may take."

Russia and the states within her sphere of influence have not participated in drawing up the report. Bevin expressed regret at their absence today and added:

"For the future, as in the past, the door remains wide open to all those of good will who will want to contribute to the healthy life of Europe and thereby end the misery which war has left behind."

He said it was "not an appeal to charity," but a "legitimate request for assistance to tide over the period of recovery and to create in turn a situation in which Europe can make its contribution to the postwar world."

V.M. Molotov photographed at the round table in the Beauvais salon at the Quai D'Orsay for the opening of the three-power foreign ministers conference on the Marshall Plan held in Paris June 27, 1947.

In emphasizing the need for immediate aid he said:

"In a matter of weeks, not to say months, we shall be facing a unique situation and immediate steps are necessary." By the "unique situation" he meant the draining away of dollar exchange.

Other statesmen joined in noting the urgency of the appeal, and Carlo Sforza, Italian foreign minister, said bluntly that if his people do not get bread within two or three months there will be "a revolution in Italy."

The total call on America came to $19,300,000,000, and a spokesman said the United States was expected to guarantee this figure.

Shortly before the final signing of the report began, Robert Margolin, chairman of the confer-

American Ambassador to France Jefferson Caffery speaks during ceremonies at Bordeaux, marking the arrival of the first boat bringing aid to France under the Marshall Plan. The ship—the John H. Quick—*carried 8,800 tons of wheat.*

ence coordinating committee, said that $19,300,000,000 was the basic sum Europe would need from America for its recovery.

If the nations manage to accumulate one or two billions of surplus foreign exchange, they might reduce the demand on America, he said. But it might be wise to let the countries keep the money thus accumulated so they would have something to keep them going beyond 1951, when the program would end, Margolin added.

Of the $22,440,000,000 laid out as the lump-sum request for materials that had to be bought with American money, $5,810,000,000 would be purchased from the United States and $5,970,000,000 from other American countries. This "deficit" in trade balance with the Americas would be matched by an additional deficit of $660,000,000 from dependent territories of European countries.

But the committee left no doubt in its report and press conference explanation that, regardless of where the goods came from, the money to make movement of goods possible would have to come from the United States.

The abstract of the report said that by 1951 the 16 European nations hoped to achieve these goals:

1. Restoration of prewar bread grain and other production.

2. Increase of coal output to 584,000,000 tons, 145,000,000 above the 1947 level and 30,000,000 tons above the 1938 level.

3. Expansion of electricity output by nearly 70,000,000,000 kwh, or 40 percent above 1947 and a growth of generating capacity by 25,000,000 kwh, or two-thirds above prewar.

4. Development of oil refining capacity in terms of crude oil throughout by 17,000,000 tons to two and a half times the prewar level.

5. Increase of crude steel production by 80 percent above 1947 to a level of 55,000,000 tons or 10,000,000 tons (20 percent) above 1938.

6. Expansion of inland transport facilities to carry a 25 percent greater load in 1951 than in 1938.

7. Restoration of prewar merchant fleets of the participating countries by 1951.

8. Supply from European production of most of the capital equipment needed for those expansions.

The British Embassy said the document would be flown to Washington possibly late tonight.
Sept. 22, 1947

COMINTERN DENOUNCES MARSHALL PLAN AS IMPERIALISM

MOSCOW, OCT. 5 (AP)—A new Communist international organization was announced today to fight the Marshall Plan and "United States imperialism."

Communist leaders of nine countries formed the organization. It is the first such grouping to which the Russians have publicly pledged support since they declared the Comintern dead in 1943.

It is aimed at uniting the chief Communist strength in Europe.

Pravda, the official Communist newspaper here, as well as Communist organs in other European capitals, said Communist leaders from the nine countries met "somewhere in Poland" last month, appraised the world as split into Russian and American orbits, and ordered an "information bureau" set up to coordinate activities.

The nine countries whose Communist foreign ministers gathered were Russia, France, Italy, Czechoslovakia, Poland, Romania, Bulgaria, Yugoslavia and Hungary.

In effect, the Communists served notice of their intention to wreck, if possible, the Marshall Plan for European aid as well as the Truman doctrine on totalitarianism, and any form of what they called United States imperialism.

Pravda said a joint resolution adopted at the conference pictured the world as split into camps led by the Soviet Union and the United States. It hit out against what was called United States "expansionism" and "imperialist lackeys."

It placed in the latter category such European leaders as Prime Minister Clement Attlee of Britain, Premier Paul Ramadier and Socialist leader Leon Blum of France and Dr. Kurt Schumacher, leader of the Social Democratic Party in Germany.

They were assailed as "traitors to the working class."

The chief danger for the working class, said the resolution, was undervaluing its own strength and overestimating the strength of the "imperialist" camp. It scoffed at the idea.
Oct. 5, 1947

TRUMAN SEEKS MARSHALL PLAN

WASHINGTON, DEC. 19 (AP)—President Truman asked a divided Congress today to vote $17,000,000,000 in the next four and a quarter years for the building of a Europe strong enough to resist "totalitarian aggression" and preserve "the civilization in which the American way of life is rooted."

This greatest relief and rehabilitation project in world history, calling for the largest peacetime expenditure ever asked of Congress, was detailed by Mr. Truman six months after Secretary of State Marshall first proposed it and three months after 16 European countries pledged their combined efforts to make it work.

First congressional comment on the "Marshall Plan" seemed to foreshadow nationwide controversy over details of the program, if not over the basic proposals, between now and Jan. 6 when Congress reassembles for its regular session.

Sen. Robert A. Taft (R-Ohio), chairman of the Senate Republican Policy Committee, came out flatly against pledging aid for as long a period as the president asked, and said assistance should be authorized on a year-to-year basis.

Sen. Alben Barkley (D-Ky.), minority leader, described Mr. Truman's figure as "conservative," however, and said he hoped that "after giving it serious consideration Congress will adopt the plan without undue delay and without material change."

In a 9,000-word message read separately to each house, Mr. Truman warned that "the Communists" will try to sabotage the recovery of the 16 countries, along with Western Germany, for which he asked aid.

"If Europe fails to recover," the president said, "the peoples of these countries might be driven to the philosophy of despair—the philosophy which contends that their basic wants can be met only by the surrender of their basic rights to totalitarian control.

"Such a turn of events would constitute a shattering blow to peace and stability in the world.

"It might well compel us to modify our own economic system and to forego, for the sake of our own security, the enjoyment of many of our freedoms and privileges."

The president asked Congress to authorize the $17,000,000,000 outlay—on top of more than $15,000,000,000 already devoted to foreign aid since the war ended—as "a major step in our nation's quest for a just and lasting peace."

With his message, Mr. Truman submitted a bill to create the entire program. It sets up a new, largely independent Economic Cooperation Administration which would, however, be responsible to the secretary of state in matters involving foreign policy.

The agency would be headed by a $20,000-a-year administrator, appointed by the president with Senate approval. He would be assisted by a $17,500-a-year deputy and a $25,000-a-year "roving ambassador" to supervise the program abroad.

Dec. 19, 1947

WASHINGTON, DEC. 19 (AP)—President Truman asked Congress today to commit America to a $17,000,000,000 European recovery program and a "bold" defense of free men against "totalitarian pressures."

Mr. Truman proposed that this vast sum be invested over four and a quarter years as "a major step in our nation's quest for a just and lasting peace."

As the first installment he asked for authority to spend $6,800,000,000 in the first 15 months. His message outlining the largest spending plan in the nation's peacetime history went to Congress in the closing hours of its special session. Mr. Truman urged swift action when the regular session starts in January, so the recovery program can begin April 1.

He predicted that the "determined opposition" already announced by European Communists will result in further incitements to strike "for the purpose of bringing chaos in the hope that it will pave the way for totalitarian control."

Even American security and the American way of life are at stake, the chief executive declared.

He asked Congress to tip its "grave and significant decision" in favor of the "Marshall Plan" to finish a job on which he said $15,000,000,000 already has been spent since the war ended. The decision, he said, will:

"Determine in large part whether the free nations of the world can look forward with hope to a peaceful and prosperous future as independent states, or whether they must live in poverty and in fear of selfish totalitarian aggression."

Along with his message, the president forwarded to Congress a bill to authorize the $17,000,000,000 expenditure and set up the machinery for carrying out the long-range recovery program. He sent along, too, a 241-page analysis prepared by experts from dozens of federal agencies.

To manage the program, Mr. Truman wants to appoint a $20,000-a-year administrator with broad powers. There would be a deputy drawing $17,500. And to run the European end of the show, there would be a roving ambassador making $25,000 a year.

In addition, the administrator would have as

his top assistants 10 men making up to $15,000 and 50 more making as much as $10,000.

However, instead of one-man control of the program, a special House Committee on Foreign Aid already has proposed an eight-man board, so the Truman proposal may be in for trouble on that score.

The president said that big as the cost will be, it is only 5 percent of the cost of the war and "less than 3 percent of our national income during the life of the program."

"As an investment toward the peace and security of the world and toward the realization of hope and confidence in a better way of life for the future," he declared, "this cost is small indeed."

Mr. Truman said he was recommending the program to Congress "in full confidence of its wisdom and necessity as a major step in our nation's quest for a just and lasting peace."

As a joint undertaking of the United States and a group of European countries, he said, the program "is proof that free men can effectively join together to defend their free institutions against totalitarian pressures, and to promote better standards of life for all their peoples."

As outlined in the documents sent to Congress, "much" of the aid would be in the form of gifts, some would be in loans.

There was no breakdown on how the $17,000,000,000 would be split among the various countries. There was no estimate, either, of how much the United States might get back.

Deals are supposed to be worked out for getting from the receiving countries supplies of scarce, strategic materials to store up in the United States. But for these, this country would pay cash.

Both in quantity and in cost to the United States the European nations would get less than they requested when they met in Paris last fall and drew up a list of needs. Already prices are up on the things they asked for.

Republicans in Congress, also concerned about higher prices, have been talking of slashing the Marshall Plan total with the idea that prices at home would come down if less money were spent to buy things for Europe.

Secretary of State Marshall figured last month that it would take $16,000,000,000 to $20,000,000,000 to hoist Europe back to her feet. As the program finally reached Congress it was only a little less.

The $17,000,000,000 is a round number.

Depending chiefly on whether prices go up or down, government experts estimate the actual cost to this country might dip as low as $15,111,000,000 or climb as high as $17,758,000,000, not including $822,000,000 for Western Germany which the administration is asking separately for 15 months.

Help from the International Bank, private financing, other Western Hemisphere nations and additional sources might up the total of outside assistance to between $20,034,000,000 and $22,685,000,000.

The most the 16 nations on the receiving end asked was $22,440,000,000 for an even four years.

These nations, which would guarantee to help themselves and each other in order to get a hand from Uncle Sam, are Austria, Belgium, Britain, Denmark, Eire, France, Italy, Greece, Iceland, Luxembourg, Netherlands, Norway, Portugal, Sweden, Switzerland and Turkey.

They took their cue from Marshall, who in a speech at Harvard University last June outlined his plan for throwing American dollars behind Europe's efforts to help herself.

Taking their cue from Moscow, Eastern European nations stayed out. But Mr. Truman left a way open for any of them—even Russia—to get into the game if they will accept the rules.

He said, too, that while the emphasis now is on helping Europe, the United States is not forgetting the importance of economic cooperation with her Latin American neighbors. And next year, he said, Congress will be handed a plan for economic help for China.

The president did not mention Russia or her satellites by name. But he let them know he doesn't like the way they have been acting.

He said the purposes of the Marshall Plan are "in complete harmony" with the purposes of the United Nations Charter, while:

"Attempts by any nation to prevent or sabotage European recovery for selfish ends are clearly contrary to these purposes."

Asserting that "aggressive" activities by Communists and Red-inspired groups have been aimed directly at barring recovery in Europe, Mr. Truman added:

"The next few years can determine whether the free countries of Europe will be able to preserve their heritage of freedom.

"If Europe fails to recover, the peoples of these countries might be driven to the philosophy of despair—the philosophy which contends that their basic wants can be met only by the surrender of their basic rights to totalitarian control.

"Such a turn of events would constitute a shattering blow to peace and stability in the world. It might well compel us to modify our own economic system and to forego, for the sake of our own security, the enjoyment of many of our freedoms and privileges."

The president said a European comeback depends on two essentials:

1. That the nations take "vigorous action" to help themselves.

2. That they get sufficient outside aid to supply the margin of victory for recovery.

While most of this aid must come from the United States, he said, total United States exports to the entire world next year are expected to be no bigger than in the past 12 months.

But even this level of shipments, Mr. Truman said, will have "an important impact on our markets." So he put in a one-sentence repeat request that Congress enact his 10-point program to fight inflation at home.

The president said the 16 recovery-program nations will finance most of the things they import themselves. In terms of value, the vital imports they cannot pay for themselves, he said, will represent only about 5 percent of their total national production. These, he said, will mean the difference between "ever-deepening stagnation and progressive improvement."

Essentially, he said, recovery is a European problem that can be solved only by increased production. America, he said, cannot supply relief indefinitely, so it is seeking practical ways to eliminate Europe's need for it.

But our deepest concern with recovery abroad, he said, "is that it is essential to the maintenance of the civilization in which the American way of life is rooted."

The first 9,000-ton wheat shipment for Greece under the European Recovery Program is funneled into holds of the SS Stanley Matthews at Port Arthur, Texas. About 30,000 bushels of Texas and Kansas wheat each hour flowed into the ship's holds during its two-day loading at the Kansas City Southern elevator docks.

"The economic plight in which Europe now finds itself has intensified a political struggle between those who wish to remain free men living under the rule of law and those who would use economic distress as a pretext for the establishment of a totalitarian state," he added.

The chances for political and economic stability in Europe may be lost, the chief executive said, if American provides "only halfhearted and halfway help."

But he left out any recommendation for special loans to Europe to help stabilize currencies there. The 16 countries had proposed something like $3,000,000,000 of this type of aid.

Mr. Truman said it might be desirable later on

but there is no way now of determining when or to what extent the loans should be made.

Furthermore, he said, the whole program has been scaled down wherever it seemed to include nonessentials or wherever supplies were too scarce to meet requirements.
Dec. 19, 1947

Editor's Note

In February 1948, a Communist coup brought Czechoslovakia under the Iron Curtain. Ten years earlier, Hitler had been able to seize the same nation without firing a shot; the Western Allies had simply given in to his demands at the Munich conference. "We are faced with exactly the same situation with which Britain and France were faced in 1938-39 with Hitler," Truman wrote to his daughter Margaret. "Things look black."

For a Congress considering the Marshall Plan, the news from Europe was ominous.

COMMUNISTS GAIN IN CZECHOSLOVAKIA

PRAGUE, FEB. 23 (AP)—Czechoslovakia apparently was headed tonight for a Communist-controlled government. This was implied in a split in the ranks of the Social Democratic Party, which had held the balance of power in the nation's political crisis.

Communists already were in control of the state government of semi-autonomous Slovakia. They threw out the non-Communists there and gave their posts to Communists. Slovakia was cut off from normal telephone communication with Prague.

The Social Democratic split and the direct action in Slovakia came after the Communists, driving for complete power in the nation, had paraded their armed police power in Prague and raided the headquarters of the Czech National Socialist Party, a bulwark of the anti-Red forces.

The raid was followed by Communist charges that the National Socialists were plotting armed revolution against the government.

Thus far the Communist actions in Prague seem to be within the letter of the law. Still to be debated is the move in Slovakia where Communist ministers assumed the state posts taken from non-Communists.

Several prominent anti-Communist political figures and student leaders were arrested. Czechoslovak citizens virtually were isolated from the rest of Europe. This was done when the Communist-controlled Ministry of the Interior issued an order requiring new stamps of approval on valid passports. The same ministry directs the security police.

Police armed with rifles and machine guns spread out through Prague. They took up posts before the nation's Parliament building, government offices and foreign embassies. Parliament, which had been scheduled to meet tomorrow, has postponed its session indefinitely.
Feb. 23, 1948

COMMUNISTS IN CHARGE

PRAGUE, CZECHOSLOVAKIA, FEB. 25 (AP)—Communists won control of Czechoslovakia today.

Communist Premier Klement Gottwald beat down President Eduard Benes' resistance after six days of crisis in this central European nation of 13,000,000 and came out with a new government of his party members and their friends.

Fifty students were arrested tonight when their columns attempted to march on Hradcany Palace to see Benes, and eyewitnesses said police used rifle butts to break up the demonstration. More than 10,000 students had gathered in the square before Charles University in a counterdemonstration against the Communists.

Benes managed to keep the appearances of representative government, for which he had battled hard, but it appeared a hollow victory.

Jan Masaryk, son of the founder of the republic, is still in the government as foreign minister. So is Bohumil Lausmann, a Social Democrat who led his party in its short revolt against pro-Communist guidance.

From a minority party, largest in Czechoslovakia, the Communists came through with complete command of every other phase of the nation's life.

They now have the Ministry of Justice, as well

On Feb. 24, 1948, thousands mass along Vaclavske Namesti bordering on Wenceslas Square in Prague, Czechoslovakia, to listen to broadcasts from Communist Newspaper rude Pravo. Traffic was stopped for five minutes during a token strike; tramways in the background came to a standstill during the strike.

as control of the police. A sympathizer remains at the head of the Defense Department, the army.

The anti-Communists were believed to have sought a showdown in the belief they could demonstrate Communist weakness in Czechoslovakia and force them into a general election before they were ready.

The strategy backfired. Gottwald counterattacked, calling them "agents of foreign reaction" and demanding that Benes give him a free hand in forming a new government. Gottwald sprang into action with organization of "action committees" throughout the country. He named members of other parties to the committee but all were his friends.

The action committees took over some of the government ministries yesterday and said they would not let the resigned ministers return to their offices. Slovak Democrat ministers in the semi-autonomous state of Slovakia were declared by the Communist deputy premier there to have vacated their posts.

Communist-directed police occupied and searched rival party headquarters in Prague. Police and action committees began taking over authority over all communications, government functions and even nationalized industries.
Feb. 25, 1948

An estimated 250,000 persons jammed a square to hear Communist Premier Klement Gottwald announce that President Eduard Benes had accepted a new Communist-dominated Czechoslovakian Cabinet.

MASARYK DEATH

PRAGUE, CZECHOSLOVAKIA, MARCH 10 (AP)—Jan Masaryk, foreign minister of Czechoslovakia, plunged to his death today after staying two weeks in his country's new Communist-controlled Cabinet.

An official government announcement said he committed suicide.

The 61-year-old diplomat was the son of a Brooklyn-born mother and a Bohemian father, who became Czechoslovakia's first president. He jumped more than 50 feet to his death on the stone flagging of a courtyard in Czernin Palace, said an announcement from the government which seized power two weeks ago today.

Vaclav Nosek, Communist minister of the interior, told Parliament Masaryk had ended his life after a night of brooding over "tendentious malicious letters and telegrams from his former friends in Great Britain and America assailing him for his manly stand" in remaining in the Communist-led government.

(In Sydney, Australia, the Czech consul, K. Tokoly, said Masaryk's death "is not suicide. It is plain murder." Tokoly said he was resigning his post.)

Masaryk's death was a blow to the Communists, who had retained him as foreign minister when they assumed control two weeks ago. His distinguished name gave prestige to their regime.

President Eduard Benes (left) of Czechoslovakia reads a statement to Premier Klement Gottwald (right) and new cabinet members at the swearing-in ceremony, Feb. 27, 1948, in Prague's Hradcany Castle. Benes gave reasons for giving in to Communist Party demands. In rear, the ministers are (left to right): Deputy Premier Bohumil Lausmann; Deputy Premier Antonin Zapotocky; Antonin Gregor, foreign trade; Zdenek Fierlinger, industry; Frantisek Krajcir, internal trade; and Alois Petr, transport.

Masaryk's death recalled that Dr. Prokop Krtina, minister of justice in the previous Cabinet with Masaryk, was recovering from head injuries suffered in what police said was a three-story plunge from his villa.

There was no word from President Eduard Benes concerning Masaryk's death. Masaryk conferred with the president only yesterday.

March 10, 1948

By John M. Hightower

WASHINGTON, MARCH 10 (AP)—The death of Jan Masaryk may help the cause of liberty by dramatizing Czechoslovakia's plight, American officials said today.

And privately voiced suspicions among diplomatic authorities found public expression at the Capitol where Rep. Stefan (R-Neb.), a native of Bohemia, told the house that Masaryk may have been murdered.

During a meeting of parliament in Prague, March 10, 1948, Gen. Ludvik Svoboda (right), Czech minister of defense; Premier Klement Gottwald (second from right) and other members of the nation's Cabinet stand in silent tribute to Jan Masaryk, Czech foreign minister, who died in a plunge from his apartment earlier that day.

"Early reports from the free radio of Europe," Stefan said, "named the cause of his death as self-destruction—suicide. It could just as easily have been murder. The Kremlin has never stopped at murder."

At the State Department, where officials are keeping as close a watch as possible on events inside the new Communist satellite country, authorities suggested that however Masaryk died his death might prove to be "the best act of his life."

Officials said they were convinced that it represented a desperate resistance against the power of the Communist government, in which Masaryk was serving as non-party foreign minister.

It adds to the tragedy of Czechoslovakia, in the State Department view, an element of high personal drama which until now had been lacking.

Authorities here are by no means certain it will be the last such incident. Concern is strongly felt about the future of President Eduard Benes, who is believed here to be little better than a prisoner of the Communist leaders of the government which he officially heads.

Benes and Masaryk symbolize Czechoslovak democracy not only to their own people but to the

British General Brian Robertson signs the charter establishing a European recovery organization under the Marshall Plan during a 16-nation meeting in Paris in July 1947.

rest of the world. The State Department sought to emphasize this fact in its official statement:

"The tragic death of Jan Masaryk has deepened the shadow cast on the observance a few days ago of the birthday anniversary of his father, Thomas Masaryk, by the extinction of Czechoslovak liberties which Thomas Masaryk founded."
March 10, 1948

VANDENBERG PLEADS FOR EUROPEAN RECOVERY

WASHINGTON, MARCH 1 (AP)—Sen. Arthur Vandenberg (R-Mich.) urged the Senate today to "light the beacon" of economic aid to Europe before "aggressive communism" knocks on the New World's door and threatens its freedom.

Beginning debate on the Marshall aid plan, the chairman of the Senate Foreign Relations Committee told his colleagues:

"This act may well become a welcome beacon in the world's dark night. But if that beacon is to be lighted at all, it had better be lighted before it is too late."

With about 50 senators listening intently, Arthur Vandenberg asked that Congress "help stop World War III before it starts" by approving the European recovery program.

Vandenberg asserted that Czechoslovakia has been "gutted by subversive conquest" directed by Moscow.

"This vast friendly segment of the earth must not collapse," he said. "The iron curtain must not come to the rims of the Atlantic by aggression or default."

The Communist Cominform, he said, is frankly calling on its adherents to wreck the Marshall Plan.

"It is indeed 'Cold War,'" he declared. "It is pressure war against the independent recovery of Europe. Obviously it also is aimed at us."
March 1, 1948

CONGRESS OKS MARSHALL PLAN

WASHINGTON, APRIL 2 (AP)—Congress roared final approval by an overwhelming margin today of a global aid bill aimed at stemming the world tide of Communism with the goods of peace and the weapons of war.

The House passed the historic measure by a thunderous 318 to 75 vote, and the Senate shouted agreement, without even bothering to call the roll, less than two hours after.

President Truman was ready to sign the bill into law almost immediately, thus starting history's largest peacetime flow of American dollars, arms and reconstruction equipment to 18 countries east, west and south of the Soviet Union.

Most of the actual funds remain to be voted later, but the Reconstruction Finance Corporation can advance right away:

$1,000,000,000 for the European recovery program—to launch the so-called "Marshall Plan" of helping 16 European countries and Western Germany work their way toward communism-proof economic health.

$50,000,000 each to China, Greece and Turkey. For Greece and Turkey, the U.S. aid is wholly military—to help them resist Communist pressure. China's share is partly military, partly economic.

The entire program—which will cost every man, woman and child in the United States an average of $42 for the first 12 or 14 months—was rushed toward the law books in a burst of speed that few would have believed possible when it started through the congressional mill three months ago.

Many veteran foes of past foreign aid programs shouted their "ayes" to this one, lining up with the majority view that the spread of communism must be halted and that all efforts must be made to stop it by means short of war if war itself is to be avoided.
April 2, 1948

Editor's Note

As the historian Robert H. Ferrell noted, "it is not easy to assess the result of the (Marshall) plan, save that Europe recovered." Two-and-a-half years after the program began, Western European industrial output was 40 percent higher than before the war. But most of the capital used for development was of European origin. The American contribution was marginal, but was it critical, like the U.S. military contribution that tipped the balance in World War I?

Ironically, just as it took the production demands of World War II to finally end the Great Depression in America, it may have been U.S. weapons orders for the Korean War that finally kicked the European economy into high gear in the early 1950s.

Chapter 4

The Cold War

Standing in the U.N. delegates lounge at Flushing Meadows, N.Y., Robert Schuman, France's foreign minister, holds a newspaper story of Russia's atomic explosion in August 1949. News of President Truman's announcement of the bomb blast reached the United Nations General Assembly shortly before Schuman spoke before that body.

- **Berlin Blockade**

  Russians Halt Traffic ... Allies Begin Airlift ... Blockade Lifted

- **NATO**

  NATO Established ... Communists React

- **Fall of China**

  Tientsin Captured ... Nanking Falls ... Nationalists Leave Mainland

- **The Red Bomb**

  Soviets Test Bomb ... Truman Talks of Hydrogen Bomb

North Atlantic defense ministers, with the aides assigned to them, stand in front of the amphitheater at Arlington National Cemetery in Virginia, where they went to lay wreaths at the Tomb of the Unknown Soldier.

Most Americans regarded the tense post-1945 standoff among the wartime allies as a bitter, unexpected consequence of World War II. But American and Russian leaders had feared and mistrusted each other since at least the 1890s, when they disagreed over which nation would develop the Chinese province of Manchuria.

The Bolshevik Revolution of 1917 overthrew Russia's monarchy but only intensified the international rivalry, for now the United States and the Soviet Union were, respectively, the world's most powerful capitalist democracy and the world's first Communist dictatorship. The two did not formally recognize each other until 1933, and they became allies in 1941—only after Nazi Germany broke a non-aggression treaty and invaded the Soviet Union.

After the war, the old tensions quickly resurfaced and took command of the relationship.

With the U.S.S.R. having been invaded twice in 20 years by Germany, Soviet leader Josef Stalin wanted to control Poland and the Balkans and limit Germany's capacity to make war. The United States, on the other hand, favored self-determination for nations such as Poland; equal economic access to Eastern Europe; and a rebuilt capitalist Western Europe, including a unified Germany.

Instead, between 1945 and 1948, Stalin clamped military control over Eastern Europe and stripped East Germany of its industrial plant.

Churchill called it an "Iron Curtain," and in 1947 columnist Walter Lippmann gave a name to the global standoff among the old allies—the "Cold War." It was a war fought to a standoff with words, and only rarely with bullets.

The Communist takeover in China sent shock waves through the United States, which had invested so much there. And the Soviets' successful detonation of an atomic bomb showed how high the Cold War stakes had become.

Berlin Blockade

During World War II the Allies had agreed to divide Germany into four zones of occupation, with Berlin deep in the Russian zone. But they never worked out exact provisions for access to the city from the Western zones. It was not a problem until after the war, as Soviet-American relations deteriorated.

In late 1947, discussions on Germany broke down over Soviet charges that the Allies were violating the wartime agreement, and on March 20, 1948, the Soviets withdrew from the Allied Control Council administering Berlin. Ten days later, guards on the East German border began slowing the entry of Western troop trains bound for Berlin. On June 7, the Western powers announced their intention to proceed with the creation of a separate, capitalist West Germany. On June 24, arguing that if Germany was to be partitioned, Berlin could no longer be the single German capital and the Soviets stopped all surface travel between West Germany and Berlin.

The move presented the United States with a dilemma: Should the U.S. risk war to maintain ties to the capital of its recent enemy? And if Berlin was to be supplied, was there an alternative short of war?

NEW MARK PLANNED

BERLIN, JUNE 18 (AP)—The Western Allies announced tonight a drastic currency reform to reduce the money in circulation in their zones of occupations and pave the way for German participation in the European Recovery Program. They set up a new mark, called the Deutsche mark, and provided for the first steps in taking old marks out of trade channels.

All old money and holdings must be registered

Inside view of a money exchange office opened in the British sector of Berlin, Aug. 2, 1948.

next week. There will be a full week's moratorium on all debts in Western Germany.

The reform is effective only in the American, British and French zones. Western sectors of the Four-Power city of Berlin are excluded.

The three military governors of the Western zones met secretly two weeks ago to set the date for changing the currency. Official informants said they had delivered letters to Marshal Vassily Sokolovsky, Soviet zone chief, advising him of the change in currency.

A few hours before the announcement, Sokolovsky said he is "ready to support any measure which would serve to accomplish a common German currency on the basis of a Four-Power decision." The Russians previously have blocked efforts to agree on such a program. This led to the decision to go ahead on a Three-Power basis.
June 18, 1948

RUSSIANS HALT TRAFFIC

BERLIN, JUNE 24 (AP)—The Russians halted all railway traffic into the Western sectors of Berlin early today. They also shut off that part of the Western sector's electric power generated in the Soviet sector.

Western circles viewed these two moves as Soviet retaliation for the refusal of the United States, Britain and France to accept the Soviet zone mark as Berlin's only legal currency.

The Russian-licensed German news agency said the Soviets halted all freight and passenger traffic between Berlin and the Western zone railhead at Helmstedt because of a "technical disturbance." It did not explain the nature of the disturbance.

British sources said the Soviets notified the Berlin electricity works that electric power used in Western sectors in the future will have to be produced in the West. Normally, power stations in the Western sectors produce only one-half of the electricity used in those sectors.

Late yesterday, Herman Rau, chairman of the Soviet zone's German Economic Commission, told newsmen that "unless supplies come by air, serious economic difficulties will develop for the Western sectors" of Berlin.

Earlier, the Russians officially threatened economic sanctions against Western Berlin if the United States, France and Britain refused to accept the Soviet zone mark as Berlin's only legal currency.

The three Western powers, however, voided yesterday a Russian decree making a new Soviet-stamped mark the only legal tender in Berlin and ordered issuance of the new Western German Deutsche mark in their three sectors. The effect was to erect a paper currency wall through the heart of Berlin, 100 miles behind the Iron Curtain.

Thus Berlin's 3,400,000 people were caught in the middle of an East-West money fight.
June 24, 1948

CLAY BACKS BERLIN

BERLIN, JUNE 24 (AP)—Gen. Lucius D. Clay served notice that no action short of war is going to force the Americans from this city.

Clay, the American military governor, said in Heidelberg that the latest moves by the Russians indicate they "are trying to put on the final pressure to drive us out of Berlin." He said this could not be accomplished "by any action short of war."

All food shipments to Berlin on rail lines from Western Germany were halted.

Clay estimated that Berliners have supplies for no more than a couple of weeks.

Berlin took on a warlike atmosphere. Steel-helmeted American soldiers in armored cars with mounted machine guns patrolled the United States sector. Military police carried rifles.

The official Soviet and German communist press demanded anew that the Western Allies quit the city.

The Russians and German communists threatened economic reprisals against any of the 3,400,000 Berliners who accept the Western Allies' new currency.
June 24, 1948

BERLIN AIRLIFT TO CONTINUE
By Lynn Heinzerling

BERLIN, JULY 3 (AP)—The Russians refused today to say they would lift their Berlin food blockade, and Allied airmen prepared to give up their Fourth of July holiday to continue the flying breadline.

An American spokesman announced that Marshal Vassily D. Sokolovsky, Soviet commander, refused to give any assurances about raising the blockade.

As top officials met, airborne supplies streamed into Berlin, and after the fruitless meeting with Sokolovsky, Gen. Lucius D. Clay, the American military governor, announced the airlift will continue and be increased.

"We will keep it up as long as the American people want to keep it up," declared Clay. "I remember that we kept one up over the hump to China for over a year."

The American spokesman said Western occupation officials went to Sokolovsky to tell him the two-week blockade of Western Berlin was becoming a serious matter and they wanted some assurance that "technical difficulties" to railway traffic would be overcome. The Russians said "technical difficulties" caused the ban on rail traffic at the start of the blockade.

As the blockade continued, hungry Berliners watched the skies for the big transport planes winging into the city with tons of food.

Lt. Gen. Curtis E. LeMay, American fliers' commander-in-chief, told them their work flying food into beleaguered Berlin was an "admirable manifestation of the principles of democracy." They will celebrate the Fourth by flying bread to Berlin.

The American Air Force claimed a new record lift. In the 24-hour period ending at 4 p.m., they flew 675 tons of food into Berlin, making 184 flights from Wiesbaden and Frankfurt.
July 3, 1948

LIFE IN BERLIN
By Richard Kasischke

BERLIN, JULY 4 (AP)—People get up at midnight when they have electric light. Factories work at night, when they have power. The dentist works his drill with a foot-pedal, and the barber has replaced his electric clippers with hand clippers and shears.

That is life these days for the 2,000,000 Germans of Berlin's American, British and French sectors since the Russians cut off electric current supplies from their surrounding occupation zone.

Without these supplies the three Western sectors can produce only about half of their needs. And even this can't last if some way is not found to bring in coal over the Russian blockade which has stopped railroad freight between Berlin and Western Germany.

To stretch power supplies, the three military governments have imposed drastic curtailments of service to industries and homes. Industry, already lamed by freight stoppages which shut off raw materials, is further crippled, and unemployment is mounting.

An official American military government estimate said the stoppage of coal shipments from the West had curtailed industrial production in Berlin's Western sectors up to 50 percent.

The ordinary German home in Western Berlin now gets only two hours electricity during daylight hours, usually provided at meal time. But the power comes on again at midnight until 6 a.m., when usage ordinarily is small.

That means that thousands of Berliners now go

Children in Berlin, Germany, had a new pastime in 1948 as they gathered on the fences around Tempelhof Airport to watch the fleets of American planes arrive with supplies for the city, now on short rations because of the land and water blockade established by the Russians. An American four-engine transport plane flies overhead.

to bed early and set their alarm clocks for midnight. Then father gets up to listen to the late news broadcast and probably trudge off to work.
July 4, 1948

BLOCKADE IN 17TH DAY
By George Bria

BERLIN, JULY 5 (AP)—American and British efforts to beat the Russian blockade of Berlin with a bridge of supply-carrying planes gained fresh momentum today.

The air forces of the two Western allies sent nearly 400 planes into the city yesterday from Western Germany and were planning to keep up the pace.

Brig. Gen. Joseph Smith, commanding the American Air Service, said he was extremely pleased with the efforts of both the flight and ground crews. Although the crews are averaging only four or five hours sleep each day, they are maintaining and flying the planes with maximum efficiency, he said.

The 400 planes sent to Berlin yesterday com-

On June 26, 1948, the U.S. Air Force in Europe began airlifting supplies into the blockaded city. The airlift operation was in operation for 15 months in all. During that time, some 2,343,300 tons of food and supplies were delivered, aboard 277,264 flights.

pared with 224 flights made during the previous 24-hour period.

Despite the giant airlift, Berlin still faced economic paralysis by the Soviet ground blockade, now in its 17th day. The stoppage of coal shipments from the West already has halved Western Berlin's industrial output.

The Western Allies are reported to be setting up a plan to fly coal into the city, but the communist press warned Berliners that a hard winter lies ahead.

British Foreign Secretary Ernest Bevin is sched-

uled to report on the Berlin crisis at a special Cabinet meeting today. At a Labor Party rally yesterday, he charged that Russia is starving innocent people to force the Western powers from Berlin.

Declaring the Western powers will not surrender the city, he said: "We are always ready to discuss Berlin if they (the Russians) are willing to discuss it, and I am not unhopeful that sanity will prevail."

"Save Berlin" campaigns were sprouting all over Western Germany. Although on slim diets

German workers unload a cargo of fresh milk from a C-47 transport plane at Tempelhof Airport in Berlin. The milk came with a consignment that included flour as part of a rations shipment for residents of the Western sectors of Berlin.

themselves, the Western Germans voluntarily were giving up one day's food rations to be flown to Berliners in the Western sectors of the city. With the gifts went messages of encouragement in "Berlin's Fight for Freedom."

Increased gifts also were reported from Sweden, Switzerland, the United States, and other countries.

Americans increased their cabled orders for CARE (Cooperative for American Remittances to Europe) food packages for delivery from warehouse stocks here.

Increases also were reported in parcel post gift shipments from America, but these ordinarily come in by rail freight from Western German ports and this route now is stopped. No provision has been made for flying in the piled-up backlog of such packages.

July 5, 1948

AIRLIFT REACHES RECORD TONNAGE
By George Bria

BERLIN, SEPT. 18 (AP)—American and British Air Forces sent 895 cargo flights into Soviet-blockaded Berlin today in an awesome demonstration of peacetime air power.

U.S. Lt. Gen. Curtis LeMay's airmen flew 651 sorties with 5,572.7 tons of "bonus" coal for the neediest of Western Berlin's 2,500,000 besieged inhabitants. The record-smashing feat dwarfed the famed wartime "hump" shuttle from India to China.

The Royal Air Force flew 244 flights with an unannounced cargo and tonnage.

The huge armada filled Berlin's skies with an endless roar. Even bad weather will not halt the lift, for the Americans flew 18 of the 24 hours ended at noon under instrument conditions.

Today's record-breaking flights were made as the Soviet ground blockade became a quarter of a year old. Exactly three months ago at midnight, the Russians closed the highway to Berlin and soon afterward severed rail and water approaches.

The American haul surpassed by 1,624.4 tons the previous record set four days ago in 498 flights. It exceeded the "hump" record by 245.7 tons.

It exceeded the target of 4,000 to 5,000 tons set by Lemay yesterday, when he called on his airmen to celebrate the anniversary of the U.S. Air Force with record-shattering flights.

The entire tonnage was loaded aboard planes in 100-pound bags. A C-74 Globemaster carried approximately 250,000 pounds of coal in six trips.

LeMay called it an "outstanding achievement that will long be remembered." He congratulated all personnel.

The total tonnage flown to Berlin by American planes since large-scale operations began June 26 exceeded 174,000 tons on more than 25,000 flights. On the first day of the lift 80 tons were flown in 32 flights.

An Air Force announcement said the coal flown today "was over and above the normal requirement for the sustenance of Berlin and will be distributed to the Germans of the Western sectors as a bonus, in effect a tribute from the Air Force to the people of that blockaded city."

About 100,000 families with two or more small children will get the coal.
Sept. 18, 1948

BLOCKADE LIFTED

WASHINGTON, MAY 4 (AP)—The Big Four powers agreed today to lift the Berlin blockade and counterblockade measures.

A State Department announcement of this gave no date for the lifting.

It said: "It can be said specifically that agreement has been reached and that all restrictions imposed in Germany which have been the subject of conversation will be mutually lifted."

The airlift grew from a baby to a giant in 10 months.

Twenty-five Americans and 22 Britons lost their lives flying food and coal to Berlin over the Russian roadblocks. American taxpayers spent more than $150,000,000 to support it; the British, too, spent millions.

Today the planes flew on, their pilots almost unmindful of the talks in New York. Next week, presumably, they can cut down on their strange adventure and turn much of the cargo-carrying over to railroads and trucks.

But the political effects of the airlift are bound to be felt for a long time. Some persons here credit it with stopping communism on the Spree River. The Russians never expected that the West could feed a metropolis by air alone. They forced the West to build and train probably the greatest peacetime air force in history.

The Russians were not the only ones who doubted the airlift would work. Some in the Western Allies' leadership felt the same way.
May 4, 1949

ON THE AUTOBAHN TO BERLIN
By George Boultwood

BERLIN, MAY 12 (AP)—Western Berlin is no longer an island. It's a peninsula.

That new geographical fact became plain with a 100-mile drive this morning down the very thin

Crowds surround the first motorcar as it leaves Berlin down the Autobahn toward the west immediately after the Berlin blockade was lifted, May 11, 1949. The barriers were lifted at 5:01 p.m. (EST) from the former Nazi capital, and about 75 automobiles began the race down the highway from that city to the west.

neck of land from Helmstedt in the British zone to Berlin.

Eddie Worth, an Associated Press photographer, and I made the trip in my 1949 model British export car in one hour and 55 minutes.

That included time at two Russian checkpoints and a brief stop for a picture at the bridge over the Elbe River.

At Helmstedt, the Russian officer stepped smartly to the car window and said, "Your papers, please." I handed over papers in English and

Russian for myself and Worth. After careful but brief scrutiny the officer said, "All right, you may go."

It was a bright moonlit night and quite cold. The smooth concrete of the Autobahn stretched ahead, and in a few minutes the speedometer needle was flickering over the 75-mile-an-hour mark.

In less than 10 minutes we passed the British military convoy which crossed the border at Helmstedt first.

We headed for the Elbe River bridge.

Paul Fuellsack, city councillor for food, distributes a box full of oranges to Berliners, who were on hand to greet the first citrus trucks to Berlin on May 14, 1949.

The bridge loomed up and the Soviet zone German police waved us on.

The bridge was one of the "technical difficulties" the Russians quoted early last year as an excuse for hampering Allied road traffic. They claimed it was unsafe, and made everyone use the ferry.

The bridge looked no different than when I last drove across it a year ago. It was a temporary structure put up by U.S. Army engineers when the Allies first went into Berlin. The wood road surface is badly worn and the planks rattle alarmingly as you drive over them. But there seemed no danger of it collapsing.

Because of our late start—we were working at the Helmstedt end of the story—we were the 12th car to reach Berlin. A Russian noncom stepped up, saluted and took our papers. He glanced at them and handed them back without a word. We got an enthusiastic welcome from the waiting crowds.
May 12, 1949

NATO

The Berlin blockade showed that U.S.-Soviet conflicts could be settled short of war. The formation of the North Atlantic Treaty Organization (NATO) signified the West's determination to hold the line against the Soviets.

NATO SIGNING

WASHINGTON, APRIL 4 (AP)—Amid solemn diplomatic pageantry, 12 North Atlantic nations today signed a treaty designed to confront any Russian aggression with a united defense.

After hearing President Truman hail it as a "shield against aggression," the foreign ministers stepped up one by one to put their names to the historic 1,040-word pact.

Previously, they, like Mr. Truman, had proclaimed to Russia and all the world that their only purpose was peace and security.

But several of them added blunt warnings to any nation contemplating violence. Britain's foreign minister, Ernest Bevin, declared:

"Our people do not want war and do not glorify war, but they will not shrink from it if aggression is threatened."

Secretary of State Dean Acheson drew on the Bible. "For those who set their feet upon the path of aggression," he said, "it (the pact) is a warning

Dean Acheson, secretary of state, takes pen to sign the North Atlantic Pact for the United States. Vice President Alben Barkley and President Harry S. Truman watch. At right is John W. Foley of the State Department.

that if it must needs be that offenses come, then woe unto them by whom the offenses cometh."

At a dinner tonight, President Truman told the foreign ministers that their children and grandchildren someday will say "we really passed a milestone in history today."

Toasting the foreign ministers at a dinner at which he and Mrs. Truman were hosts, the president asserted:

"May I offer a toast to the Atlantic Treaty and its success. And I think your children and your

grandchildren will tell you that in the days to come."

A crowd of 1,500 which jammed the government's gray and gold departmental auditorium included representatives of most of the nations with envoys in Washington. But there were several notable exceptions. These were the representatives of Russia and the Soviet bloc. They did not ask for tickets, the State Department explained.

Projecting American defense frontiers into the heart of Europe, the treaty would pledge all 12

Foreign ministers and ambassadors of 12 signatory nations meet in Washington, Sept. 17, 1949, to perfect organizational operation of the new North Atlantic Pact.

nations to take measures to resist an attack on any of them.

Mr. Truman termed "absolutely untrue" the charge that the treaty is aggressive in intent, a charge which Russia made in formal notes on the eve of the signing.
April 4, 1949

WASHINGTON, JULY 21 (AP)—The Senate vote approving the Atlantic Pact tonight empowered President Truman to establish America's defensive frontiers against Russia in the heart of Europe.

That is exactly what he now proposes to do as quickly as possible—not only to keep the Soviets at arm's length but also to spread the cloak of American power over the borders of weaker states.

The United States is thus embarked on a revolutionary new course in its foreign policy. It is pledged—or in a legal sense shortly will be—to act in case any one of 10 European-area nations, or Canada, is attacked.

It is committed to a program of mutual aid and expects to share a single grand strategic plan for the defense of the whole Western world.

Treaty supporters believe greater assurance of world peace will result from all these actions and arrangements; critics have denounced the alliance and its companion rearmament program as a new incitement to Russia.

The pact brings together the United States and Canada (with defense lines running far into the Pacific as well as Europe); the five members of the Western European Union—Britain, France, Belgium, the Netherlands and Luxembourg; two Scandinavian states—Norway and Denmark; one southern European nation—Italy; and two countries with key positions in the Atlantic—Iceland and Portugal.

The Truman administration wants $1,130,000,000 to supply arms to Atlantic allies in Europe, plus $320,000,000 for Greece, Turkey and other "free nations."

The arms program, administration leaders will tell Congress, should have two purposes: to boost Western European morale and actually to strengthen the defenses of this nation's European allies.

July 21, 1949

Editor's Note

Membership in NATO was a decision of great significance for the United States. Not since the pact with France during the time of the American Revolution had the nation in peacetime been bound by a treaty of alliance.

The outbreak of the Korean War in 1950 led to an even deeper commitment. Convinced that the Soviet Union was responsible for the attack in Korea, the Truman administration considered it likely that the Russians would soon be on the move in Europe as well. To counter this perceived threat, the administration led the way in creating a strong military force in Western Europe, a NATO army. In late 1950, Gen. Eisenhower, then the president of Columbia University, was dispatched to Europe to organize and command the new force. Truman also planned to contribute as many as four divisions of American troops to the NATO forces.

The president's initiative ran into considerable opposition. In December 1950, former President Herbert Hoover argued for the complete defense of the "Western Hemisphere, Gibraltar of Civilization," but suggested protection of Europe by naval and air forces only—not ground troops. Sen. Robert A. Taft sided with Hoover. The Ohio senator doubted that the president had the constitutional authority to commit military forces without prior congressional approval. And he wondered what good the troops would do. "The thing about Europe," he wrote, "is can you defend it? If Russia has the atomic bomb, can't they knock the devil out of Europe?"

Hoover and Taft revealed the lingering strength of isolationism in American opinion. They were fighting a losing battle. "We will probably be defeated," Hoover observed in March 1951, "but we can at least hope that posterity will realize we did our best in their protection."

He was right about their being defeated. By the end of 1952, NATO forces in Europe included 25 combat-ready divisions, more than one-third of them American.

By Arthur Gavshon

BRUSSELS, BELGIUM, DEC. 19 (AP)—A historic international army was established today to keep the peace in Europe, and Gen. Dwight D. Eisenhower was named to head it.

The army was set up by the 12 countries of the North Atlantic Treaty Organization. Early next month Gen. Eisenhower, from a headquarters likely to be located at Versailles, France, will begin forging the forces supplied by these nations into an integrated army of around a million men. Their immediate task will be to defend a line from the Arctic to the Mediterranean against any aggressor.

Eisenhower, at 60, goes back into active duty to head another great allied undertaking—but this time with the help of the Germans he subdued in 1945. His chief of staff will be Lt. Gen. Alfred M. Gruenther, U.S. Army deputy for plans and operations.

Eisenhower said today in St. Louis that he was hopeful of maintaining peace.

"But it's not going to be easy and it's not going to be quick," he added.

The commander of Supreme Headquarters Allied Powers in Europe will be on leave of absence from Columbia University, where he has been president. In Washington, President Truman said Eisenhower will have the same position in Europe that Gen. MacArthur has in the Far East. MacArthur is supreme commander in the area of Japan and also supreme commander of U.N. forces fighting in Korea.

President Truman said additional armed forces will be sent to Europe as soon as possible. The president would not say how many American troops will be included in the new command.
Dec. 19, 1950

COMMUNISTS REACT TO IKE APPOINTMENT

LONDON, DEC. 19 (AP)—Diplomats of non-Communist countries saw in the designation today of Gen. Eisenhower as commander of the North Atlantic defense forces a powerful stimulus to Western European unity. The first Communist reaction included a statement that Eisenhower would suffer the same fate as Hitler.

East German press chief Albert Norden, in a statement in Berlin, said: "Eisenhower depends on the same forces which formed Hitler's entourage—Eisenhower will suffer the same fate as Hitler."
Dec. 19, 1950

Fall of China

The United States appeared to have contained communism in Europe, but it was on the march in the world's most populous nation.

For Chiang Kai-shek's Nationalists and Mao Tse-tung's Communists, World War II never really ended; they simply turned their weapons on each other. Indeed, some of Chiang's U.S. wartime advisors, frustrated by his unwillingness to take vigorous action against the Japanese, had believed all along that he was holding back his forces for just such a postwar showdown.

Thanks to U.S. military aid, Chiang in 1945 possessed the best-armed force in the history of China. But his government was inefficient and corrupt, and never really gained control of the country. Communist armies advanced steadily from their northern bases and by late 1948 Mao's armies had overrun Manchuria and were pushing south. In December 1949, Chiang proclaimed a new government in Taiwan (Formosa), an island off China's south-eastern coast.

THE AMERICAN DILEMMA
By John M. Hightower

WASHINGTON, NOV. 24 (AP)—The Communist sweep in China appears certain to cost the United States billions more in foreign aid over the next few years—whether or not this country decides to give grand-scale help to Generalissimo Chiang Kai-shek.

As policy planners here see the picture, two points stand out:

1. If President Truman and Secretary of State Marshall determine that China still can be saved from communism—and decide to go ahead with an aid program—they will have to ask the new Congress for several hundred million dollars at least. And that would be just a starter, since any new China program is regarded as a long-term undertaking.

2. If—in spite of American help or without it—all China falls to the Communists, the task of rebuilding Japan and providing it with a stable economy will be much more costly. That is be-

cause Japan would find trade relations with Communist China more difficult.

In addition, if a Communist China should prove actively hostile to the West in the Cold War, military leaders might consider it essential to strengthen American defenses in the Western Pacific. That, however, is no more than a speculative possibility at the moment.

These factors, as well as the impact of a Red victory in China or the whole anticommunist struggle, are believed to be before Mr. Truman and Marshall as they cope with the problem of developing their China policy to deal with the present crisis.

Marshall was scheduled to meet the president again today for their second foreign policy conference in three days. Their first talk took place on Monday shortly after the secretary returned from the United Nations meeting in Paris.

But if any decisions were reached then they were not disclosed. Secrecy even covered the question of whether Marshall will continue as secretary of state or soon retire.

Meanwhile, it is understood that Chiang, in connection with his appeal to President Truman for urgent assistance, proposed that a prominent American military leader—someone with great prestige—be sent to head this country's military mission in China.

Some Chinese informants claim the Generalissimo would like to have Gen. Douglas MacArthur, but there is no evidence that such an assignment has been seriously considered here for the supreme commander of the Allied occupation in Japan.

One military estimate made here is that a greatly enlarged American mission, numbering about 10,000 officers and men, would have to be set up in China to make any major aid program effective. Moreover, the belief is that it would have to take considerable responsibility for running Chiang's war against the Communists. The present 1,000-man mission is limited to rear area training activities.

Still another factor bearing on the whole aid question is what Russia might do if this country went all out to help China and the Communists there began taking a beating.

On this point, some authorities say there is a real risk of building up an indirect clash of Soviet and American military powers.
Nov. 24, 1948

MME. CHIANG VISITS WASHINGTON

WASHINGTON, DEC. 1 (AP)—Mme. Chiang Kai-shek flew here today seeking new aid for China's hard-pressed government but made no immediate engagements to see top American officials.

The Chinese first lady went to the home of Secretary of State and Mrs. George C. Marshall at Leesburg, Va. Reporters there were told that she planned to rest for two days before undertaking any appointments.

At the White House, Charles G. Ross, press secretary, said that Mme. Chiang had no engagement to see President Truman and, so far as he knew, had not asked for one. Undersecretary of State Lovett told reporters that he knew of no request from her to talk with any official at the Department of State.

At Leesburg, Mme. Chiang permitted newsreel photography. During the picture-taking, she remarked to Mrs. Marshall: "This is my wedding anniversary."

Mrs. Marshall said: "We must have a celebration."

Mme. Chiang said: "It is enough of a celebration just being here."

Mme. Chiang and Generalissimo Chiang Kai-shek were married in Shanghai in 1929 in a Christian service.

Mme. Chiang arrived at 10 a.m. from San Francisco aboard President Truman's former personal plane, the Sacred Cow.

Top American administration officials were missing. The State Department sent Walter Butterworth, chief of its office of Far Eastern Affairs.

While American officials undoubtedly will show Mme. Chiang every courtesy due the wife of a nation's leader, behind their smiling welcome they are not too happy about the visit. They expect Mme. Chiang not only to appeal to government officials for aid against the Communist armies, but also to try to stir up greater popular interest in the Chinese cause.

Her mission comes at a time when Mr. Truman

Gen. George C. Marshall (left), special presidential envoy to China, prepares to leave Nanking airport with Generalissimo Chiang Kai-shek and Madame Chiang, Dec. 28. 1945.

and Marshall apparently have concluded that any aid which would involve this country deeply in the Chinese war is out of the question. Some new program of carefully limited help still seems probable.

There were strong indications also that Congress may adopt a "let's see what has been accomplished" attitude on all foreign spending. *Dec. 1, 1948*

TIENTSIN CAPTURED

NANKING, CHINA, JAN. 15 (AP)—The Chi-nese Communists captured Tientsin today, sharpening the urgency of the government alternatives to yield to harsh peace terms or flee.

The Cabinet and other government bodies were holding tense conferences, and the policy-making executive committee headed by Ma Ching-yuan scheduled an emergency session Sunday to discuss the Red conditions.

Those conditions, broadcast Friday night by the Communist radio, amounted to a demand for unconditional surrender of the Chiang Kai-shek government. Nanking hopes that they might be eased went glimmering as the fall of Tientsin demonstrated the Reds' dominant military position.

Deepening the government gloom was authoritative word that both the United States and Britain had declined to use their good offices to seek peace talks. There appeared no reason to believe that France or Russia would heed similar pleas. Conquest of Tientsin after a month of siege and a day of artillery bombardment cost the government another 60,000 of its dwindling troops and freed an estimated 150,000 Reds for new operations.

The Communist radio stressed the obvious fact that the capture cleared a rail route all the way from Manchuria down to the Yangtze River front before Nanking.

This hurried the continuing flight of government offices from this dejected capital.

It was learned authoritatively that the bulk of government gold and foreign currency already had been moved to the island of Formosa, more than 500 miles by air southeast of Nanking. Generalissimo Chiang Kai-shek was reported also to have sent many of his personal possessions there.

Semiofficial Chinese sources said Foochow, more than 400 miles by air south of Nanking, had been chosen as a temporary capital when Nanking should become untenable. Formosa is being saved as an ultimate refuge if the government finds itself unable to stay on the mainland, these sources reported.

Antipathy of the residents plus a well-developed Red guerrilla movement were said to have forced abandonment of plans to move to the great southern center of Canton.

Every indication pointed to Formosa as the final retreat of Chiang. It was believed that, with the protection of army, navy and air units already being sent there, he hoped to wait for future world events to provide him with the necessary support for a comeback.

The universal reaction was that the Red terms left no room for bargaining. Broadcast by the Red radio last night, they included punishment of "war criminals," destruction of "reactionary elements," and abandonment of the constitution.

Radio reports from Tientsin indicated the Communist seizure at noon Saturday was practically

Communist troops entering Nanking in the early morning of April 24, 1949. They marched through the west gate of the former Nationalist capital and moved up the main boulevard, Chungshan Road, to the center of the city.

bloodless, but it followed a day of heavy shelling that damaged many of the city's large buildings and took an unknown but high number of civilian lives.
Jan. 15, 1949

NANKING EVACUATED

NANKING, CHINA, APRIL 23 (AP)—This tottering capital of Nationalist China was abandoned by its officials and its garrison today as Communist troops smashed across the river and reached its gates.

Red troops, apparently cracking the Nationalist defenses on a wide front, seized broad areas on both sides of the capital.

Looting began in Nanking, from which all high

Chinese in the city of Peiping raise their clenched fists in a welcoming salute for Chinese Communist troops entering the city after driving out the Nationalist forces. Behind them are portraits of the Chinese Communist leaders, with General Mao Tse-tung, commander-in-chief, in the center.

government officials presumably had fled along with the garrison. The city was a no-man's-land, with both soldiers and police withdrawn.

Mobs broke into shops and carried all manner of merchandise to their homes and the country-side.

Dirty and disorganized troops, believed withdrawn from Fukow, streamed through the city.

An estimated 100,000 Nationalist troops reportedly clogged the roads in disorderly retreat from Nanking. They fled south along four main highways.

In the hour of Nationalist China's extremity, "retired" President Chiang Kai-shek joined in

Hangchow yesterday with acting President Li Tsung-jen in declaring that they were resolved to "fight to the end."

Hangchow, the meeting place for Nationalist leaders, is 50 miles southeast of Nanking. Li's home in Nanking was among those looted by Chinese mobs.

The flight of government soldiers led to belief that their commanders temporarily had lost control. Military quarters said the 26th Army, which was ordered to move into Nanking last night to defend the capital, never arrived.

The city gates are open and unguarded. Desertion of Nationalist troops was reported at many points. The defecting troops simply sat down and waited for the Communists.

Volunteer militia seemed to be bringing the looting slowly under control.

Chiang, president and for 22 years the No. 1 man in China, "retired" Jan. 21 to let Vice President Li try to negotiate peace with the Communists.

April 23, 1949

'WE DON'T HAVE ENOUGH TROOPS'

By Seymour Topping

NANKING, CHINA, APRIL 24 (AP)—In a dingy back room of Nanking's dilapidated Cairo Hotel sits a weary old man who had the task of handing over this Nationalist capital to the victorious Communists.

He is 60-year-old Gen. Ma Ching-yuan, a former divisional commander who is chairman of Nanking's emergency peace preservation committee.

A telephone call aroused him shortly after midnight yesterday morning. It was Gen. Chang Yao-ming, garrison commander, who told Ma hastily that his troops were evacuating the city. Chang asked Ma to take charge during the transition period and promised him enough police and security detachments for the job.

Ma Ching-yuan bitterly recalled that conversation as he sat on the edge of his chair this morning, his hands folded between his knees, and shaking his head as he repeated:

"We don't have enough troops. We don't have enough troops to protect the city against looters."

Rifle shots in the street underlined his fears. In the old city section of Futzemiao, looters already had done their work. In the new part of town, with its embassies and large homes, only the mayor's house and that of Premier Hoying-chin, acting President Li Tsung-jen, and other high officials had been stripped and looted.

Earlier, I had seen Ma's committee at work in the broken down, dowdy Nanking Hotel. In the dining room they sat around small tables, composing welcome slogans for the Communists—to be posted and printed in the papers.

The Nanking Hotel was the nerve center of the

few men which Ma had to keep order in this sprawling city of a million people.

His few hundred soldiers, volunteer militia and police could not handle the job if serious rioting broke out. His police, with their white arm bands, huddled near their stations, flying the white flag of the committee. They looked frightened by the artillery fire audible on the south.

Beyond the south edge of town on Blue Dragon Hill, two battalions of Nationalist artillery were firing at Chinese Red forces on the north bank of the Yangtze.

A member of Ma's committee said they were firing aimlessly and without effect, in an effort to cover the retreat of government troops.

Ma was worried about the city's key installations, the embassies, and the civilian population.

In his small bedroom, which is painted a ghastly pea-green, he was debating what to do about the small airfield inside the city walls. He was looking for enough men and trucks to take away the gasoline stored there. He said his committee was afraid the Nationalists would bomb it and destroy all installations there.

He had heard that all dumps had been blown up at the military field outside the city wall and had heard the explosions beginning at 9 o'clock last night. He wasn't reassured when Bill Kuan, of Agence France Presse, and I told him we had driven over it and found it deserted, except for a half a dozen planes burning on the field.

"You were lucky," he said. "The air force left time bombs on that field, just as they did along the water front."

He said his committee had tried to send a man across the river to contact the Communists and offer to surrender, but that the man was turned back by explosions and artillery fire.

Returning to The Associated Press house, just down the street a couple of blocks from Li Tsung-jen's looted residence, Bill Kuan and I passed through dark and deserted streets. Off to one side soldiers were firing now and then, apparently at looters.

It had not been like that on the ride to Ma's hotel. Then we had been stopped by a line of eight soldiers who wanted a ride on our jeep. They were polite but firm and pointed their rifles at us. They piled on the jeep and somehow the 10 of us made t up Chung-shan Road to the center of town, where a statue of Sun Yat-sen stared off into the darkness.

The soldiers said they were going to the south gate. We said we had to turn off to go to the Nanking Hotel. They climbed off reluctantly. Their sergeant said they were the last sentries to leave the Yangtze water front.
April 24, 1949

Editor's Note

AP coverage of the historic entry of Chinese Communist troops into Shanghai is described here by Fred Hampson, AP chief of the Shanghai bureau, who directed the coverage.

By Fred Hampson

SHANGHAI, CHINA, MAY 25 (AP)—My wife, Margaret, and I spent Tuesday night atop the Broadway Mansions, a 17-story skyscraper north of Soochow Creek, as Red troops began moving into Shanghai.

She remained there when I made my way to The Associated Press office across the creek in the old settlement. Throughout this morning, she telephoned developments seen from her vantage point.

While looking down on the creek's bridges from a balcony, she heard three rifle bullets whine past. She said the barricades still were being held by Nationalists on the Garden Bridge and that armored vehicles stood on Szechuan Bridge, two blocks up the creek.

Communists could be seen on the bund at Edward VII Avenue.

Looking down from the office window, I can see them too.

The last time Margaret telephoned, she ended her message by saying: "Everything is fine here, except I forgot my compact and powder puff, but I suppose we must expect these hardships in war."

Meanwhile, correspondent Amos Landman doffed his khaki shirt so that he would not be taken for a battle participant. He crept to the Cathay Hotel and watched fighting from the roof.

Landman reported that shots rang out from rooftops, where evidently a few Nationalists were holding out.

(Later, at noon Shanghai time, Hampson continued his description.)

Just below me, on Edward VII Avenue, a group of Communist soldiers came down the street carrying stacks of rifles they took from soldiers who barricaded themselves in the China Press-China Tribune Building but later surrendered.

The Reds examined the rifles with great interest.

These are the most professional-looking Chinese soldiers I ever saw.

Everybody connected with The Associated Press is covering the changeover from some vantage point. My house boy, Koo, just telephoned from his spot near the top of Hamilton House, which is across Fuchow Road from the city hall.

Koo said: "Master, just now I see through window mayor's office many Communists go in, open desk, take many papers. Just now many Communists reading papers."

For a while, the Great Northern Cable Building, where The Associated Press office is located, was blocked off by Red troops.

Correspondent Landman solved the problem by climbing over a high fence, scurrying behind a service station into an alley and reaching Szechwan Road. There, he got into the government radio office, where he stayed while developments were phoned to him.

An Associated Press local news editor, Eddie Crighton, who lives in the western part of the city, started for work at 6 a.m. He finally reached the office at 11 a.m. Eddie explained:

"Everyplace I went, they told me it was not safe to cross the street. So I walked around the block the other way. I walked around about 100 blocks getting here."

Eddie said the Communist troops were polite but firm, wherever he met them.

My wife, Margaret, who telephoned me play-by-play accounts of the fighting along the bund from her vantage point in Broadway Mansions, likely will have to spend the night there, along with 25 other foreigners trapped by the fighting.

American and British consulate employees were trapped in their buildings too.

The *Russian Daily News*, the pro-Soviet, independently owned Russian newspaper, was hit by a shell. But editor V. A. Chilikin telephoned The

Chairman Mao solemnly proclaims the founding of the People's Republic of China on the Tiananmen Gate rostrum on Oct. 1, 1949.

Associated Press office, which is barricaded, and worriedly asked for news stories.

"We were shelled but are publishing," he said.

Amos Landman, correspondent, and courier coolies crawled over a back fence and delivered the incoming report to him. Landman went on to the government cable office.

May 25, 1949

TRUMAN ADMINISTRATION CONCEDES CHINA

By John M. Hightower

WASHINGTON, AUG. 5 (AP)—The Truman administration today publicly abandoned all hope of saving China from the Reds by aiding its Nationalist government.

In an unprecedented blast, it labelled that government as a dismal failure in the war against communism.

Instead of aiding it, the administration laid down a policy of encouraging the Chinese people to throw off the "foreign yoke" of a Red regime which, Secretary of State Acheson charged, serves Russian imperialism.

The new turn in American policy was announced in a letter from Acheson to President Truman, presenting him with the long-awaited white paper on American relations with China. It was amplified in a statement which Acheson made in a news conference an hour after the white paper was made public.

In the statement Acheson laid down five "basic principles" for American relations with China, with emphasis on rebuilding "an independent" Chinese nation.

Criticism of the white paper sent by Acheson to President Truman today crossed party lines. One Democratic congressman called it an "alibi" for American failure.

A Democratic senator, Pat McCarran of Nevada, forecast that Acheson's proposed policy of giving only one arm's-length encouragement to internal Chinese resistance would bring all Asia under communist control "in a short time."

Republicans were almost unanimously critical. But the State Department course was defended by some Democrats, who saw it as the only "realistic" one to follow. Said Sen. Johnson (D-Colo):

"To intervene in the civil war in China would be reckless beyond description. The State Department in this instance is being realistic and sensible."

Mr. Truman had endorsed the Acheson letter at his own news conference yesterday and there was no doubt that it represented the considered views of the administration. It accepted the Communist conquest of China as an accomplished fact. Acheson argued that the Nationalists are militarily incapable of blocking the forward march of the Red armies into those areas of China which they do not yet actually control.

The 1,054-page official record of Chinese-American relations is probably without parallel in U.S. diplomatic history for its criticism of another friendly government. It bluntly blamed China's

114

fall to communism on Generalissimo Chiang Kai-shek and other Chinese Nationalist leaders. It said their unwillingness to win popular support for

their leadership was the root cause of their "failures."

Aug. 5, 1949

The Red Bomb

On the morning of Sept. 23, 1949, just 49 days after the administration had virtually written off China to the Communists, reporters were summoned to the office of Charles Ross, President Truman's press secretary. Ross was standing behind his big walnut desk. After ordering the doors locked, he passed out mimeographed sheets with Truman's announcement: The Soviet Union had detonated an atomic bomb.

The information had been gathered earlier that month. A reconnaissance plane had detected an unusually high level of radioactivity in the upper atmosphere. That was on Sept. 3; two days later another plane registered a far higher reading. After studying the evidence, a government panel in Washington decided the Soviets had deliberately exploded an atomic bomb sometime between Aug. 26 and Aug. 29 in the Asian part of the Soviet Union. On Sept. 19 the five members of the Atomic Energy Commission gave the president the news. He kept asking, "Are you sure?"

Truman had been counting on a U.S. nuclear monopoly. When he received word of the first successful American test detonation during the Potsdam conference in 1945, his demeanor shifted perceptibly. Churchill later described Truman as "a changed man. He told the Russians just where they got off and generally bossed the meeting." Indeed, Truman had told aides before the bomb test that if all went as expected, "I will certainly have a hammer on these boys"—the Soviets.

After the war the bomb became even more important, as the Soviet threat grew and American conventional armed strength waned. Truman believed the American monopoly would force the Soviets to be more cooperative. He accepted the most pessimistic estimates of the Soviet nuclear timetable, be-

lieving the Soviets simply did not have the technical know-how to build such a complicated weapon.

Indeed, most American scientists predicted that the Soviets—largely dependent on captured Nazi experts—would not be able to perfect the weapon until 1952. Some had not expected it until 1955.

For Truman, the Russian bomb was the worst possible news. "Don't overplay the story," Secretary of Defense Louis Johnson told reporters.

EVIDENCE OF RED BOMB

WASHINGTON, SEPT. 23 (AP)—The United States has evidence of a recent atomic explosion in Russia—news indicating the Communists have learned to make an A-bomb.

President Truman disclosed this in a statement today. He then held an hour-long session with his Cabinet about it.

Mr. Truman said the development emphasizes the necessity for "truly effective, enforceable international control of atomic energy."

The United States has sought that through the United Nations, but has been unable to get together with Russia on how it should be carried out.

With a note of reassurance to the American people, the president said the probability that some other nation might develop an atomic bomb "has always been taken into account by us."

American scientists have been ready with delicate instruments for months to record an atomic explosion anywhere in the world.

One competent source said he believed whatever apparatus reported the atomic explosions in Russia was probably located in the western zones of

Members of the Joint Congressional Atomic Energy Committee talk with Commissioner Sumner T. Pike as they started meeting to discuss ways and means of producing the hydrogen bomb approved by President Truman.

Austria or Germany rather than in the British Isles.
Sept. 23, 1949

TRUMAN'S DECISION TO DEVELOP H–BOMB

WASHINGTON, JAN. 31 (AP)—Congressional leaders tonight swung quickly behind President Truman's fateful decision to speed development of the hydrogen "super bomb."

Members of both Senate and House said they felt the president had no other choice in the Cold War with Russia, but they said fervently they hoped it would never be necessary to use such a fearsome weapon.

In announcing his decision, Mr. Truman said he acted to bolster this country's defenses "against any possible aggression."

He said the United States will drive ahead in the production of atomic weapons until international control is tightly safeguarded.

Reputedly 8 to 1,000 times more devastating that the atomic bombs dropped on Japan during

A view of the cloud formation after the H-bomb explosion by the United States. Photo taken at a height of approximately 12,000 feet, 50 miles from the detonation site. Two minutes after zero hour, the cloud rose to 40,000 feet, the height of 32 Empire State Buildings. Ten minutes later, as it neared its maximum, the cloud stem had pushed upward about 25 miles deep into the stratosphere. The mushroom portion went up to 10 miles and spread for 100 miles.

World War II, the H-bomb has been the subject of behind-the-scenes debate for at least four months.

Mr. Truman's announcement clearly took Senate-House Atomic Energy Committee members by surprise. The president had said last week that he alone had the power of decision—a statement which ruffled some lawmakers—and there were indications today that the committee had not expected a presidential announcement before next week.

Jan. 31, 1950

BEHIND THE DECISION

WASHINGTON, JAN. 31 (AP)—President Truman's decision to develop a hydrogen super bomb climaxes one of the greatest and most shadowy arguments in the peacetime history of this quarrelsome capital.

It also indicates Mr. Truman's own answers to some of the questions thrown up for public debate: Is it actually possible to make such a weapon? Is this weapon necessary to maintain America's supposed lead over Russia in the arms race? Is it morally right to develop a bomb that may be up to 1,000 times more destructive than bombs made from uranium?

The chief executive's answers to these questions appear, on the basis of his statement, to be:

1. The bomb is at least theoretically possible, and probably scientists are now convinced that it will work, with a terrible devastating force. This is shown by Mr. Truman's order to the Atomic Energy Commission "to continue its work on all forms of atomic weapons, including the so-called hydrogen or super bomb."

Unless his experts had advised him that the work would probably pay off, there would have been little if any basis for such a directive.

2. Since the bomb is possible, its manufacture is necessary in the defense of the country. The president emphasized he was issuing the order as commander in chief of the armed forces with the responsibility of seeing that "our country is able to defend itself against any possible aggressor."

In terms of today's world, his comment on this point has a wider meaning. The only possible aggressor foreseen by Washington officials at this time is Russia. Also, through the Atlantic Treaty the United States is committed to defense actions far beyond its own shores so that this nation's lead in the arms race may be regarded as a protection for Western Europe as well as North America.

3. As to the issue of morality, whether it is right to make the super bomb, Mr. Truman declared that the work "will be carried forward on a basis consistent with the overall objectives of our pro-

gram for peace and security." And he reaffirmed his desire for a "satisfactory plan for international control of atomic energy."

Judged in the light of information available from some top advisers, the president's statement suggests he may hold to the view that the morality of a weapon lies in questions of its use rather than its manufacture; and that in war the basically immoral act is the act of aggression which touches off the conflict.

In the atomic arms race, the United States takes the position that responsibility rests on Russia's unwillingness to agree with proposals for the control system already accepted by a majority of nations on the United Nations Atomic Energy Committee.

Both Secretary of State Dean Acheson and Defense Secretary Louis Johnson are reported to have advised the chief executive that in the absence of world controls for atomic weapons, the United States has no choice but to develop the most effective weapons it can.

Jan. 31, 1950

Editor's Note

The Soviet nuclear test, the historian Eric Goldman would write, had the effect of "stripping the American people of whatever security they felt behind their atomic stockpile, jangling nerves still more because the timetable of the trusted scientists had been wrong."

"There is only one thing worse than one nation having the atomic bomb," said Harold C. Urey, the Nobel Prize-winning atomic researcher. "That's two nations having it."

But the nuclear arms race was only beginning. After the Soviet bomb test, the United States began a crash program to build the "super bomb," or hydrogen bomb, which it first tested in 1952.

Election of 1948

Left: Republicans demonstrate for Gov. Thomas E. Dewey after his name was placed in nomination for the presidency.

Below: President Truman holds up a copy of the **Chicago Tribune** published early election night in 1948.

The election of 1948 was one of the most memorable in American history, from rambunctious campaign to startling conclusion. Years later, everyone of a certain age could still remember where they were and what they were thinking the moment they heard the news—Truman had beaten Dewey.

It was the year Franklin Roosevelt's New Deal coalition splintered, Southern Democrats, or Dixiecrats, stormed out of the Democratic convention after it adopted a strong civil rights platform plank. They formed the States Rights Party and nominated South Carolina Gov. Strom Thurmond for president. The new, left-wing Progressive Party, representing another part of the New Deal coalition, nominated former Vice President Henry Wallace for president.

WALLACE ANNOUNCES

CHICAGO, DEC. 29 (AP)—Henry A. Wallace, stormy petrel of politics, who has been a Republican Party member and later a Democratic vice president, tonight announced his candidacy for president as an Independent.

Wallace, in an address over the Mutual Network, said he would campaign for his third party on a platform advocating "peace and prosperity."

The former Cabinet member under the late President Roosevelt accused the Democratic and Republican parties of standing "for a policy which opens the door to war in our lifetime, and makes war certain for our children."

He declared that the menace to peace was greater than ever before and "that menace can be met and overcome only by a new political alignment in America which requires the organization of a new political party."

Republicans, whose comments largely welcomed Wallace's announcement, reasoned that the Iowan has a following which could swing away some votes from the Democrats.

The Democrats, who anticipated the announcement, advanced the theory that if the former secretary of commerce pulled no punches in criticizing the administration of President Truman, his candidacy actually will work for Mr. Truman's benefit.

The Democrats reasoned that if Wallace attacks Mr. Truman, the public would be led to believe he is acting out of personal bitterness toward the president who dismissed him from the secretaryship for interfering in foreign affairs.

Wallace, whose group at the radio studio tonight included singer Paul Robeson, Negro baritone once named by the House Committee on Un-American Activities as one of a group of persons "which are invariably found supporting the Communist Party and its front organizations," said "thousands of people had asked him to engage in this great fight."
Dec. 29, 1947

DAILY WORKER BACKS WALLACE

NEW YORK, DEC. 30 (AP)—The *Daily Worker*, official organ of the Communist Party, said editorially this morning of Henry A. Wallace's announcement:

"Every honest American must know that the Truman Democratic Party and the Taft-Dewey GOP are at bottom a single party, united on the same platform of reaction, profiteering and war.

"Wallace's declaration should be studied for what it is—a historic challenge to a vast and sinister conspiracy against the true interests of the United States.

"Wallace's candidacy and the platform on which he makes his fight, sounds the call for a national fight for peace which will show where every progressive really stands, for peace and democracy, or for witch hunts and war."

Mrs. Eleanor Roosevelt, informed last night that Henry A. Wallace had announced his candidacy for president, said:

"Does he really thing he's going to win?"

Told that Mr. Wallace had said in his Chicago speech that a vote for him would be a vote for peace and against a policy which he charged was leading to war with Russia, Mrs. Roosevelt said:

"Oh dear, oh dear."
Dec. 30, 1947

IKE SAYS NO

WASHINGTON, JAN. 23 (AP)—Gen. Dwight D. Eisenhower today told his supporters for the presidency: "I am not available for and could not accept nomination to high political office."

His letter was addressed to a New Hampshire Republican backing him for the party's 1948 presidential nomination, but it was made public generally, the Army's press department said, "because Gen. Eisenhower hopes through this means to inform every interested person or group that he is not in politics and that he would refuse the nomination if offered."

Then, as if to squelch any remaining doubt that he is pulling out of the presidential running, Eisenhower closed his letter to Leonard V. Finder, publisher of the *Manchester Evening Leader*, with these words:

"My decision to remove myself completely from the political scene is definite and positive. I know you will not object to my making this letter public to inform all interested persons that I could not accept the nomination even under the remote circumstances that it were tendered me."

Finder had written the chief of staff that his name had been entered in the March 9 New Hampshire presidential primary. He said, "We are deeply confident that you will not resist or resent a genuine grass roots movement."

Eisenhower's announcement is expected to increase activity on the part of followers of the four avowed candidates now in the Republican field—Gov. Dewey of New York, Sen. Taft of Ohio, former Gov. Harold E. Stassen of Minnesota and Gov. Warren of California.
Jan. 23, 1948

THE TRUMAN PROGRAM

WASHINGTON, FEB. 2 (AP)—President Truman asked Congress today to pass federal laws against lynching and against discrimination in voting or employment on grounds of race, creed or color.

In a 4,000-word message, the president outlined a 10-point program to correct what he called "flagrant" offenses against the American faith—that "all men are created equal and that they have the right to equal justice."

Mr. Truman replied in advance to the objection, frequently raised in the South, that this is a matter for state and local governments to deal with, in keeping with local problems and traditions.

"The federal government has a clear duty," he said, "to see that constitutional guarantees of individual liberties and of equal protection under the laws are not denied or abridged anywhere in our union."

Taking a stand on two questions charged with political dynamite in the South, the president:

1. Called for anti-discrimination laws covering election of state as well as federal officers.

2. Asked Congress to end the requirement, in some states, that residents pay a poll tax before voting in federal elections.

Mr. Truman called for re-establishment of the wartime Fair Employment Practice Commission—a step certain to be fought by some Southern legislators to the point of filibuster if necessary.

He also proposed:

Establishment of a permanent commission to study civil rights questions, a joint committee of Congress for the same purpose and a civil rights division in the Department of Justice.

Home rule, and the right to vote in presidential elections, for residents of the District of Columbia—now voteless and governed by Congress and a commission appointed by the president.

Statehood for the territories of Hawaii and Alaska, and a larger degree of self-government for our island possessions.

An end to discrimination in interstate travel—"Jim Crow" separation of whites and Negroes.

Removal of racial or national barriers which prevent U.S. residents from becoming citizens.

The setting up of machinery to pay the damage claims of the more than 100,000 Japanese-Americans evacuated from Pacific coast states during the war.

Insuring equality for all our citizens, the president said, will make us "stronger in our leadership, stronger in our moral position," as we strive with the free nations of the world to create a lasting peace.

He declared that this country will not achieve the ideals on which it was founded "so long as any American suffers discrimination as a result of his race, or religion, or color, or the land of origin of his forefathers."

Members of both houses of Congress and the Cabinet hear President Truman (extreme left) deliver his State of the Union address in the House chamber, Jan. 7, 1948. Members of the Cabinet, seated in first row at left center, are, from the left: Secretary of Labor Lewis Schwellenbach, Secretary of Commerce W. Averell Harriman, Secretary of Interior Julius Krug, Postmaster General Jesse Donaldson, Attorney General Tom Clark, Secretary of Defense James Forrestal, Secretary of Treasury John W. Snyder and Secretary of State George Marshall.

He said the recent report of his commission on civil rights shows that there is "a serious gap between our ideals and some of our practices."
Feb. 2, 1948

THE DIXIECRATS REBEL

WASHINGTON, FEB. 18 (AP)—A group of Southern Democrats tonight cancelled plans to attend the annual party dinners tomorrow night because of a "no segregation" policy.

Mrs. Olin D. Johnston, wife of the junior South Carolina senator, told a reporter she would not show up for the Jefferson-Jackson Day dinner "because she might be seated next to a Negro."

Mrs. Johnston is vice chairman of the dinner committee.

Earlier it was revealed that Gov. and Mrs. Strom Thurmond of South Carolina also had cancelled their reservations to attend the party's fund-raising festivities. An address by President Truman will climax the evening.

Gov. Thurmond is chairman of a group of five Southern governors who will meet with national

Democratic leaders here Monday to discuss the Dixie revolt against President Truman's civil rights program.

Mrs. Johnston said she had asked Democratic National Chairman J. Howard McGrath to arrange it so her party of approximately 45 would not be seated next to Negroes. She herself was to have been seated at the speakers' table. She said the party now has dwindled to about 30 and some of these may still decide to stay away "because of the race issue."

Mrs. Johnston said "Senator McGrath has made it impossible for us to go. He would not give an inch."

She declared the "whole dinner-seating issue is symbolic of party leaders' efforts to get minority votes through 'civil rights' proposals that led to threats of a Southern bolt."

McGrath refused to comment on Mrs. Johnston's remarks. But he did say that some dozen or more Negroes would attend the $100 per plate party. He added that he could not impose any policy of segregation at the party.

Mrs. Johnston said some Southerners are "demanding their $100 back." It could not be learned from party officials if the request will be granted.
Feb. 18, 1948

WASHINGTON, FEB. 23 (AP)—A group of Southern governors tonight called on "Democrats everywhere" to join the revolt against President Truman's civil rights program.

Declaring that the South is no longer "in the bag" for the Democratic Party, they said "strong and effective" action is needed to "save" the party and to "preserve American democracy."

The call was issued by the governors of North Carolina, South Carolina, Texas and Arkansas after they and Gov. W. Preston Lane Jr. of Maryland held a showdown session with Democratic National Chairman J. Howard McGrath.

McGrath gave a flat "no" to their request that he work for withdrawal of Mr. Truman's anti-discrimination proposals.
Feb. 25, 1948

DEWEY ANNOUNCES

ALBANY, N.Y., JAN. 16 (AP)—Gov. Thomas E.

At a 1948 Lincoln Day dinner before Massachusetts Republican leaders in Boston, Gov. Thomas E. Dewey of New York stresses a point as he lashes out against the foreign policies of the Truman administration.

Dewey late today announced his candidacy for the Republican presidential nomination through a "surprise" statement by a member of his staff.

The New York governor, 1944 GOP standard bearer, broke his long official silence on his availability by authorizing his executive assistant, James C. Hagerty, to issue a statement saying he "would accept" if nominated.

Dewey was in seclusion at his farm in Pawling. He is expected back here tomorrow.

Hagerty said the statement resulted from "queries" about the entry yesterday in Oregon's pref-

erential primary in May of a full state of convention delegates pledged to the Empire State executive."
Jan. 16, 1948

TRUMAN ON WESTERN TOUR

SPOKANE, WASH., JUNE 1 (AP)—President Truman lambasted the GOP-controlled Congress yesterday as the worst one we've ever had.

And House Speaker Martin fired back that there are people who have said the same thing about the president.

The president, bidding openly for votes in November, demanded overthrow of the Republican majority on Capitol Hill. He ripped into the GOP legislative record at Spokane, Wash., on his Western tour.

First he reached for the labor vote by telling a union group that if it wants to do something about the Taft-Hartley labor law, the "only remedy is November 1948."

"If you continue that law, in effect, that is your fault and not mine, because I didn't want it," the president said in an unscheduled talk to the national convention of the Communications Workers of America.

Then, before a civic celebration he told citizens that they deserve a continuance of the present Congress if they fail to vote.

He brought out his most heated criticism of the lawmaking body in a scathing exchange with a newspaper reporter from the *Spokane Spokesman-Review* as the president stood on the rear platform of his train.

He called the *Chicago Tribune* and the *Spokesman-Review* "the two worst papers in the country."

And then, the president added that the *Tribune* got what it wanted: "the worst Congress we've had since the first one met."

Reaction was immediate on Capitol Hill. Said Sen. Wherry (R-Neb.), acting Senate Republican leader:

"That's a curious statement from the nonpolitical, bipartisan investigation trip that the president said he was making. That's just ward politics."
June 1, 1948

A lei about his shoulders, Gov. Thomas E. Dewey of New York smiles at cheering delegates as he appears on the speaker's stand in Convention Hall, Philadelphia, June 24, 1948, to acknowledge his nomination as the GOP standard bearer in the forthcoming elections.

DEWEY NOMINATED

CONVENTION HALL, PHILADELPHIA, JUNE 24 (AP)—The Republican National Convention unanimously placed its presidential banner for a second time tonight in the hands of Thomas E. Dewey.

And proudly he accepted the nomination, with a pledge to work for "freedom of men" everywhere in these times of "grave challenge."

The New York governor walked away with his personal victory on the third ballot of the 24th GOP convention—1,094 to 0.

"Hallelujah," cried Mrs. Dudley Hay, convention secretary, as she finished the roll call.

The party had decided to try to make a winner in 1948 of its 1944 loser. Exactly four years ago,

Sen. Robert A. Taft (R-Ohio) speaks with emphasis during a radio discussion in Washington, May 18, 1948. The candidate for the Republican presidential nomination said that "we cannot outlaw communism" but should drive it into the open and expose it. Seated on the platform are (from left, first row): Thurman Arnold, former assistant attorney general; G.V. Denny, program moderator; Rep. Richard M. Nixon (R-Calif.), co-author of an anti-communism bill; and Ralph E. McGill, editor of the **Atlanta Constitution.**

lacking a day, the GOP gave Dewey his first fling at the White House. He lost to the old master, Franklin D. Roosevelt.

But this time, the Republicans were cockily proclaiming, it will be different against Harry S. Truman—or anyone else the Democrats might put up.

Again, as at Chicago in 1944, Dewey had things his way almost from the start. He romped out ahead on the first ballot. On the second he raided opposition camps, lassoed stray votes from dele-

gation after delegation and pulled to within 33 votes of the glittering goal of 548.

A coalition had tried frantically to stop him. In it were other candidates, men of stature within the party. They never had a chance, but they were late finding it out.

Included among them were Sen. Robert A. Taft of Ohio, former Gov. Harold E. Stassen of Minnesota, Gov. Earl Warren of California, Sen. Arthur H. Vandenberg of Michigan.

Dewey even gave them time in a two-and-a-half hour recess to reorganize their strategy. The best they could do was meekly submit to the pressure of rank and file delegates who saw the New Yorker walking away with the nomination. Those delegates wanted to be with him when he won.

So the anti-Dewey boom collapsed dramatically and completely.

One after another emissaries for the faltering candidates—and Stassen in person—hustled to the convention platform. One after another they surrendered. Each in turn promised to pitch in and help guarantee a Republican election in November.
June 24, 1948

DEMS IN PHILADELPHIA

PHILADELPHIA, JULY 9 (AP)—There is a for-whom-the-bell-tolls atmosphere in Philadelphia today.

The Democratic convention opens Monday, and, according to the sign on the depot, this is the same city that entertained the Republicans two weeks ago. But it doesn't look or feel or sound the same. Registering at the hotel today was like checking in at a haunted house.

The difference lies in this:

The Republicans came here convinced that they were nominating the next president. Hence, theirs was a joyous session of skull-crushing and shin-kicking, a boisterous battle-royal that left even the vanquished with much to expect next November. They were alive, lusty and vital.

The Democrats act as though they have accepted an invitation to a funeral.

Old-timers say they have never seen a convention start under such a cloud of plain depression.

The trappings are all here. The city is beflagged and bedizened. The red, white, and blue signs denoting headquarters and offices are gleaming in the lobbies and corridors.

A jaunty handout announces that the marquee of the Bellevue-Stratford, this time, will have a more durable party symbol than the Republicans were able to display.

The rubber Republican elephant developed a slow leak early in the other proceedings. His knees buckled and his trunk became softer and

softer, and finally completely limp, a very depressing sight.

The Democrats are erecting an electrical donkey that will snort out smoke, waggle its head and kick.

The party has placed a large portrait of Franklin D. Roosevelt in Convention Hall. Mr. Truman's portrait smiles down from the wall at headquarters.

Some delegates speak wistfully of Gen. of the Army Dwight D. Eisenhower, and when they mention his name it takes on the quality of a magic word.

"If only Ike would…."

In trying to find some delegates last night, a reporter questioned a hotel desk clerk. He looked puzzled, so the newsman explained he meant delegates to the convention.

To which the clerk replied, "What convention?"
July 9, 1948

WOMEN SEEK EQUALITY PLANK
By Relman Morin

PHILADELPHIA, JULY 9 (AP)—They fought another round today in the battle of the sexes, and gentlemen—I mean you brutes—you took an awful beating.

Eighteen militant ladies, members of the National Women's Party, appeared before the Democratic Convention Resolutions Committee. Their purpose was to get an "equal rights" plank into the party platform, now in process of construction. Rolling up in relays, they talked for 66 minutes.

And they had nothing good to say for that half of the human race that wears suspenders.

For example, do you know why, in some places, women are not permitted to work after 10 o'clock at night in an ice cream parlor?

The question was asked by Mrs. Emma Guffey Miller, leader of the party.

She waited in vain for an answer from the committee.

"I'll tell you why," said Mrs. Miller. "Because after 10 o'clock, the tips are bigger, that's why."

She paused a moment to let this sink in. Then she added, "That's why the men are so chivalrous… won't let women work late at night… so-called protective legislation for women." Mrs. Miller sniffed. "It's because the tips are bigger."

Nobody asked the explanation for this phenomenon, and Mrs. Miller did not volunteer it. The inference was that, after 10 o'clock, as those ice-cream sodas and double chocolate malts begin to take effect, the customers are more generous with their tipping.

Nevertheless, at the press table, we all lowered our eyes, blushing. Hard-boiled reporters leaned down to tie a shoelace, or sidled toward the door, mumbling something about a glass of water.

Mrs. Miller then summoned the other 17 ladies.

The majority of them seemed to be professional women, doctors, lawyers, politicians. No housewives appeared. They had gray or graying hair. And they wore floppy hats, print dresses and glittering spectacles. One of them declined to sit before the microphone, asserting, "Everybody can hear what I'm going to say."

Briefly, their argument is that discrimination against women is practiced, generally, in business. They proposed to end this by legislation.

Among their opponents on the issue is the CIO, which argues that the special privileges for women, now guaranteed by many laws, will be lost if equality on all points is written into the statutes.

In the course of this, some interesting facts and statements went into the record, such as:

"Every man has his woman on a pedestal anyway, and this would make it legal."

"During the war, women went right on giving life and bringing children into the world."

"The women of Italy and Japan held their countries together in spite of everything the enemy could do." The witness did not specify whether she meant men in general, or just the United States armed forces.

And finally, to illustrate what a serious matter this is, one testified: "I spent many a sleepless night in the legislature."

July 9, 1948

THE DEMOCRATIC CONVENTION

By Relman Morin

PHILADELPHIA, JULY 13 (AP)—This is about a raw steak, held aloft in the dainty hands of a lady wearing diamonds.

The Democrats are feeling a little stronger today because of this steak, plus some salty oratory and 28 minutes of strenuous exercise in the steam room.

Of course, they still lack a presidential candidate who will be acceptable to all sections of the party. But they may have found the nominee for vice president, of whom more will be said here.

First of all, the steak.

It was a real one, a medium-sized sirloin, raw, red, limp and damp. It was introduced in evidence, so to speak, by Mrs. India Edwards, chairman of the women's division of the National Committee. She was proving a point with it.

Mrs. Edwards, handsome and fashionable in after-dinner black, brought a market bag with her when she made her speech, blaming the Republicans for the high cost of food. The bag contained a quart of milk, a pound of margarine—and the red meat.

The price of each was stated by the speaker. And if her object was to startle her hearers with the steak, she achieved it in full measure. They gasped, gulped, then laughed and cheered.

It hung in her hand, oozing limply down between her fingers, and partly obscuring the diamond rings that glittered and twinkled in the bright klieg lights. It looked, somehow, like a red jellyfish stuck on a trident encrusted with jewels.

Mrs. Edwards told her audience how much she had paid for it. Then she put it down on the rostrum beside her. Because of the slant in the rostrum, the steak began to creep downhill until it was dripping partly over the edge.

She retrieved it, to the delight of the photographers, who asked her to hold it up again "for just one more." Mrs. Edwards complied.

This could not have continued much longer. The Convention Hall was so hot that, very shortly, the steak would have begun to broil. She tossed it into a large white box with green stripes that also housed a large toy balloon. The balloon was supposed to symbolize inflation.

Mrs. Edward's steak and the rolling periods of Sen. Alben W. Barkley's keynote speech, delivered just before, put the Democrats in a mood they have not known since the convention began.

The senator is a square-set, barrel-bodied man

with white hair and a flinty, fighting face. He delivered a fighting speech, and it was just what the strife-torn Democrats wanted to hear.

He was wearing whites. And as he thundered through 69 minutes of oratory, waving his arms and beating the air with his big fists, a great brown patch of sweat began to stain the white coat. It spread downward, from the middle of his back to his hips. When he had finished, even his trousers were flecked with wet.

The crowd gave him an ovation.

It was partly genuine, but in the opinion of many observers it was assisted, here and there, by a little assiduous needling.

Unquestionably, Sen. Barkley had made an impression. The delegates poured out of their chairs into the aisles, spontaneously.

The fact that they had been sitting for two hours on hard wooden chairs, and that Sen. Barkley had been rumored as a vice-presidential possibility, and that the band was playing the thrilling, blood-lifting songs of Dixie—these things may have had something to do with it, too.

They were happy, excited, jubilant people as they struggled down to the rostrum, sweating and stumbling in the 92-degree heat of the hall.

The senator looked happy, too. He stayed right there for 28 minutes, shaking hands with some, shaking the state standards of those he could not reach.

The band blared on. Democratic bigwigs were summoned to the platform to embrace him. And as each new embrace was made, the demonstration received a new impetus.

It was a fine 28 minutes for everybody—and the Democrats needed it badly.

July 13, 1948

DEMOCRATS REVEAL PLATFORM

CONVENTION HALL, PHILADELPHIA, JULY 14 (AP)—The Democratic National Convention handed the South a double-barreled defeat on the race issue today. It slapped down Dixie's states rights plank and then amended the platform to stamp endorsement on President Truman's civil rights program.

Mr. Truman's civil rights program, that has split the party, calls for federal anti-lynch, anti-poll tax,

anti-discrimination and fair employment practices legislation. Southerners contend these are matters for the states to handle.

The crucial convention action on the race issue came in the face of a solemn warning from one Dixie spokesman that it would mean destruction of the Democratic Party in the South.

Some Southern delegates quickly made plans to call a separate convention, nominate their own candidate for president and write their own platform.

The history-making political development, that may determine whether Democrats will be one party or two, rocked the convention just before a majority of delegates shouted approval of a 5,000-word 1948 "Roosevelt-Truman" platform.

First the convention refused, 925 to 309, to put a states rights plank in the platform. This plank, offered by former Gov. Dan Moody of Texas, would have declared that states have the right to run their own internal affairs and police powers. Thus, the South had sought, while joining in support of a general civil rights plank, to have the convention declare that states have jurisdiction over the legal processes governing those rights.

Then, to rub it in, the convention adopted an amendment to the platform sponsored by Mayor Hubert H. Humphrey of Minneapolis and former Rep. Andrew Biemiller of Wisconsin, endorsing the president's civil rights stand. The vote was 651½ to 582½.

Rep. John Bell Williams, Mississippi delegate, issued a statement saying:

"It drives a knife into the heart of the party and reads the South out of the party."

Mayor Humphrey shouted to the convention that the words "all men are equal" in the Declaration of Independence mean equality without regard to race. He demanded a "new emancipation proclamation" with a party declaration on "human rights" instead of states rights.

July 14, 1948

TRUMAN NOMINATED

CONVENTION HALL, PHILADELPHIA, JULY 15 (AP)—Harry S. Truman was nominated for president early today by a Democratic Party facing its worst split since before the Civil War.

At Philadelphia's Convention Hall on July 14, 1948, delegates applaud as President Harry S. Truman accepts the Democratic Party's nomination to head his party's 1948 ticket. Behind the president are Rep. Sam Rayburn (hands on hips), convention chairman, and Sen. Alben W. Barkley (hand to head), vice-presidential nominee.

The president won the nomination on the first ballot, after one Southern delegation and half of another one stormed out of the convention in rebellion against the 1948 platform endorsement of Mr. Truman's civil rights program.

And as the president made ready to accept the nomination in person, angry Dixie rebels called a convention of their own at Birmingham, Ala., next Saturday—to discuss forming a new party with an anti-Truman states rights candidate.

Mr. Truman romped home handily in his race for the nomination. He got 947½ votes to 263 for Sen. Richard Russell of Georgia and one-half a vote for Paul V. McNutt, former governor of Indiana.

Russell was thrust forward as a candidate in a final gesture of defiance by Dixie rebels—against the president many of them now are vowing to beat in the November election. McNutt got into the edge of the picture the same way.

Some of the Southerners shouted in the convention: "Truman can't win."

One rebellious Southerner, Charles J. Bloch of Georgia, shouted to fellow delegates:

"You know—and if you don't know you'll learn it now—the Democrats can't elect a president without the votes of the South."

Dixie delegates, almost without exception, tossed their ballots to Russell in futile protest against Mr. Truman and his demands for federal laws against lynching, poll taxes and racial discrimination in jobs.

But ironically for the South, and its spectacular but losing battle, it was 13 of North Carolina's 32 votes that pushed Mr. Truman beyond the 618 total he needed to win on the first ballot.

July 15, 1948

DIXIECRATS NAME NOMINEES

By Leroy Simms

BIRMINGHAM, ALA., JULY 17 (AP)—Defiant Dixie Democrats named two Southern governors today to head a campaign to defeat Mr. Truman in the solid South in November.

J. Strom Thurmond, 45, of South Carolina, was chosen as presidential candidate. Fielding L. Wright, 53, of Mississippi, was named for vice president.

Angered over what both candidates termed "a stab in the back" at the Democratic Convention earlier this week, the tumultuous meeting gave shouting agreement to assertions the South will never surrender local control on racial issues.

Neither candidate made any claim of victory, but both promised to show the national party "the real Democratic Party is in the South."

Campaigns were planned in 15 states, including Missouri, home of Mr. Truman.

Birmingham's city auditorium was unable to hold the crowds.

It seats 6,000, but the manager of the hall said at least 7,500 were inside for the afternoon session and many others outside, listening through loudspeakers.

The statement of principles, similar to the usual party platform, devoted major attention to civil rights.

"We stand for segregation of the races and the racial integrity of each race," the committee reported.

Pickets bearing pro-Henry Wallace placards paraded briefly before the municipal auditorium

A highlight of the 1948 Democratic National Convention in Philadelphia was the July 14 walkout of the Alabama and Mississippi delegates over the controversial states rights issue.

shortly before the start of the meeting this morning. They were led by Robert Travis, chairman of the Peoples' Progressive Party of Alabama. He said "we just want the decent people of the South to know there are some opposed to such actions as these here."

July 17, 1948

PROGRESSIVE PARTY MEETS

By Relman Morin

PHILADELPHIA, JULY 24 (AP)—This is the same political convention mixture as before.

Henry Wallace's new party, "Progressive" as it calls itself officially, is in formal convention.

Except for a mite more enthusiasm, a more sustained "yay-yay, yay," and a somewhat marked difference in delegate dress, this conclave

On July 24, 1948, Henry A. Wallace formally accepts the Progressive Party's 1948 presidential nomination at the new party's noisy, outdoor rally at Shibe Park in Philadelphia.

is pretty much like the other two—Republican and Democratic—that met here during recent weeks.

It is a polo-shirt convention, and a conclave of bare shoulders. You see more of both than you saw when the Republicans and Democrats were in session.

It seems to have attracted more women, many more, than the major parties brought to Convention Hall. For the most part, they are young women, and they wear spectacles, with those oddly shaped rims that induce an unusually owlish look.

The two possibly notable differences between this convention and the others are in intensity and the amount of music.

These people hiss their villains, in the manner of a Gay '90s melodrama, whereas there was never a boo from the Republicans when they mentioned a Democratic villain, or vice versa. It was a new experience to hear a speaker interrupted, and forced to pause, while people hissed and booed.

They applauded with equal vigor.

Some of the speakers, notably the sleek and electric young congressman from New York City, Leo Isaacson, was forced to halt after virtually every sentence last night. A tall, heavy-chested young man in a yellow polo shirt, standing near the rostrum, would yell "Oh, boy, Leo—yay-yay, yay—give it to 'em, Leo!" A fat woman rose from her chair, waving her handkerchief and throwing kisses.

The Progressives are miles ahead of the two major parties in the field of music. It is a singing convention, and they have cheerful, melodious songs, many of them lifted from spirituals and the folk music of back-country America.

Pete Seeger, of New York, is the maestro.

He is a thin and gangling young man with an enormous haystack of brown hair and a banjo that he beats unmercifully. He took possession of the rostrum and its microphones last night for a collectively greater amount of time than any other one person.

He first appeared in a wine-colored coat and brown trousers. Later, he put aside the coat, whanging his banjo, and, calling for chorus after chorus, Seeger faced a larger audience, and whipped it into greater enthusiasm than many a more celebrated musician.

But apart from these minor variations, the theme was the same, and the pattern was virtually identical.

The Progressives have a wider field of criticism because they can attack both the Republicans and Democrats. They tore into President Truman and the Republican-dominated 80th Congress with equal eagerness. And like both the Republicans and Democrats, they confidently announced a victory in November.

On the appropriate occasions, they demonstrated in the aisles, leaving their seats and milling around the hall, waving banners, while the band played and the galleries howled.

It is a mixture as before—people having a high old time.

July 24, 1948

DEMS BAN STAFF SEGREGATION

WASHINGTON, AUG. 4 (AP)—The Democratic National Committee has banned race segregation in its headquarters staff in a new bid for Negro support in the presidential election.

Confirming the change, National Chairman J. Howard McGrath said the committee "merely is being consistent" by putting into effect a policy urged by President Truman for government jobs and the armed forces.

McGrath said he expects to announce later the appointment of a Negro assistant to the chairman.

McGrath said the committee is abolishing its Negro division as such and distributing its Negro workers among other units. He said there will be no race discrimination in the hiring of stenographers, clerks or other employees.

The Republican National Committee maintains a Negro division with Val Washington, of Chicago, former Illinois state official, as its head. William Murphy, GOP publicity director, said several Negroes are employed on the headquarters staff.

McGrath's move was looked on by some Dixie Democrats as a further sign that the administration is more interested in Negro support from the big-vote states than it is in patching up the party row in the South.

Aug. 4, 1948

THE CAMPAIGN BEGINS

WASHINGTON, SEPT. 17 (AP)—The presidential campaign began yesterday to bloom into vigor, with President Truman saying he was going to give the opposition "hell" and Gov. Dewey accusing the Democrats of lying to the farmers.

Mr. Truman rolled today toward Iowa for the start of a 100-speech campaign planned by the Democrats to harvest the votes he needs to keep him in the White House four more years. It was, in the president's own words, a "Give 'em Hell" campaign tour.

Mr. Truman showed no signs of being daunted.

"I'm going to fight hard and give them hell," he said, as his 17-car special train left Washington for a 9,500-mile trip to the West Coast and back. He agreed with Sen. Alben Barkley of Kentucky, his running mate, who came down to see him off: "It's a victorious trip."
Sept. 17, 1948

THE PRESIDENT AND THE FARMERS

DEXTER, IOWA, SEPT. 18 (AP)—President Truman ate a country dinner in his shirtsleeves today.

Sitting down to a chicken dinner with a group of farmers and dignitaries after making a major campaign speech, the president removed his coat and set the example for others at the table.

The table, covered with a red-and-white checkered cloth, was set up in a large tent. Folding chairs were placed around it for 32 persons, including Mrs. Truman and their daughter, Margaret.

The president shook hands and chatted with those seated nearby. He was flanked at the table by Howard Walker and Ralph Mortimer, Iowa farmers.

Next to Walker was Mrs. Lois Agg, on whose farm the speech was delivered. Mrs. Truman and Margaret were each a couple of seats removed from the chief executive.

The president ate heartily of fried chicken, mashed potatoes, buttered corn, baked beans, tomatoes, relish, cheese and coffee.

A few yards away, plowmen with tractors and plows were turning furrows for $1,500 in prizes offered to the National Plowing Match.

Hundreds of cars stood hub to hub in nearby fields, and one level plot was reserved for the planes used by dozens of flying farmers.

After lunch the president drove out to look over some conservation projects in nearby fields.

Walker and Mortimer said Mr. Truman expressed amazement at the size of the crowd (an estimated 80,000) and commented on the "excellent" dinner, but did not discuss politics.

Miss Jean Carter, 22, of Dallas Center, Iowa, queen of the plowing festival, was photographed with the president.

"I have been fussed all day, so meeting Mr. Truman didn't fuss me any more," she commented. She added that he was "much more handsome than I had expected, and charming."

The president viewed a demonstration in dam

President Truman speaks from the train platform in Pocatello, Idaho, while on the 1948 campaign trail.

building but didn't do any plowing because, he said, "there weren't any mules."

Later he made a second speech to the crowd, remarking that he had a pleasant time at Dexter. He said he had looked for crooks and jumps in the plowed furrows and found only two such spots.

Then the president said that in making a second speech he felt like a fellow who went to his wife's funeral and was asked by the undertaker to ride with his mother-in-law. The fellow protested, Mr.

Truman said, that having to do that would spoil his whole day.

Mr. Truman reminisced about his own experiences on the farm and how he used to get behind a gang plow. He said plowing is easier now.

"I don't want to go back to those horse-and-buggy days," he said, "although some of our Republican friends do."

Sept. 18, 1948

President Harry S. Truman, off on his cross-country campaign tour, waves from the rear coach of his special train at Harrisburg, Pa., Sept. 17, 1948. The crowd is largely composed of representatives from a railroad brotherhood.

TRUMAN ON THE ATTACK

ABOARD TRUMAN CAMPAIGN TRAIN, SEPT. 22 (AP)—President Truman today asked Western voters to "fire" the Republican 80th Congress, which he said is led by "a bunch of old mossbacks."

Welcomed to Reno by a crowd the police estimated at 25,000, the president said a Republican victory would return to control the "Wolcotts, the Tabers, the Allens and Martins."

He referred, respectively, to the Republican chairmen of the House Banking, Appropriations and Rules Committees and to Speaker Martin.

The men who lead the Congress and who head its committees, he said in an address to a throng outside the Nevada State Building, are "a bunch of old mossbacks" living as though it were 1890.

Earlier, in a talk to another crowd at Sparks, Mr. Truman referred to his Republican opponents as exponents of "double talk."

"You know where I stand," the president declared from an improvised stand off a main street.

"Everybody knows where I stand. You don't get

any double talk from me. I hope you can find out what the other people stand for when they come out here. But I greatly fear you won't for a long, long time."

He carried his campaign into Nevada and California on the theme that a Democratic victory in November will mean "a glorious West with wealth and security for our people."

A major address before a cheering overflow crowd in Salt Lake City's Mormon Tabernacle set the tone for rear platform speeches at "whistle stops" en route to addresses in Oakland and San Francisco tonight.
Sept. 22, 1948

DEWEY IN CALIFORNIA
By Marvin L. Arrowsmith

LOS ANGELES, SEPT. 24 (AP)—Gov. Thomas E. Dewey pledged tonight to wage a war of truth against communism—a "mighty worldwide counteroffensive"—if he wins the presidency.

The Republican candidate made the promise in addressing a near-capacity crowd in the 20,000-seat Hollywood Bowl.

Dewey told the applauding, whistling throng that what he has in mind is a counteroffensive of truth and hope, free of "aggressive acts."

The New York governor slapped back at President Truman's "red herring" tag on the congressional inquiry into Communist spy activities.

In using that phrase, Dewey said Mr. Truman—without mentioning his name—was jeering at the Communist threat.

The GOP candidate also accused the Democratic administration of "giving aid and comfort to the enemies of our system" of government.

The setting for Dewey's speech was in the Hollywood tradition. Huge spotlights played on the flag-draped speakers' stand.

A line of baton-twirling chorus girls entertained the big crowd before Dewey arrived. The turnout was the largest Dewey has had since he started his Western tour.

The film colony was well represented.

George Murphy served as master of ceremonies. Jeanette MacDonald sang "The Star Spangled Banner." Also on hand were Gary Cooper,
Ginger Rogers, Dennis Morgan, Barbara Stanwyck and others.
Sept. 24, 1948

TRUMAN IN KENTUCKY
By Ernest B. Vaccaro

ABOARD TRUMAN CAMPAIGN TRAIN, OCT. 1 (AP)—President Truman moved through Kentucky today like a trouper doing 10-minute stands, mingling campaign issues with historical chitchat on the Truman ancestry.

He wowed 'em at Shelbyville with the story of Grandfather Truman, who ran off and got married in that town, and Grandmother Young's brother, who escaped jury duty by living in a house astride the county line.

It was early, but Police Chief Roy Jones estimated that 4,000 persons were in the crowd that thronged around the rear platform of the president's car. Mr. Truman talked to the descendants of his grandfather's neighbors in a homespun way.

"My Grandfather Truman ran off with Mary Jane Holmes and was married here in Shelbyville, and lived on an adjoining farm out here west of town," he said. "Then he went to Missouri—was afraid to go back home.

"And about three or four years after that, why, his father-in-law sent for him to come home, he wanted to see the first grandchild; so that settled things and they got together."

And, in the same vein of levity, after introducing his daughter, Margaret, the president quipped: "You all know my daughter, Margaret. She was down here several years ago looking up the records to see if my grandparents were legally married."

The president said he was proud of his Kentucky ancestry, "naturally."

At Lexington, in the heart of the Bluegrass Country and famous racehorses, Mr. Truman said he was trying to do in the presidential race "what Citation did in the horse race."

It isn't important who is ahead at one time or another in either an election or a horse race, he said:

"It's the horse that comes in first at the finish that counts."

Ten thousand persons overflowing the Jefferson County Armory at Louisville roared applause last night, as he unleashed a bare-knuckle attack on the National Association of Manufacturers.

He was welcomed to Louisville by a howling, screaming, whistling populace.

With the help of Republican congressmen, he said, the NAM killed price controls with a "vicious" organized campaign it financed with $3,000,000.

Using language as homespun as a calico dress, the chief executive talked of living costs in terms of "hamburgers" and "chuck roasts."
Oct. 1, 1948

DEWEY CONFIDENT OF VICTORY

ALBANY, N.Y., OCT. 4 (AP)—Gov. Thomas E. Dewey—awaiting a detailed report on the international situation—was described today as so confident of victory he will not alter the measured pace of his presidential campaign.

Back at the New York capital after a 60-speech Western campaign tour, the GOP nominee expects to meet tomorrow with John Foster Dulles, his foreign-affairs adviser.

The presidential nominee would not comment on his 14-day Western trip, but an aide said Dewey regards his prospects so highly four weeks before the election that he has no intention of altering his present campaign course to trade punches with President Truman or any other Democrat.

Dewey has been discussing the issues on what his assistants call "a high plane," while Democrats have contended that the GOP nominee talks only in generalities, never gets down to brass tacks.

Taking this criticism in stride, the Dewey camp said it will continue its same course in forthcoming campaign tours.

A poll conducted by Lucian Warren, of the *Buffalo Courier-Express*, showed that of 47 newsmen aboard the candidate's campaign train who were willing to express their views, all think Dewey will win.

Large crowds which turned out to hear the Republican nominee at train-stop speeches in President Truman's home state of Missouri also

encouraged the Dewey aides, who summed up the results of his Western trip this way:

Ed Jaeckle, one of his campaign managers, predicted the Republican nominee would carry all of the 14 Western states in which he spoke. They have 129 electoral votes.
Oct. 4, 1948

TRUMAN IN CHICAGO
By Douglas B. Cornell

CHICAGO, OCT. 25 (AP)—President Truman, wildly acclaimed by cheering Chicagoans, said tonight forces he implies are akin to those that built up Hitler, Mussolini and Tojo now operate "through the Republican Party."

He said the threat is "serious," that American democracy and freedom are in jeopardy.

Mr. Truman spoke in Chicago's huge stadium, the scene of many a political rally and convention. He got there as part of a parade that brought out people by the hundreds of thousands, fireworks that would dim a Hollywood spectacle and an ocean of waving political banners.

William Horstman, stadium manager, estimated more than 24,000 persons had jammed the stadium to capacity. He said "about 200,000 people were milling around (outside) the stadium during the speech."

It was the most tremendous demonstration for the president in the whole campaign.

In his speech, Mr. Truman didn't say right out that a Republican election victory would bring a totalitarian dictator to America. But he did say:

"In our own time we have seen the tragedy of the Italian and German peoples, who lost their freedom to men who made promises of unity and efficiency and security."

Unity and efficiency have been almost a theme song in the campaign of Republican presidential candidate Thomas E. Dewey.
Oct. 25, 1948

TRUMAN ENDS CAMPAIGN
Ernest B. Vaccaro

ST. LOUIS, OCT. 30 (AP)—President Truman brought his campaign to a fiery climax tonight before a roaring home state audience and said

Voters of the tiny mountain hamlet of Hart's Location, N.H., show how they voted for Gov. Dewey, 11-1, as they stand outside the voting place. Left to right: Mrs. Macomber, Town Clerk Douglas Macomber, Joseph Burke, Preston Burke, Town Treasurer Mrs. Alice Burke, Peter King, Mrs. George Morey and George Morey. The town was the first to report complete returns in the 1948 presidential race.

Gov. Thomas E. Dewey was conducting a "fake" campaign.

To shouting, screaming, whistling Missourians, who interrupted him at the end of nearly every sentence to voice approval, the chief executive declared:

"Of all the fake campaigns, this is the tops as far as the Republican candidate is concerned. He has been following me and making speeches about home, mother, unity and efficiency. He won't talk issues, but he let his foot slip and endorsed the 80th Congress."

Mr. Truman, striving to make himself heard above the crowd, which packed Kiel Auditorium's Convention Hall, declared he was "on the road to victory" despite all the efforts of "character assassins" to ruin his standing with the people.

The president was interrupted repeatedly throughout his address by roars of approval from upward of 12,500, persons in Kiel Auditorium.

The convention hall seats 12,500, and many persons were standing outside. The rally topped in enthusiasm all the receptions of the president's campaign.

Remarks had been prepared by the speechwriting staff for the president's delivery tonight. But Mr. Truman threw them away to substitute his own rough-and-tumble speech, glancing from time to time at a sketchy draft typewritten just before his train arrived.

And the crowd responded to the mostly extemporaneous remarks with vigor.

They shouted "Pour it on, Harry," as he went down the line with his attack on the Republican-controlled 80th Congress. This time he called it a "do-nothing idiot Congress."

As he "poured it on," waves of yells, whistling and screams of encouragement swept over the packed assembly, which welcomed him home from a two-month campaign covering more than 270 speeches, in addition to more than 70 speeches made in a pre-convention tour in June.

He said Gov. Thomas E. Dewey won't talk about the issues, "but he did let his foot slip when he endorsed that good-for-nothing 80th Congress."
Oct. 30, 1948

DEWEY STILL CONFIDENT

NEW YORK, NOV. 2 (AP)—Gov. Thomas E. Dewey's campaign manager said at 1:45 a.m. (EST) today: "We now know that Gov. Dewey will carry New York state by at least 50,000 votes and will be the next president of the United States."

This appeared to give the New York governor the state, since most upstate areas are Republican. All of the votes in Democratic New York City had been tabulated.

In saying the Democratic majorities in practically all cases have been "substantially smaller" than necessary for the Democrats to win, campaign manager Herbert Brownell added:

"A case in point is the city of Philadelphia. In 1944 Republicans lost the city by about 150,000. The complete returns are just in for Philadelphia, and the Dewey-Warren ticket carried the city.

"So we conclude here at Republican headquarters that Dewey and Warren are elected."

Brownell declined to comment on an 11:08 p.m. (EST) Associated Press report that Mr. Truman was leading in 21 states with 284 electoral votes, while Dewey was leading in 20 states with 191 electoral votes.

The Brownell statement was one of a series issued during the evening. In one at 9:30 p.m. (EST), he claimed at least 24 states with a total of 295 electoral votes.
Nov. 2, 1948

TRUMAN WINS

NEW YORK, NOV. 3 (AP)—Scrappy, underrated Harry Truman captured the presidential election yesterday in one of the biggest upsets in America's political history.

And in the hour of his greatest triumph, the Democratic Party gave him a solid, comfortable majority in both Senate and House.

It was a triumph which the little man from Missouri, standing almost alone against the flood-tide of pre-election forecasts, had predicted with unswerving confidence.

Down to defeat went Thomas E. Dewey, trying for a comeback along the road to the White House, which invincible Franklin D. Roosevelt blocked four year ago.

Down with him went Republican candidates in key congressional races and gubernatorial contests.

They went down fighting, in the toughest presidential battle since Woodrow Wilson squeezed out Charles Evans Hughes in 1916. Dewey conceded defeat at 11:15 a.m., Eastern Standard Time, yesterday. Later in the day Truman's margin of victory widened.

And at the moment of decision by tens of millions of American voters, victor and vanquished alike cried out their hopes for peace in a troubled world.

For himself, Mr. Truman pledged anew that he would give all his efforts "to the cause of peace in the world and the prosperity and happiness of our people."

In those words of the president and the men who want to be president, there was new notice that America's foreign policy will remain bipartisan, that it will remain one of unwavering firmness toward Russia.

All through his campaign, as he trudged up and down and across the country, the president prom-

The combined radio-television newsroom of the American Broadcasting Company in New York's Radio City at the height of reporting the 1948 presidential election returns. This was the center of ABC's Election Night coverage.

ised that a Democratic Congress and a Democratic president would give the people:

Price controls, housing, more Social Security, a higher minimum wage, repeal of the Taft-Hartley labor law, benefits for farmers, development of the West, medical insurance, strengthened civil rights.

The political dopesters still were in a daze trying to figure out how it all happened. Adjectives like "stunning," "amazing," "astounding" were on every tongue.

The grit and never-give-up spirit of the man who inherited the White House from Roosevelt couldn't be discounted. And Mr. Truman could say "I told you so." He had told the poll takers they would be red-faced today. They were.

Even the cards had been stacked against him.

Presidential candidates aren't supposed to win without the big electoral votes of New York and Pennsylvania. Truman did.

And he did it with his own party split, without the solid South, without any bulging money bags to finance the campaign, without the big total vote that is supposed to favor the Democrats.

Progressive Party candidate Henry A. Wallace, fired from the Truman Cabinet, got even in part in New York, Connecticut, Maryland and Nevada. The votes Wallace collected there would have been enough to swing those states to the Democrats.

Thurmond captured only Alabama, South Carolina, Mississippi and Louisiana.
Nov. 3, 1948

TRUMAN'S TRIUMPH

NEW YORK, NOV. 3 (AP)—President Truman proved today he was the nation's best forecaster. He had the country's highest office to prove it.

His victory over Gov. Thomas E. Dewey settled the dispute between him and the pollsters on whether the national surveys—which predicted his defeat—were right or wrong.

"Sleeping polls," the president termed them.

Then he proceeded to give them the worst lacing since 1936, when the *Literary Digest* picked Alf M. Landon to beat Franklin D. Roosevelt.

At least one pollster got a laugh out of the results. He was Wilfred F. Funk, the *Literary Digest's* last editor, who said:

"I got a very good chuckle out of this—nothing malicious, mind you. I think that national political polls will be nonexistent for a long time."

Dr. George Gallup, whose American Institute of Public Opinion predicted Dewey would get 49.6 percent of the vote and Mr. Truman 44.5 percent, had this to say:

"Why did all the polls underestimate Truman's strength? The answer to this question will likely be found in an analysis of voting statistics when they are all available.

"Here are the pertinent questions of which we are seeking the answer:

"1. Which voters stayed home? Only 47,000,000 voters went to the polls Tuesday. Another 47,000,000 stayed home. Was it the Republicans or the Independent voters who failed to show up at the polls?

"2. What about the undecided vote? As late as the final week of the campaign some 3,000,000 voters had not yet made up their minds. Since many of these voters who were undecided had voted the Democratic ticket in earlier elections, many of them must have decided to cast their vote for Truman the last few days of the campaign.

"3. Did the Wallace strength early in the campaign return to Truman? Unquestionably the sharp decline in the Wallace vote was a great help in many pivotal states. Wallace insured the Dewey victory in New York. On the other hand, the absence of the Wallace ticket on the ballot in Illinois undoubtedly made the difference there between victory and defeat.

"4. How much help did the national ticket get from local and state candidates? Early returns show many local candidates leading the vote in a number of close states.

"All polls must analyze these problems and work toward their solution to make certain that the same errors do not occur in future election surveys."

Another pollster offering an explanation was Archibald Crossley, director of the Crossley poll, which forecast 49.9 percent of the vote for Dewey and 44.9 for Truman.

He said:

"The Crossley poll showed that the Truman and the Dewey vote would be even if all adult citizens voted. In its final interviewing three weeks before the election it indicated considerable apathy toward both candidates, but somewhat more toward Truman than toward Dewey.

"I am convinced that the widespread publicity given poll findings served to redouble Democratic efforts to bring out the vote and may have created overconfidence among Republicans. The results clearly show what happens when one gets out its vote and the other does not.

"The final poll in mid-October indicated a definite trend toward Truman and a falling off in the Wallace vote. Experiences in the last three national elections, however, led us to believe that in the final weeks this trend could not be sufficiently accelerated to overcome the five-point lead Dewey had at the time.

"Polls can and do register the temper of public opinion, but cannot infallibly predict how opinion will be depressed at the last minute in terms of relative turnout."

Elmo Roper, director of the *Fortune* magazine

New York's Gov. Thomas E. Dewey, unsuccessful Republican candidate for the presidency in 1948, chats with newsmen in the Roosevelt Hotel, New York City, a short time after he conceded the election to President Harry S. Truman. Gov. Dewey said he would not consider running a third time for the presidency. He called a published report that he planned to resign as governor "pure fiction."

poll, who predicted 52.2 percent of the vote for Dewey and 37.3 for Truman, said:

"On September 9 I predicted that Mr. Dewey would win Tuesday's election by a wide margin and that it was all over but the shouting. Since then, I have had plenty of changes to hedge on that prediction. I did not do so.

"I could not have been more wrong.

"The thing that bothers me most," Roper said, "is that at this moment I don't know why I was wrong.

"But I certainly propose to find out," he said.

Roper offered several "possibilities" of why he was wrong.

"Perhaps," he said, "the abnormally high 15 percent 'don't know' vote we received last August did not distribute equally to both major candidates as it has in the past, but this time it all went to Mr. Truman."

"It has been suggested," Roper said, "that the labor vote, brought out to the polls more quietly but more efficiently this time, turned the tables."

"Or it might be," he added, "that, as we found out in a poll done late in the campaign, the people are strongly pro-New Deal, and perhaps they see the objectives of the Roosevelt program imperiled."

In the dying days of the presidential campaign, Mr. Truman had derided the results of the surveys, terming them "sleeping polls."

Sen. J. Howard McGrath, Democratic national chairman, had urged the poll takers "to properly adjust" their figures. If they did so, he said, Mr. Truman would be shown in the lead, not Dewey.
Nov. 3, 1948

CAPITAL ACCLAIMS VICTORIOUS TRUMAN

By Douglas B. Cornell

WASHINGTON, Nov. 5 (AP)—The capital proudly poured forth its people and its plaudits today in roaring acclaim of a returning president who wouldn't be beaten.

From the north portico of the White House he will occupy for four more years, Harry S. Truman responded simply and humbly:

"I thank you from the bottom of my heart."

He looked across swarms of people on the White House lawn, crammed along broad Pennsylvania Avenue and overflowing Lafayette Park. His warm smile disappeared for a moment. He remarked gravely:

"I shall look forward to the help and cooperation of all the people, because we are faced with great issues now which I think we can bring to a successful conclusion."

Sharing the tumultuous welcome, as he shared the triumph of Tuesday's election, was Sen. Alben W. Barkley of Kentucky, the next vice president.

But mostly Washington and the folks of nearby Maryland and Virginia turned out to thrust out a friendly hand to the man who almost alone carried the Democratic banner to an upset victory.

Three-quarters of a million strong, the little people and big men of government and the diplomatic corps shrieked out their welcome to the chief executive.

With Barkley by his side, sitting on the folded top of a long, black car, Mr. Truman paraded slowly along the historic Pennsylvania Avenue route from Union Station to the White House. His hat and grin were going strong.

Ten and 20 deep, men and women—and school kids waving a sea of miniature American flags—packed the sidewalks. More of them hung from government buildings, perched on rooftops, dangled like oversized acorns from oak trees at the station plaza.

They waved banners and balloons and tossed torn paper by the fistful. Some sported blue "I told you so" buttons. Maids in hotels fluttered sheets and towels from upper windows.

Signs along the way jeered at poll takers and political experts who had predicted that Republican Thomas E. Dewey would capture the White House. A sample: "Truman Gallup-ed to Victory."

Spread across the front of the *Washington Post* building was a picture of a crow on its back on a platter.

"Welcome home from the crow eaters," the *Post* said.
Nov. 5, 1948

Chapter 5

Sen. Joseph McCarthy talks to newsmen in his office after being ousted from a closed-door session of a Senate subcommittee questioning Louis Budenz, a former Communist, about the activities of Owen Lattimore. Lattimore, who is charged by McCarthy with being a "top Russian spy in the U.S.," also was excluded from the proceedings.

Anticommunism, Alger Hiss & Joe McCarthy

- **Hiss and Chambers**

  Chambers Names Hiss a Spy ... Who's Lying? ... Hiss Indicted ... Hung Jury ... Hiss Convicted of Perjury

- **Sen. Joseph McCarthy**

  McCarthy Talks of Card-Carrying Communists ... McCarthy Says Marshall a Liar

Ronald Reagan, film actor and president of the Screen Actors Guild, listens to testimony at the Oct. 22, 1948, session of the House Un-American Activities Committee in Washington, D.C. The committee was probing Communist activities in Hollywood.

The rise of the Cold War turned anticommunism from a fringe political impulse into one of the strongest movements in American public life. The potential for conflict between nationalist, capitalist democracy and international communism had long been obvious, but World War II had made the United States and the Soviet Union allies of convenience. After that war ended and the Cold War began, American Communists came to be regarded by many as a threat to national security because of their Soviet links.

Whatever the strength of those links, the federal government led the charge against domestic communism. In 1947 the Truman administration initiated a loyalty-security program that barred Communists or those who associated with them from government jobs. The Department of Justice sought the deportation of foreign-born Communists and indicted and obtained convictions of party leaders under the Smith Act, a 1940 law prohibiting the "teaching and advocating" of subversive doctrines. Several hundred Communists went to jail. The House Un-American Activities Committee, known as HUAC, investigated alleged Communist subversion throughout society.

The Supreme Court placed few restrictions on the anticommunism campaign, clearing the way for the use—and often, the misuse—of anticommunism by politicians. Communism became an all-purpose rallying cry for all sorts of causes.

In such an atmosphere, civil liberties became an afterthought. There was a rationale: If the national security was threatened by an enemy within, needn't individual rights take a back seat to dealing with that threat? Moreover, direct government action against suspected Communists often was unnecessary; after an individual had been "identified" by a congressional committee or federal agency, private employers would fire them or not hire them. The risk of being branded a "Red" was chillingly clear, from Hollywood to Harvard.

Although communism had merely been part of a larger left-wing movement that had flourished in depression and war, non-Communist left-wingers—"fellow travelers," in the term of the day—risked being tarred by the anti-Communist brush. The definition of "Communist activity" expanded quickly and widely to fit the needs of various investigators and politicians.

Hiss and Chambers

Alger Hiss personified establishment respectability in Washington. A Harvard-educated lawyer, Hiss had been a high-ranking State Department official who had played a significant role in planning the United Nations. Hiss also had been an aide to President Roosevelt at the wartime summit conference at Yalta, albeit a junior one. In 1948 he was president of the Carnegie Endowment for International Peace.

That same year Whittaker Chambers, the man whose accusations would destroy Hiss, was an editor of **Time** magazine and a confessed former secret member of the Communist Party. Over three decades, Chambers had changed from Coolidge Republican to doctrinaire Communist to anti-Communist intellectual.

Hiss and Chambers were an odd pair: the former was handsome, self-confident, well-mannered, strikingly patrician in bearing. His professor at Harvard Law School, Felix Frankfurter, had arranged a Supreme Court clerkship for him with the great Justice Oliver Wendell Holmes. Chambers, in contrast, was unusually sloppy in dress and personal hygiene. His ideological odyssey made even some of his supporters uneasy.

But as the case of Alger Hiss evolved, the historian Eric Goldman has observed, "Whit-

Alger Hiss and Whittaker Chambers (standing, right) face each other before the House Un-American Activities Committee in Washington, in August 1948.

taker Chambers receded into the background; Alger Hiss, the individual, blurred. Everything was turning into Alger Hiss, the symbol."

CHAMBERS NAMES HISS

WASHINGTON, AUG. 3 (AP)—Whittaker Chambers, who said he once served in the Communist underground in Washington, swore today that it was headed by a number of U.S. govern-

ment officials, including Alger Hiss, a State Department official who later rose to be secretary general of the San Francisco Conference at which the United Nations was launched, and Nathan Witt, who served successively as attorney and executive secretary for the National Labor Relations Board.

Chambers also declared a number of other government officials were among the leaders of the Red network in the capital during his life as a Communist Party member from 1924 to 1937

Chambers, now a senior editor for *Time* magazine, testified before the House Un-American Activities Committee as it dug into stories of a widespread spy ring in the federal government.

The witness also told of seeking unsuccessfully to get Hiss to "break away from the party."

Hiss, now president of the Carnegie Endowment for International Peace, said in New York: "I don't know Mr. Chambers. As far as I know I never met him. And there's no basis for the statement which has been reported to me that he made to the committee." Chambers named other cell leaders of the Red network here as Lee Pressman, Donald Hiss, Victor Perlo, Charles Cramer or Kramer (also known as Krivitsky), John Abt and Henry Collins. Tonight, Donald Hiss, now a Washington lawyer, denied "every statement made by Mr. Chambers with respect to me," except the allegations that he has an older brother named Alger, that he once worked for the State and Labor departments, and that as an employee of a law firm he once gave legal service to the Polish Supply Mission in connection with an export-import bank loan.

Robert E. Stripling, committee counsel, described Donald Hiss as a brother of Alger and a State Department employee from 1938 to 1945.

He said Pressman formerly was general counsel for the Works Progress Administration and other agencies.

Abt, general counsel for Henry Wallace's Progressive Party, said in New York tonight "the cloak and dagger tales to which the Thomas Committee is now giving currency were told to the FBI as long ago as 1945."

Chambers, a short, husky man, said he dropped communism in 1937. He felt, he said, that "its triumph means slavery to men and spiritual night to the human mind and soul."

The purpose of the underground group as he knew it was "infiltration" of the government, the witness said.

Aug. 3, 1948

WHO TO BELIEVE?

WASHINGTON, AUG. 5 (AP)—House investigators said today they have located a witness who may "crack wide open the whole Soviet spy case."

Acting Chairman Karl Mundt (R-S.D.) declined to say who or where this "mystery witness" is, but announced the House Un-American Activities Committee is sending a subcommittee out of town to question the witness.

Alger Hiss, former State Department official, told the House committee under oath that "I am not and never have been a member of the Communist Party." Hiss appeared at his own request after Whittaker Chambers, a previous witness, had testified that Hiss was a member of the "Red underground" here. Hiss now is head of the Carnegie Endowment for International Peace.

Rep. Mundt told reporters that in his opinion Hiss certainly "made a rather convincing case." Chambers issued a statement saying he has "no change whatever to make" in his testimony concerning Hiss.

Hiss acknowledged that he knew a few of the other persons Chambers said belonged to the underground. Otherwise, he declared, "the statements about me made by Mr. Chambers are complete fabrications."

Rep. Mundt wondered aloud "what possible motive a man who edits *Time* magazine would have in coming here and giving testimony which you now completely deny." Hiss said he wondered too.

"I have no understanding of what might have motivated him." Hiss denied that he even knew Chambers.

After he left the stand, Mundt remarked to reporters: "One of them lied. There's no question about that."

Aug. 5, 1948

NIXON: HISS KNEW CHAMBERS

WASHINGTON, AUG. 17 (AP)—Rep. Richard M. Nixon (R-Calif.) said tonight that Alger Hiss has identified Whittaker Chambers, his accuser in the congressional spy hearings, as a man he had known under a different name.

Nixon gave this information to a reporter by telephone from New York, where three members of the House Un-American Activities Committee said they had brought Hiss and Chambers face to face for the first time for purposes of identification.

Alger Hiss (left), former State Department official, holds a press conference at his New York City home. Hiss told newsmen he had been brought face to face with Whittaker Chambers, his accuser in the congressional spy hearings, and that he identified Chambers as a man he knew in Washington, D.C., 15 years ago under another name. Hiss and Chambers met with three members of the House Un-American Activities Committee in a New York City hotel room. Hiss said he had denied Chambers' charge that he (Hiss) had been a Communist.

Nixon said Hiss testified that he had known Chambers, who has accused Hiss of being part of a prewar Communist underground in Washington, as a man named George Crosley.

Chambers testified here under oath that he used to be Communist from 1924 to 1937, serving as a courier for the underground in Washington.

He named Hiss as one of the members of that underground.

"The impression given to the public," Nixon said, "was that he (Hiss) had never known this man at all. This identification today is a direct contrast with that impression." Nixon said Hiss told the committee members today he had known

Chambers under the name of Crosley during the period that Chambers claims to have known Hiss. Nixon said that Chambers maintained, however, that Hiss knew him under the Communist Party name of Carl.

Chambers, Nixon said, could not recall having used the name of George Crosley.

The two men, Nixon said, were brought together at the Commodore Hotel today. The entire purpose, he said, was to make sure there was no case of "mistaken identity" in advance of appearance in public hearings by Chambers and Hiss together.

Later tonight Hiss called a news conference at which he said he had known "Crosley" as a freelance journalist. He said "Crosley" came to him in Washington 15 years ago when Hiss was a legal assistant to the Senate Munitions Investigation Committee. The writer, he said, asked him for material for a series of magazine articles.

Hiss said he saw Crosley 10 or 11 times during the winter of 1934-35 and that he later sublet an apartment to him. "Crosley," Hiss said, failed to pay the rent, and he never saw any of his articles in print.

He said they parted on "not very pleasant terms."

Hiss said that when he was shown photographs of Chambers in Washington there was "something vaguely familiar" about them. Tonight, he said, he noted a change in the facial appearance of the man he knew as Crosley.
Aug. 17, 1948

A HISS-CHAMBERS FACE DOWN

WASHINGTON, AUG. 25 (AP)—Alger Hiss and Whittaker Chambers, face to face in the congressional spy hearings, took turns today at stinging charges and denials revolving around a tale of a prewar Red underground in Washington.

Accused and accuser, they brought their utterly conflicting stories into the open at hearings before the House Un-American Activities Committee. And the hearings went on into the night. After eight hours and 37 minutes of intense questioning, the probers called a halt. Neither man had yielded an inch. The problem of who lied is still

before the committee. It called a closed session tomorrow morning.

Chambers has accused Hiss of being a leader in a Communist underground back in the middle '30s. He repeated the accusations tonight, again under oath.

Hiss listened in a few feet away, while hot lights of television and movie cameras bore down on him in the jammed caucus room of the old House office building.

Earlier it was Chambers' turn to listen. He stared stolidly up toward the lofty ceiling as Hiss questioned his "sanity" and accused him of being a "self-confessed liar, spy and traitor."

At one point, Chambers asked to be excused from saying publicly where he lives now.

Asked if he objected to letting Hiss know where he lives now, the chunky, graying witness replied:

"I believe that is tantamount to telling the Communist Party."

Right at the start this morning, Hiss and Chambers confronted each other a few feet apart, and said, yes, they knew each other.

At the very opening of the hearing Chairman J. Parnell Thomas (R–N.J.) announced that "certainly" one or the other of the men "will be tried for perjury."

Chambers' voice broke and tears glistened in his eyes when he told about his relationship with Hiss.

"I don't hate Mr. Hiss," he said. "We were close friends. We were caught in the tragedy of history. Mr. Hiss represents a concealed enemy against which I am fighting and we are all fighting."
Aug. 25, 1948

CHAMBERS REPEATS CHARGE

WASHINGTON, AUG. 27 (AP)—Whittaker Chambers paved the way for a possible court fight with Alger Hiss tonight by stating publicly, without congressional immunity, that Hiss "was a Communist and may be now."

Chambers, who renounced communism in 1937 and now is a senior editor of *Time* magazine, had stated before the House Un-American Activities Committee that Hiss, former top State Department executive, was a Communist.

Alger Hiss listens to a question during testimony before the House Un-American Activities Committee in Washington. The former State Department official was the lead-off witness as the committee called him and Whittaker Chambers, magazine editor, to discuss their relationship in the 1930s.

Last Wednesday Hiss, now head of the Carnegie Endowment for International Peace, challenged Chambers to make the statement outside the committee, where he could be sued for libel or slander.

Chambers repeated the statement tonight on the "Meet the Press" radio program broadcast by the Mutual network.

He added: "I do not think that Mr. Hiss will sue me for slander or libel."
Aug. 27, 1948

HISS SUES

BALTIMORE, SEPT. 27 (AP)—Alger Hiss, holder of several federal government posts for four years, asked $50,000 damages today because Whittaker Chambers' statements about his alleged Communist Party membership were false.

Hiss filed suit for slander and libel in the U.S. District Court here because Chambers has a farm residence at Westminster, Md. Hiss, a former Baltimorean, now resides in New York.

Hiss' suit claimed that Chambers, a senior editor of *Time* magazine, made "untrue, false and defamatory statements" about him in five appearances before the House Un-American Activities Committee and on a radio broadcast Aug. 27.

After appearances of both before the committee, Hiss challenged Chambers to repeat his statements publicly beyond protection of congressional immunity.
Sept. 27, 1948

THE PUMPKIN PAPERS

WASHINGTON, DEC. 3 (AP)—The House Un-American Activities Committee declared tonight that a bunch of microfilms, found in a hollow pumpkin on a Maryland farm, offers conclusive evidence that national security information was "fed out of the State Department" before the war.

Rep. Mundt (R-S.D.), who made the announcement on behalf of the committee, said the microfilms were obtained from Whittaker Chambers.

In a statement, Mundt said the copied documents were given to Chambers by "a member of the Communist underground" who was not identified.

Robert E. Stripling, chief investigator for the committee, told reporters that Chambers was subpoenaed yesterday to produce the documents.

Then, according to Stripling's account, Chambers took two committee agents to his farm near Westminster, Md. He led them to a spot in back of the farmhouse and showed them a pumpkin, hollowed out, jack-o'-lantern fashion, but minus a face. Chambers lifted the top off the pumpkin and fished out the microfilms, Stripling said.

Mundt's statement said:

"There is now in the possession of the committee, under 24-hour guard, microfilmed copies of documents of tremendous importance, which were removed from the offices of the State Department and turned over to Chambers for the purpose of transmittal to Russian Communist agents.

"These microfilms are of such startling and significant importance and reveal such a vast network of Communist espionage within the State Department, that they far exceed anything yet brought before the committee in its 10-year history.
Dec. 3, 1948

HISS INDICTED

NEW YORK, DEC. 15 (AP)—A spy-hunting grand jury tonight indicted Alger Hiss, former State Department official, on two counts of perjury.

It accused Hiss of lying when he denied he gave secret State Department papers to Whittaker Chambers, confessed Soviet courier.

United States Attorney John F. X. McGohey said he expected Hiss to give himself up to authorities. Hiss probably will be arraigned tomorrow or Friday, McGohey said.

Attorney General Tom Clark said here he was "not surprised" by the indictment. He said he though Hiss would be brought to trial some time in January.

Clark was asked whether he thought the indictment would affect President Truman's "red-herring" condemnation of the committee inquiry.

Clark replied: "I don't think it will alter it."

Hiss is liable to a $2,000 fine and five years' imprisonment on each count of the indictment if convicted.

Specifically the indictments said Hiss "unlawfully, knowingly and willfully" lied when:

1. He denied that either he or his wife, Priscilla, gave any documents of the State Department or any other government agency to Chambers.

2. Testified he did not talk to Chambers during February and March 1938.

The jury, which had been sitting for 18 months, earlier indicted 12 top Communist Party leaders on charges of advocating violent overthrow of the government.

Hiss and Chambers had appeared daily before

the grand jury since it began its espionage inquiry December 6.

Three days previously, Chambers had produced five rolls of microfilms from a hollowed-out pumpkin on his Maryland farm in connection with his charges. The microfilms purportedly bore approximately 200 pictures of classified documents, three of which allegedly were in Hiss' handwriting.
Dec. 15, 1948

Editor's Note

On Dec. 15, 1948, Hiss was indicted for perjury. His trial began in late May 1949.

NEW YORK, JUNE 1 (AP)—An old typewriter stole the first scene at the perjury trial of Alger Hiss today.

The government charged that on it Hiss or his wife, Priscilla, copied State Department documents which he then turned over "in wholesale fashion" to Whittaker Chambers, self-styled courier for a Soviet spy ring a dozen years ago.

Government counsel said, however, that 25 to 30 FBI agents scoping the nation's capital had been unable to find the machine.

Then Hiss' attorney stirred the crowded federal courtroom with the announcement the defense had the typewriter. Under certain conditions the FBI could look at the machine "all they want," the attorney said.

Hiss, 44, former high-ranking State Department official, went on trial Tuesday on two counts of perjury because he denied before a federal grand jury last December that he ever turned over department documents to Chambers.

Assistant U.S. Attorney Thomas F. Murphy charged in his opening address to the jury of 10 men and two women that Hiss, with his wife, was responsible for making 65 typewritten sheets of 47 department documents, all dated in the first three months of 1938.

One of the documents, Murphy told the jury, "is secret to such an extent that we will ask the judge not to permit you to see it."

He said the government would develop its case

in this way: FBI experts will prove that 64 of the 65 typewritten documents were made with a Woodstock, pica type machine. Then the government will prove its case if it can show that Chambers got the typewritten papers from Hiss and that the documents came from the State Department.

Defense attorney Lloyd Paul Stryker, on the other hand, based his opening remarks to the jury before federal Judge Samuel H. Kaufman largely on a comparison of the characters of Hiss and Chambers.

He characterized Hiss as a man of "trust and confidence" and Chambers as a "moral leper."

The heavy-set, white-haired Stryker said the case boiled down to whether Hiss testified truthfully when he said he had not given restricted documents to Chambers.

"The whole story rests on Chambers," he declared. "If you do not believe Chambers, the government has no case."

Even before Chambers joined the Communist Party (from which he resigned several years ago) he was "a furtive, secretive, deceptive man," Stryker said.

He traced Hiss' career, saying he was highly trusted in the State Department and handled "more important secrets" as Secretary General of the United Nations Planning Conference at San Francisco.

Stryker said the missing typewriter was located by a defense associate, Edward C. McLean, a Harvard Law School classmate of Hiss, after an exhaustive search. McLean bought it from a mover, whom he did not further identify.

Murphy, a tall, bulky, mustached man, told the jury in his opening remarks:

Chambers asserted the typewritten sheets were given him "pursuant to an arrangement between the defendant and his wife, she to type them when he brought them from the State Department so that he could bring them back to the State Department in the morning."

Murphy said Chambers testified that in 1937 he, Hiss and a Col. Bykov, identified by a House Un-American Activities report as a member of the "Soviet espionage system," met in New York.

There Murphy said, they decided Hiss "should extract documents from the State Department chiefly relating to Germany and the Far East."

Under the plan, Murphy said, Chambers would call at the Hiss home "every week or 10 days" but would take for copying only those documents Hiss brought home from the State Department that day.

The method proved "not fast enough," Murphy said, so it was decided Mrs. Hiss would copy or paraphrase department documents in the intervals between Chambers' visits and that he would take them and original documents for copying.

During the attorneys' remarks, Hiss and his wife sat on a bench within the court well appearing composed. Both wore subdued gray suits. While Murphy spoke, Hiss occasionally jotted notes on a small card.

June 1, 1949

HISS TAKES THE STAND

NEW YORK, JUNE 23 (AP)—Point by point, Alger Hiss today denied the charges that he sold out his State Department office to a Soviet spy ring.

"I've been waiting a long time for this," he said as he went to the witness stand in a climax to his federal perjury trial. Hiss took the stand shortly after a surprise defense witness quoted Whittaker Chambers as once saying that former assistant Secretary of State Francis B. Sayre was a leader of a prewar Communist underground in Washington.

The witness, Malcolm Cowley, a Sherman, Conn., writer, said Sayre was so described in 1940 by Chambers, Hiss' chief accuser and a self-styled courier for the Russian spy ring. Defense attorney Lloyd Paul Stryker immediately told the court he did not believe Chambers' purported description of Sayre. But he introduced it, Stryker said, in a further effort to prove Chambers a liar.

Hiss, tall and slender, was gravely serious as he raised his right hand to take the witness' oath before the jury of 10 men and two women upon whose verdict his honor rests.

For 17 days he has been sitting in federal Judge Samuel H. Kaufman's courtroom listening to the

government brand him a tool of Russian spies during his brilliant prewar career in Washington.

Hiss denied Chambers' accusations and denied he even had seen him since Jan. 1, 1937. As a result, a New York grand jury indicted Hiss on two counts of perjury.

Hiss took the witness chair wearing a light tan summer suit, a white shirt and a gray, checked tie. He folded his arms. He nodded occasionally in answering questions put to him by Stryker. His even voice dropped so low at times that Stryker prodded him to speak louder. Hiss identified four data slips introduced by the government and said he wrote them.

"In February or March (1938) or any other time in your life did you ever furnish, transmit or deliver those exhibits to Whittaker Chambers?" Stryker asked.

"I did not," Hiss replied.

Stryker then pointed to 42 other government exhibits, data slips of State Department information which Chambers said he got from Hiss.

"Did you ever furnish, transmit or deliver them to Whittaker Chambers?" Stryker went on.

"I did not, Mr. Stryker," the witness said.

Q: "Mr. Hiss, are you now or have you ever been a member of the Communist Party?"

A: "I am not, and never have been."

June 23, 1949

HISS, CHAMBERS AND A RED RUG

NEW YORK, JUNE 27 (AP)—Alger Hiss admitted today that Whittaker Chambers once gave him a bright red rug but said he never considered it a gift from the prewar Communist underground.

He said he accepted it as part payment for money borrowed but never repaid by Chambers, self-styled former courier for a Soviet spy ring.

Chambers testified early in the 20-day-old trial that he gave Hiss the rug as a tribute from the spy ring for Hiss' underground work when he was a high State Department official. Hiss, who has denied he ever was a Communist or tool of the ring, recalled he received the rug from Chambers in 1936. He said he thought the rug was in part payment for what Chambers owed him.

"He implied it and I inferred it," the 44-year-old

Hiss testified. However, the witness said he did not "specifically ask" Chambers why he offered him the rug. Hiss added:

"I now have a very definite and clear recollection of his (Chambers) bringing the rug to the P Street (Washington) house."

Hiss said Chambers carried the rug into his home.

"Did he come through the door—I thought you said he came to the door," Murphy asked.

"That's the way he entered the house," replied Hiss with a smile.

When spectators began to laugh, Murphy turned to federal Judge Samuel H. Kaufman and demanded:

"Your honor, will you ask some of the clowns to stop laughing?"

Judge Kaufman said Murphy's comment was not justified. However, the court ordered a five-minute recess at that point. Although Hiss continued his composed attitude on the witness stand for the third successive court day, he and Murphy exchanged remarks with some heat at times.

At one point in the questioning on minor details, Hiss brushed off a question by asking what difference it made.

June 27, 1949

A HUNG JURY

NEW YORK, JULY 8 (AP)—The Alger Hiss perjury trial ended at 8:01 p.m. (EST) tonight in a jury disagreement.

The jurors were split eight to four in favor of convicting the former State Department official after weighing his fate for nearly 29 hours.

U.S. Attorney John F.X. McGohey announced that Hiss would be tried again.

James F. Hanrahan, one of the jurors who voted for conviction, said, "eight of us pounded the hell out of the four since last night but we could not get anywhere."

Hiss was smiling faintly when he left the courtroom following discharge of the jury by federal Judge Samuel H. Kaufman. His wife, Priscilla, however, appeared close to tears.

July 8, 1949

CHAMBERS' RESPONSE

WESTMINSTER, MD., JULY 8 (AP)—Whittaker Chambers, weary after a day of toil on his farm, tonight calmly received the news that the Alger Hiss perjury trial resulted in a hung jury.

In shirtsleeves and slacks and puffing a pipe, the chief prosecution witness said: "In view of what has happened, no statement seems necessary."

The confessed former courier for a Communist spy syndicate, who has become a full-fledged farmer, maintained the air of detachment he had displayed all day while doing his chores.

During the day, he and his family wasted no time waiting around to hear word of the trial.

"Cows have to be milked," he explained. His son and daughter, both in their early teens, helped Chambers and his wife as they tended to their duties in the fields and kitchen.

Occasionally he passed newsmen on his way to and from the frame farmhouse. "Anything yet?" he would ask.

But he left the actual vigil up to the newsmen. After hearing the news and issuing his brief statement, he posed for a few photographs, then prepared for bed. He arises at 5 a.m.

July 8, 1949

Editor's Note

The divided verdict permitted the government to try Hiss a second time. That trial opened on Nov. 17, 1949, and concluded in January 1950.

HISS CONVICTED

NEW YORK, JAN. 21 (AP)—Alger Hiss was convicted today of perjury charges.

Thus the jury found it believed Hiss' chief accuser, Whittaker Chambers, who said the former high State Department official gave him secret papers for a Soviet spy ring.

The jury received the case at 3:10 p.m. yesterday, spent five hours and seven minutes in deliberations before it was locked up for the night, then resumed consideration of the case at 9:20 a.m. today. The jury spent nine hours and 13 minutes in deliberation.

Hiss and his wife, Priscilla, gave no indication of emotion immediately.

A moment after Hiss heard the verdict, his chin went up and his lips tightened. He folded his arms akimbo.

Jan. 21, 1950

THE CONGRESSIONAL RESPONSE

WASHINGTON, JAN. 21 (AP)—The perjury conviction of Alger Hiss was greeted with approval in Congress today, especially among administration critics.

Rep. Velde (R-Ill.) said the New York verdict "cooks President Truman's 'red herring,' and I hope he enjoys eating it."

Velde, a member of the Un-American Activities Committee, referred to the label Mr. Truman pasted on the group's investigation of Communist activities in the Republican 80th Congress.

Sen. Bridges (R-N.H.) called the jury's decision "an important milestone in our fight against Communism," adding: "Only last January Dean Acheson issued a statement to the effect that he was a friend of Alger Hiss. What does Dean Acheson have to say of his friend Alger Hiss now?"

Sen. Karl Mundt (R-S.D.), who was acting chairman of the House committee at the time the original "pumpkin papers" testimony in the case was taken, declared that the conviction shows what can be accomplished by "an alert and energetic House Committee on Un-American Activities, supported by the investigative machinery of the FBI and the prosecution personnel of the Department of Justice."

Rep. Clarence Brown (R-Ohio) praised "the tenacious and highly diligent efforts of congressman Richard Nixon of California, who almost single-handedly cracked the case wide open, after Hiss had apparently satisfied the committee of his innocence on the basis of a preliminary inquiry."

Nixon, a Republican, said: "I consider this verdict a vindication of congressional methods of investigation when they are accompanied by adequate staff work and fair procedures."

Jan. 21, 1949

NEW YORK, JAN. 25 (AP)—Alger Hiss was sentenced today to five years in a federal penitentiary after his conviction on two perjury counts.

He will appeal his case.

Ashen-faced but composed in manner, the former State Department official denied to the end that he ever slipped secret state documents to Whittaker Chambers, self-styled courier for a prewar Soviet spy ring.

Before federal Judge Henry W. Goddard sentenced him, Hiss was granted permission to speak.

Rising from his seat beside his gray-haired wife, Priscilla, the man who was an adviser to President Roosevelt at Yalta walked to the bar between two United States marshals and declared in a firm voice:

"I would like to thank your honor for your consideration and for this opportunity again to deny charges against me.

"I am confident that in the future all the facts will be brought out to show how Whittaker Chambers was able to carry out forgery by typewriter."

The next step for appeal beyond the circuit court would be to the United States Supreme Court. Should it go to the highest tribunal, at least three justices are expected to disqualify themselves. They are: Felix Frankfurter, Stanley Reed and Tom C. Clark. The first two testified as character witnesses for Hiss at the first trial last June. Justice Clark was United States attorney general while the government worked up its case against Hiss.

Jan. 25, 1950

'I DO NOT INTEND TO TURN MY BACK ON ALGER HISS'

WASHINGTON, JAN. 25 (AP)—"I do not intend to turn my back on Alger Hiss," Secretary of State Dean Acheson said today.

He delivered that dramatic pledge of continued loyalty to his former State Department associate a few hours after Hiss was sentenced to five years in prison as a perjurer.

He advised people acquainted with Hiss to take counsel of the Sermon on the Mount in deciding their attitude toward the convicted man. He cited chapter and verse of the fable to show exactly what he meant.

Thus Acheson hammered home a somewhat similar statement he made a year ago, when Hiss was under indictment but had not been brought to trial. On Jan. 13, 1949, while up for confirmation to his present high post, Acheson told a Senate committee: "Alger Hiss and I became friends and we remain friends. My friendship is not given easily and it is not easily withdrawn."

Today's renewed commitment was given at a news conference. Acheson later gave permission to be quoted directly.

In a matter of minutes his words were relayed to the Senate floor by Sen. McCarthy (R-Wis.), who called the secretary's statement "fantastic."

McCarthy said he wondered whether Acheson was saying, in effect, that he also would not turn his back on others who—as McCarthy put it—had aided the Communist movement.

Sen. Mundt (R-S.D.) told his colleagues that the Hiss case should spur Congress into extending the statutory time limit for trying men and women for serious crimes which involve the nation's security.

"We must not blandly assume that by the arrest, conviction and punishment of Alger Hiss we have rid the State Department of all its foreign-minded operatives or Communist sympathizers," Mundt said.

"We must keep in mind that many employees in that department were brought into positions of responsibility and importance through their connection with Hiss and his misguided friends, mentors and associates."

Acheson seemed fully prepared for the question propounded at his news conference by the New York *Herald Tribune*'s Homer W. Bigart.

"Do you have any comment on the Hiss case?" Bigart asked. Reporters thought Acheson's voice sounded more tense and emotional than usual as he replied.

He said the Hiss case is now before the courts and "I think it would be highly improper for me" to discuss any aspect of the evidence or any other matters pertaining to the conduct of the trial.

The secretary said he supposed the questioning reporter had in mind something more than what he had just said. Then he elaborated:

"I should like to make it clear to you that whatever the outcome of any appeal which Mr. Hiss or his lawyers may make in this case, I do not intend to turn my back on Alger Hiss.

"I think every person who has known Alger Hiss or has served with him at any time has upon his conscience the very serious task of deciding what his attitude is and what his conduct should be. That must be done by each person in the light of his own standards and his own principles.

"For me, there is very little doubt about those standards or those principles. I think they were stated for us a very long time ago. They were stated on the Mount of Olives and if you are interested in seeing them, you will find them in the 25th chapter of the gospel according to St. Matthew beginning at verse 34."
Jan. 25, 1950

Editor's Note

The debate over Alger Hiss has never ended. As journalist David Halberstam would observe, "even those who were unbiased and who tried to separate the record from their own political biases always had a feeling that there were missing pieces and that each of the principals was holding back something…. More than 40 years later, the pieces still did not add up."

The Hiss case helped trigger a decade of Red-baiting, a campaign that would subside only after the rise and fall of a demagogue far more ambitious than Whittaker Chambers or Alger Hiss.

Sen. Joseph McCarthy

After four years in the U.S. Senate, Joe McCarthy, Republican of Wisconsin, was arguably the chamber's least distinguished member. His career had been marked by opportunism and little else. He started out as a Democrat, switched parties, and lied about his military service to win Wisconsin's Republican senatorial nomination in 1946. Elected in a national GOP landslide, he latched onto anticommunism.

On Feb. 9, 1950, McCarthy gave a speech in Wheeling, W.Va., for a Lincoln Day weekend celebration. Almost casually, he claimed that there were Communists in the State Department and that they controlled American foreign policy. McCarthy had consciously chosen anticommunism as an issue, but he apparently did not realize his speech would prove so explosive.

It started with a line in the middle of his speech: "While I cannot take the time to name all of the men in the State Department who have been named as members of the Communist Party and members of a spy ring, I have here in my hand a list of 205 that were known to the secretary of state as being members of the Communist Party and who nevertheless are still working and shaping the policy of the State Department."

A reporter for the **Wheeling Intelligencer** *included the statement in his story, and the newspaper relayed it to The Associated Press bureau in Charleston, the state capital. An AP editor called the paper to check the number: 205? Yes, the* **Intelligencer's** *editor and reporter said, 205. The AP moved the story on its news wire that night.*

McCarthy flew to Denver, where he told reporters he would like to show them his list, but that he had left it in one of his suits, which was still on the plane. Then he moved on to Salt Lake City, where he made new charges.

THE NAMES OF 57 CARD-CARRYING COMMUNISTS

SALT LAKE CITY, UTAH, FEB. 10 (AP)—Sen. McCarthy (R–Wis.) said tonight that, under certain conditions, he would give Dean Acheson, secretary of state, the names of "57 card-carrying Communists" in the State Department.

He said he would give Acheson the names if he telephoned him, and if "Acheson would show his sincerity by having a presidential order revoked," at least insofar as the 57 are concerned. The order prohibits government departments from turning over loyalty records to congressional committees.

In Washington today, Lincoln White, press officer of the State Department, said of McCarthy's charge:

"We know of no Communist member in the department, and if we find any they will be summarily discharged."

McCarthy said: "It would be a waste of effort to give Acheson the names, then have him deny they are Communists and we cannot get the records."

He added that "there are some very high-type people in the State Department and they are infinitely disturbed about this whole thing."

McCarthy declared the president loyalty board screened about 3,000 persons in the State Department. It described 289 of them as "bad risks," he said.

He declared 207 of these are still in the department and that this group includes "57 card-carrying Communists."

The Wisconsin senator said the sources of his information were varied, that he would not reveal them. In this connection, he added, "the House Un-American Activities Committee should get credit for the initial work."
Feb. 10, 1950

WASHINGTON, FEB. 20 (AP)—Sen. McCarthy (R-Wis.) told the Senate tonight that a White House speech writer, whom he did not name, is a member of Communist-front organizations. McCarthy made his charge at an angry session during which the Senate sergeant-at-arms was

Sen. Joseph McCarthy listens to testimony by Owen Lattimore before a Senate Foreign Relations subcommittee. Lattimore denied being a Communist or Communist sympathizer and called McCarthy's accusations "base and contemptible lies."

instructed to go out and arrest absent senators to provide a quorum.

Sen. Lucas of Illinois, Democratic leader, repeatedly tangled with McCarthy, who also said he has case histories of 81 subversives—including what he called a "big three"—who are working in and with the State Department.

Lucas challenged McCarthy to name names. McCarthy refused, saying Lucas or any other

interested authorities could get the names at McCarthy's office.

McCarthy complained that few senators were present and accused Lucas of tipping off Democrats to leave. Lucas hotly replied that senators often leave when there are no votes coming up. When a quorum call failed to turn up a quorum, Lucas moved to adjourn. This failed to carry, and Lucas snapped out a motion that the sergeant-at-

Owen Lattimore (far lower left), object of "Soviet agent" charges, and Sen. Joseph McCarthy, R-Wis. (top right, light suit), who made the charges, hear Louis Budenz (center, light suit, back to camera) tell a Senate subcommittee that Lattimore was a member of a "Communist cell" in the Institute of Pacific Relations.

arms be told to arrest absentees. This motion was passed, giving the sergeant-at-arms the task of rounding up senators at home, at the theater, parties and dinners.

Forty-nine senators were rounded up and the senate stayed in session, listening to McCarthy, until 11:43 p.m. EST. Then it recessed until 11 o'clock Tuesday morning.

Concerning the White House speech writer,

McCarthy said: "Both he and his wife are members of Communist-front organizations."

He added that the man "has a relative who has a financial interest in the *Daily Worker*," the official publication of the Communist Party in this country. But the senator said that "cannot be held against him."

McCarthy said he was "doing Mr. Truman a favor" in telling him about the speech writer.

Sen. Joseph R. McCarthy puts papers in his briefcase after saying that he has decided to make public copies of "pertinent parts" of government loyalty files having a bearing on the Owen Lattimore case.

"I do not think he knows it," McCarthy said. "I do not think he would have this individual writing speeches for him if he knew it."

At one point, Sen. McMahon (D-Conn.) interrupted to ask McCarthy if he had in the files he brought to the Senate anything but derogatory information about the persons he was describing.

McCarthy said he hadn't. McMahon suggested that maybe all McCarthy had was gossip and rumor about the people concerned. McCarthy said maybe some of them weren't Communists.

"But you can be dead sure that some of them are," he added. McMahon said, "We've got to be careful we don't imitate the very thing we are against." He added that "Star Chamber" proceedings are not the American way.

Sen. Brewster (R-Maine) jumped up to say that "after the revelations" in the Hiss and Klaus Fuchs (espionage) cases, Congress has a right to know what is going on in the executive departments.

McCarthy said he believes Mr. Truman "will not clean house until it becomes politically inexpedient" for him to fail to do so.

Sen. Withers (D-Ky.) said that by not naming names McCarthy was reflecting on the reputation of every State Department employee.

McCarthy replied that was entirely possible, but that this country "is in a situation so close to war" that he feels justified in the course he is taking."
Feb. 20, 1950

By Marvin L. Arrowsmith

WASHINGTON, MARCH 26 (AP)—Owen J. Lattimore, one-time State Department associate, was named tonight as the man Sen. McCarthy has identified as Russia's top secret agent in the United States.

His name was first mentioned publicly by Drew Pearson on his weekly radio broadcast. This coincides with information given privately to The Associated Press by McCarthy.

Lattimore is in Afghanistan.

Mrs. Lattimore and associates of the Johns Hopkins University professor and Far Eastern expert hotly denied McCarthy's public charges, made March 13, that Lattimore was "pro-Communist" and "an extremely bad security risk."

Pearson, on his broadcast, said that Lattimore has not had an opportunity to defend himself, and he added: "I happen to know Owen Lattimore personally—and I only wish this country had more patriots like him."

When McCarthy turned over the name in a secret session, Chairman Tydings (D-Md.) of the Senate subcommittee inquiring into his charges said McCarthy produced no "primary evidence" to back up his accusation.

McCarthy has said he is willing to let his whole case against the State Department stand or fall on the basis of the one principal charge—that of Lattimore.

Lattimore, 49, is now director of the Walter Hines Page School of International Relations at Johns Hopkins University in Baltimore. A Harvard graduate, he served as political adviser to

Gen. Chiang Kai-shek in 1941-42 and was a deputy directory of the U.S. Office of War Information from 1942 to 1944.
March 26, 1950

By Ernest B. Vaccaro

KEY WEST, FLA., MARCH 30 (AP)—President Truman today bitterly denounced Sen. McCarthy for trying to "sabotage the bipartisan foreign policy of the United States."

He described McCarthy, instigator of an investigation of alleged communism in the State Department, as the Kremlin's greatest asset in this country.

But it was mostly on foreign policy, and on the series of attacks on Secretary of State Acheson and the State Department, that the president devoted most of the 25-minute news conference on the lawn of the "winter White House" here, where he served newsmen hot dogs and hamburgers.

A reporter wanted to know if Mr. Truman thought McCarthy was "getting anywhere" with his charges that Communists and spies infest the State Department.

The president looked grave and stern. He said he thinks the greatest asset the Kremlin has is Sen. McCarthy.

Did he care to elaborate? "I don't think it needs any elaboration," he replied.

Mr. Truman said the real reason for McCarthy's attacks is political, that the Republican Policy Committee is backing them, and that they are trying to find an issue on which they can win control of Congress this year.

Sharply, he added that the Republican Policy Committee of the Senate had endorsed McCarthy's antics, but without the support of level-headed Republicans like senators Vandenberg and Saltonstall and Mr. Stimson and others.

Then, he told the newsmen they could quote these words:

"The greatest asset that the Kremlin has is the partisan attempt in the Senate to sabotage the bipartisan foreign policy of the United States."

Dean Acheson, Mr. Truman said solemnly, will go down in history as one of the greatest secretaries of state. The president said McCarthy's charge that Owen Lattimore, former State Department

Louis Budenz talks with Sen. Millard Tydings (D-Md.) (right), chairman of the Senate Foreign Relations subcommittee probing charges of Red influence in the State Department, after Budenz testified about his knowledge of Owen Lattimore. Sen. Bourke Hickenlooper (R-Iowa) is at center.

associate, is a top Russian agent, is silly on the face of it.
March 30, 1950

WASHINGTON, APRIL 6 (AP)—Sen. Tydings (D-Md.) said today that FBI records clear Owen Lattimore "completely" of Communist spy charges preferred by Sen. McCarthy.

Tydings, chairman of the Senate Investigating

Committee, said furthermore that four members of the committee hold the same opinion after inspecting a "complete summary" of FBI files on Lattimore, a Far Eastern expert.

The fifth member, Sen. Hickenlooper (R-Iowa), who was out of town when the committee visited FBI Director J. Edgar Hoover, will view the records next week.

Hardly had Tydings made his announcement when McCarthy told reporters that "either Tydings hasn't seen the files, or he is lying. There is no other alternative."

The chairman had referred to a summary prepared for the committee by Hoover from the FBI files on the accused Johns Hopkins University professor.

McCarthy said he didn't know what Hoover had compiled for the committee, "but I know what is in the files."

In reply to McCarthy's statement, Tydings said:

"I'll let my reputation for accuracy stand. It is significant that no member of the committee contradicted the statement when I made it in the presence of the committee."

Tydings told reporters that Hoover and Attorney General McGrath agree with his estimate of the information on Lattimore.

The chairman saved his statement until Lattimore had completed before the committee his defense against McCarthy's charges. The witness told the committee, and McCarthy to his face, that McCarthy is a contemptible liar, the tool of discredited fanatics, and a violator of senatorial responsibility who ought to resign.

Lattimore, in his formal reply to McCarthy, scornfully told the committee: "He (McCarthy) has dredged up and slung at me all the mud that he could accumulate from all sources, however polluted."

The Wisconsin Republican sat impassively looking on behind the members of the committee conducting the inquiry.

Afterward he told reporters: "I am not changing anything I have said."

Lattimore, sitting with his wife and two attorneys, read for an hour and 45 minutes from the statement. The big Senate caucus room was packed with spectators and blazing with lights of movie and television cameramen. Sen. Lodge (R-Mass.) wore dark glasses.

As the witness finished reading, there was prolonged applause from the visitors.
April 6, 1949

WASHINGTON, JUNE 1 (AP)—Sen. Margaret Chase Smith (R-Maine), the Senate's only woman member, today delivered a blistering attack in the Senate against both Republicans and Democrats for their tactics in the furor over charges of communism in the government. "The American people are sick and tired," she said, "of seeing innocent people smeared and guilty people whitewashed."

Both sides, she said, are "playing directly into the Communist design of 'confuse, divide and conquer.'"

Without mentioning Sen. McCarthy (R-Wis.), she said the Republicans can find enough campaign issues in the record of the "ineffective" Truman administration without resorting to "political smears."

The nation sorely needs a Republican victory, she said, "but I don't want to see the Republican party ride to political victory on the four horsemen of calumny—fear, ignorance, bigotry and smear."

Hitting out in one of her rare Senate speeches, the gray-haired Maine legislator read a statement signed by herself and six fellow Republican senators decrying the "techniques" employed by both sides.

"We are Republicans, but we are Americans first," the statement said. "It is as Americans that we express our concern with the growing confusion that threatens the security and stability of our country."
June 1, 1950

By Marvin L. Arrowsmith

WASHINGTON, JULY 17 (AP)—Republican Sen. McCarthy's Communists-in-government charges were labeled "a fraud and a hoax" tonight in a report by the Democratic majority of a Senate inquiry committee.

It accused him of "perhaps the most nefarious campaign of half-truths and untruths" in the nation's history.

McCarthy fired back with a statement calling the action of the three Democratic committeemen "gigantic in its fraud and deep in its deceit."

"The Tydings-McMahon report is a green light to the Red fifth column in the United States," McCarthy said.

The three senators, Tydings (Md.), Green (R.I.) and McMahon (Conn.), declared McCarthy failed to prove a single basic accusation. They declared he used "the totalitarian technique of the big lie." The report ranks as one of the bitterest denunciations by senators of a colleague Congress has ever seen.

Republican Sen. Lodge of Massachusetts, however, filed a minority report which said the stormy four-month investigation "must be set down as superficial and inconclusive..." a tangle of loose threads... of leads which were not followed up." Lodge said that too frequently the tone of the inquiry, as set by the Democrats, lacked impartiality.

But unlike the Democrats, Lodge said there was an incomplete investigation regarding Lattimore, who is a Johns Hopkins University professor and occasional consultant to the State Department. Lodge added that under the circumstances his conclusion dealing with Lattimore was "inescapably tentative."

The Democrats asserted they found "no evidence to support the charge that Owen Lattimore is the 'top Russian spy' or, for that matter, any other kind of a spy." The majority also cleared Lattimore of "Communist" charges fired at him by ex-Communist Louis F. Budenz. Lodge also said the allegation was not proved.

The Democrats' 350,000-word report bristled with declarations that McCarthy lied time and again. The document contains this summarizing castigation by the Democrats: "At a time when American blood is again being shed to preserve our dream of freedom, we are constrained fearlessly and frankly to call the (McCarthy) charges, and the methods employed to give them ostensible validity, what they truly are: a fraud and a hoax, perpetrated on the Senate of the United States and the American people."
July 17, 1949

Sen. Joseph McCarthy (R-Wis.) is busy in his office with telegrams he said he received congratulating him on an encounter with columnist Drew Pearson. Both McCarthy and Pearson have agreed that the incident at the swank Sulgrave Club involved physical violence when the two met in the men's cloakroom.

By Raymond J. Crowley

WASHINGTON, DEC. 13 (AP)—Sen. Joe McCarthy of Wisconsin hauled off at columnist Drew Pearson in the plush Sulgrave Club last night and slapped, punched or kicked him, depending on whose version you accept.

The senator and the columnist-commentator do not fancy each other. Pearson has been critical of McCarthy, who has been conducting a campaign for months against persons he calls Reds in high government posts.

The senator, taking note of Pearson's writings, has been circulating the word that any day now he will arise in the Senate and take the hide off Pearson.

Last night they met at a party in the club, which is just off Dupont Circle and is frequented by many well-known Washingtonians.

McCarthy's version—"I slapped him hard."

Pearson's version—"He kicked me below the belt."

Radio commentator Fulton Lewis's version—

"McCarthy punched Pearson and lifted him about three feet off the floor."

Sen. Richard Nixon (R-Calif.), who was there, viewed the proceedings in a different light.

"I have no comment except that this incident occurred at a private party. I do not believe such foolishness should be bandied about in times like this."

McCarthy told a reporter he met Pearson in the men's cloakroom after the party, and he gave this account: "Pearson said to me: 'McCarthy, if you talk about personal things regarding me on the Senate floor, I'll get you.' So I slapped him in the face. I slapped him hard."

McCarthy said that when Pearson first approached him he said: "McCarthy, you are going to make a speech about me, aren't you?" "I said," McCarthy related, "'Pearson, you laid down the rules. Don't be disturbed if I get a bit rough.'"

McCarthy said Pearson replied: "You get rough and I'll get you, McCarthy. I've got more circulation than you have."

McCarthy: "Then I smacked him with my open hand and knocked him down on his hips. I didn't punch him."

Commentator Lewis gave his account in his broadcast tonight, and his aides elaborated on it in talks with reporters.

They said there had been an exchange of remarks and that Pearson got up from his table and walked over to McCarthy, whispering something in the senator's ear.

Lewis said McCarthy was sitting down and jumped up to strike Pearson, lifting the columnist about three feet off the floor. He commented that McCarthy is an ex-Marine and is pretty powerful. Pearson denied he was knocked down.

"The senator kicked me twice in the groin," he said. "As usual he hit below the belt. But his pugilistic powers are about as ineffective as his Senate speeches. I was not hurt."
Dec. 13, 1949

WASHINGTON, DEC. 15 (AP)—Sen. McCarthy (R-Wis.) said in the Senate today that Drew Pearson is a "Moscow-directed character assassin" who serves as "the voice of international communism."

Pearson promptly retorted in a statement that his record in fighting Communism is well known to everybody but "the headline-happy senator from Wisconsin." He threatened to sue McCarthy.

McCarthy studded his attack on the columnist-commentator with such epithets as "unprincipled liar and fake," and "this twisted, perverted mentality."

He said, however, "it appears that Pearson never actually signed up as a member of the Communist Party and never paid dues."
Dec. 15, 1950

McCARTHY CALLS MARSHALL A LIAR

WASHINGTON, JUNE 14 (AP)—Sen. McCarthy (R-Wis.) denounced secretaries Marshall and Acheson today as monumental liars and accused Acheson of taking part in "a great conspiracy" to deliver the U.S. to communism.

He said in a Senate speech that Secretary of Defense George C. Marshall is "steeped in falsehood" and described him as a "mysterious, powerful" figure who sided with Russia in historic decisions which "lost the peace" for America.

McCarthy said there is now afoot "a conspiracy of infamy so black that, when it is finally exposed, its principals shall be forever deserving of the maledictions of all honest men." "Who constitutes the highest circles of this conspiracy?" McCarthy asked. He added that he couldn't be sure, but Acheson "must be high on the roster," and President Truman "is their captive."

McCarthy had announced that he would talk for six or seven hours. But he skipped large portions of his 60,000-word speech, talking for a little less than three hours and inserting the whole speech in the *Congressional Record*. Galleries, crowded at the start, thinned out progressively, and, at times, only three senators were on the floor. Sen. Kenneth Wherry (R-Neb.), congratulating McCarthy, said many more people would read the speech than heard it.

Democratic senators made no comment and indicated they planned to let the speech pass without a reply.

The Defense Department countered by making public excerpts of pronouncements from famous men picturing Marshall as a great soldier and statesman.

In accusing Marshall and Acheson of being liars, McCarthy said Marshall wrote "blatant untruths" to the late Sen. Arthur H. Vandenberg about why a report on China was suppressed in 1947. He raised these questions:

Marshall "lied" to Vandenberg, McCarthy said, by telling him that one reason for keeping the report secret was because it was "replete with quotations" from prominent Americans and Chinese who gave their opinions "under the seal of confidence."

He called Acheson's testimony before the Senate Inquiry on China Aid "a piece of organized fabrication on so vast a scale as to have excited the envy of the prince of liars, Ananias." Of Acheson's report in 1949 that "nothing was left undone by this country" to avert the fall of China to the Reds, McCarthy said: "I hope that I never have an angry God with a lie of that enormity."

June 14, 1951

Chapter 6

War in Korea

Maj. Thomas P. Mulvey (left) of Wenonah, N.J., and Master Sgt. Russel Brahmi of Detroit raise the Stars and Stripes at paratroop headquarters after the area had been secured behind enemy lines in North Korea.

- **The War Begins**

  North Korea Invades ... U.N. Responds

- **The Tide Turns**

  Marines Storm Inchon... Across the Han

- **The Chinese Intervene**

  Red Chinese Enter War ... U.S. Abandons Seoul ... Seoul Recaptured ... 'Wonju Shoot' ... Across 38th Parallel ... Gen. Ridgway

Shortly after arriving in Korea from Japan, men of a U.S. 40th Division regiment move into position on Jan. 13, 1952.

The Korean War was two wars. One was the last war in which superpowers fought each other with the conventional tactics and weapons of World War II. The other was a Cold War conflict, in which the United States and its allies fought a vigorous but limited and ultimately inconclusive battle to contain communism.

As in the case of Germany, the division of Korea reflected the positions of Allied armies at the end of World War II. Southern Korea was under American control, northern Korea under Soviet control. Unable to agree on elections for a new government, the allies-turned-rivals stood their ground on a divided peninsula.

The Soviets wanted a unified, Communist Korea under their influence; they felt it was only a matter of time until the Americans left Japan and the Japanese walked back into Seoul. They were probably not as sure about what the United States wanted. In 1947 the U.S. Joint Chiefs of Staff had agreed South Korea was not worth fighting for, and two years later General of the Army Douglas MacArthur described to reporters a Pacific defense line that did not include the peninsula.

On Jan. 12, 1950, Secretary of State Dean Acheson, apparently referring to Korea and Formosa (Taiwan), said in a speech that certain nations would have to defend themselves in case of invasion, at least at first. "It must be clear," he said, "that no person can guarantee these areas against military attack." A week later, the House defeated by one vote money for 500 U.S. Army officers to advise the South Korean army.

The War Begins

It may have looked to Soviet leader Josef Stalin as if Korea was ready to be taken, but the Truman administration could not afford such a loss. After the fall of China, which had shocked the American public, the issue of Communist expansion was placed on the table for full partisan debate.

Meanwhile, North Korea and South Korea had repeatedly declared their intention to unify the country—by force, if necessary. But North Korea's 120,000-man army was twice as large as South Korea's, and much better equipped and trained. It was also more experienced—some of its soldiers had fought at Stalingrad.

Dismayed by the belligerent pronouncements of South Korean President Syngman Rhee, the Truman administration had done little to develop his military forces. And when President Truman proposed $60 million for military aid to South Korea in his 1950-51 budget, Congress cut that amount in half.

Nor was the United States particularly ready to fight. Following the rapid military demobilization after V-J Day, the Army had about 600,000 men, less than half the number at the beginning of World War II. The nearest U.S. forces were under MacArthur, who was commander of the Allied occupation of Japan. He had four Army divisions, the Fifth Air Force, and units of the Seventh Fleet.

By 1950 the North Koreans were regularly crossing the 38th parallel with patrols, some with as many as 1,500 troops, and had deployed nine divisions along the border. The U.S. Central Intelligence Agency warned that the buildup looked like preparation for an invasion. A CIA report dated March 10 predicted that North Korea "will attack South Korea in June, 1950."

And that was when, as MacArthur later put it, "North Korea struck like a cobra."

NORTH KOREA INVADES

SEOUL, SUNDAY, JUNE 25 (AP)—North Korean Communist troops, backed by tanks and artillery, swarmed across the border into South

Korea today and ran into furious resistance after penetrations up to three miles.

U.S. military advisers said the attackers were virtually stopped, and there was no indication of a massed buildup of troops which would be expected in a full-fledged invasion. They emphasized, however, that the situation was fluid and a full invasion still was possible.

A government spokesman said North Korea had declared war at 11 a.m.

The radio at Pyongyang, the Communist capital, added to the confusion by a series of conflicting broadcasts. One said the invaders intended to drive south of the border for one kilometer (.621 of a mile), establish positions and hold.

The radio also asserted that the South had invaded the North for the distance of a kilometer. There was no confirmation of this report.

The North Korean attacks rolled up at 11 points along the 38th parallel.

One U.S. military adviser said the attack was launched during heavy rain, preventing air support.

U.S. Ambassador John J. Muccio would not comment on the possibility of surplus planes from Japan being sent here. "Government forces," he said, "are giving a good account of themselves."

The ambassador insisted there was "no reason for alarm" because "as yet it cannot be determined whether the North intends to precipitate all-out warfare."

June 25, 1950

TRUMAN PROMISES U.S. SUPPORT

By Francis J. Kelly

WASHINGTON, JUNE 26 (AP)—President Truman threw the "vigorous" support of the United States government today behind the United Nations effort to end the sudden weekend war in Korea.

The overshadowing—and as yet wholly unanswered—question was whether this nation is prepared to dispatch its fighting men to the trouble zone if the U.N. should decide on a showdown test of strength to enforce its peace orders.

No, said the Conference of Republican Senators, in effect. Unanimously they declared that the assault of North Korean Communists on the Republic of South Korea must not be allowed to involve the United States in war. The Republicans said, however, that this nation should provide military supplies and other assistance.

Republicans began speculating immediately whether the United States had been caught napping by the surprise attack on the little country this nation has sponsored and befriended. Officials were silent.

Sen. Wherry of Nebraska, the Republican floor leader, likened it to the unheralded assault on Pearl Harbor eight and a half years ago.

"Where was our intelligence service?" the Republican asked.

Mr. Truman cut short a weekend in Missouri to fly back to the capital yesterday.

The president sternly called the Communist onslaught a case of "unprovoked aggression," and a "lawless action."

He praised the speed with which the United Nations Security Council acted Sunday to order withdrawal of the invaders, and promised that this nation will "vigorously support" the council's effort to end what he called "this serious breach of the peace."

Russia ignored the council meeting. She has been boycotting it because the Chinese Nationalists still have a delegate on the council.

Accordingly, anything the council does about Korea is presumably illegal in Russian eyes.

June 26, 1950

UN BACKS U.S.

LAKE SUCCESS, N.Y., JUNE 27 (AP)—President Truman's bold act in dispatching military aid to South Korea and drawing the line on communism in East Asia won the backing of the U.N. Security Council tonight.

The 11-member council voted 7 to 1 for an American resolution endorsing the president's decision. India and Egypt said they were not participating in the vote because they had not received instructions. Yugoslavia voted against it.

The Soviet Union was absent from the council. Its chief delegate, Jakob A. Malik, insisted at a secret luncheon talk with U.S. Ambassador Ernest A. Gross that the council decision Sunday for a cessation of hostilities in Korea was illegal.

Marines of the Fifth Regiment First Division, carrying camouflaged battle packs and rifles, go aboard the Navy transport Henrico. *The first division was completing loading operations in preparation for departure for the Korean war zone.*

The council voted little more than 10 hours after President Truman announced in Washington that the U.S. is putting ships and war planes into protective combat against Red invaders from North Korea.
June 27, 1950

By Roger D. Greene
WASHINGTON, JUNE 29 (AP)—President Tru-

man today expressed full confidence that Red-invaded South Korea will be saved as a free nation, and he denounced the Communist attackers as a "bunch of bandits."

Mr. Truman told his news conference the United States is "not at war." "We are simply supporting the United Nations in a police action," he said.

With a firm "no comment," the president declined to say whether American ground troops will be thrown into the far Pacific conflict or whether the atomic bomb might be used.

At the president's order, U.S. planes and warships are already blasting at the Russian-trained invaders.
June 29, 1950

By Russell Brines

TOKYO, JULY 1 (AP)—The first U.S. ground troops today flew in to South Korea in an attempt to stem a Communist armored drive threatening to overrun all resistance before the refugee capital of Taejon.

They evidently were being rushed into position 25 to 35 miles north of Taejon to hold bridgeheads across the Kum River. Taejon is 90 air miles south of Seoul, the fallen South Korean capital.

The number of troops involved was not given. They previously were identified as a battalion of the 24th Infantry Division (possibly 1,000 men).

Reports from the front said Suwon and its strategic air strip 20 miles south of Seoul had fallen. They indicate the North Koreans, with from 40 to 50 tanks, had driven possibly 40 miles south of Suwon.

Despite these reports, Premier Sinn Sung Mo insisted in Taejon that the South Koreans had stopped the invaders from the Communist North short of Suwon. The American accounts said the South Korean army had collapsed and had about quit fighting. Reports reaching here said the American troops landed under a thunderous air cover that ranged far northward, looking for the North Korean armored column.

The airborne landings of American troops were made at Pusan, on the southeast coast 163 road miles southeast of Taejon.

It was a swift, well-organized operation across the 120-mile-wide Tsushima Strait between Japan and Korea.

Brig. Gen. John H. Church, commanding the headquarters, told AP correspondent Tom Lambert in Taejon today that the first battalion would be flown to Pusan, a southern port, and taken by train to defend Bruges 25 to 30 miles north of Taejon.

Lambert reported the South Koreans, hard pressed ever since the Reds invaded last Sunday, had virtually quit fighting by 6 p.m. Friday (3 a.m. Friday, EST). He described the defense as in a state of collapse after Red tanks broke through the Han River defenses, north of Suwon.

The Reds were officially reported to have gotten 40 to 50 armored vehicles across the broad Han River, crossing at several points south of Seoul, the fallen southern capital.

A column of 50 Northern trucks then moved infantry southward against almost no opposition.

Reliable sources in Taejon said the South Koreans refused to mine roads and walked away from the fight after having told the Americans they would keep battling.

These disastrous developments came as President Truman in Washington ordered use of American ground forces to bolster the then-faltering defense. Word of the Southern collapse came several hours later.

There was no word when the first American combat infantry would arrive. They were reported already en route, however. Pusan is a southeast Korean port—the only spot remaining in the south which has an airstrip long enough to handle big transport planes. It is 162 miles southeast of Taejon, with which it is linked by rail.
July 1, 1950

By O.H.P. King

ADVANCE AMERICAN COMMAND HEADQUARTERS IN SOUTH KOREA, JULY 5 (AP)— Here is a picture of war's desolation in South Korea:

Thousands of South Korean army troops in retreat—some call it a rout.

More thousands of bewildered civilian refugees, some trudging in one direction, others going the opposite way. All are laden with pitifully small bundles.

War planes have passed this way, their gunfire raking the road.

The dead still lay along the roadway, and the wounded cry for aid and are ignored.

Scores of abandoned vehicles are along this highway. I have just traveled 180 miles through the nightmare area. Some had been strafed and burned, others had been run off the road and still others were left because of mechanical or fuel difficulties.

Newly organized and equipped Republic of Korea troops march toward the front lines in South Korea to take up the battle against the invading North Korean forces.

(Amid this scene of refugee turmoil, Gen. MacArthur's headquarters communique warned that numbers of North Korean troops in civilian clothes were slipping south on missions of sabotage and espionage.

(The flight of civilians also was occurring north of the front, in areas already seized by the invaders. American fliers returning to bases in Japan said they saw the highways east of Red-conquered Seoul jammed with thousands of refugees. Whether they were trying to escape the Reds and the new terror of the "people's courts" or feared U.S. air raids was uncertain.

(A city which had swollen to nearly 2,000,000 in the past five years—twice its previous population—Seoul is largely of insecure wood, plaster and straw construction.)

The American engineers had instructed the South Korean troops how to blow up bridges to hinder the Communist North Korean columns. Three bridges had been destroyed during the afternoon, and a fourth was slated for destruction at night.

We saw bombs drop on a front-line city and black columns of smoke arise.

A wounded man lay moaning by the road, his ox and cart not far away on a rice paddy field. Nobody paid any attention to him until we stopped. He had wounds in the head, back, shoulder and body.

We saw several battalions of completely uniformed South Korean troop trainees all carrying rifles that used to belong to the Japanese army. But the rifles all were minus their vital bolts.

Sometimes trains on a nearby track stopped to pick up military stragglers and refugees, then proceeded slowly south, their rooftops crowded with civilians, and soldiers packed within the cars.

We bucked a tide of military vehicles driven by frantic South Korean reserve troops.

No matter what their retreat is called officially, military men would call it a rout.

July 5, 1950

By Tom Lambert

WITH U.S. FORCES IN SOUTH KOREA, JULY 9 (AP)—The line of stout Americans halted North Korean Communist advances on the ground today while the allies pounded the Reds from the air. The Communist thrust, which forced Americans Saturday to abandon some positions, was blunted by artillery and aircraft, which chewed impartially at Red infantry and tanks.

American positions today (Sunday) were stretched across the top of a long ridge some miles south of Chonan, which is 60 road miles south of Seoul and is the deepest major penetration the Reds have made since they invaded South Korea two weeks ago today (June 25).

In foxholes and rifle pits on the brow of the hill, the Americans looked north over a small village to a line of low ridges among which the Reds were reported massing.

Mortar shells passed overhead, bursting in one of the shallow valleys.

Suddenly the throatier whistle of artillery volleys took over, pouring in on the same targets as the mortars were firing on. "Boy, listen to that! My morale is 300 percent higher than this morning!" exclaimed a grimy, bearded sergeant as he leaned back luxuriously in his foxhole.

(This indicated the mortar and artillery fire was American.) Down the slope, a thin-faced captain asked an artillery liaison man, "Did that do it, Joe?"

"Yup," Joe replied. "The observer says he can see them now. They're confused and running."

Another volley roared in. As the artillery and mortars slammed into the enemy positions, three GIs were discussing a story in the Army newspaper, *Stars and Stripes*.

"Listen to this," read Sgt. Edward Stellans of 1156 West 48th Street, Chicago. "The Association of Veterans of the 82nd Airborne approves Truman's decision on Korea."

"Maybe they'd like to come over," offered Cpl. Joe Marcinko of Windber, Pa. "Maybe it'd be another Bastogne again if they did."

Then a U.S. jet, sweeping widely, poured a short burst of machine-gun fire into our positions.

This endeavor elicited profane indignation. The pilot's ancestry was questioned cursingly and his ability and eyesight condemned as the GIs spilled back into their holes.

The muttering continued until a laconic officer reported to headquarters by telephone, "One of our aircraft strafed our position, no damage or injuries."

July 9, 1950

By Tom Lambert

WITH AMERICAN FORCES IN SOUTH KOREA, JULY 11 (AP)—One week ago today U.S. armed forces went into action in the South Korean war against communism. The week has been one of American withdrawal and losses. This is not to say that the war here is lost—far from it. But it is to say that for one week surprisingly strong North Korean forces have mauled one of the most powerful nations on earth.

A review of Gen. MacArthur's communiques and the statements of an advanced headquarters spokesman discloses that the Americans have been pushed back and back since they went into the lines.

There are various reasons for this. Some of them sound unpleasantly like those advanced for early American defeat in the last war.

We were not prepared for this fight. In fact it is extremely doubtful that we knew the Red invasion was coming. One must ask if we know about and are prepared for any other possible Communist attacks.

We have not yet been able to muster the strength and weight which gave us victory over Germany and Japan. This question then arises:

Could we muster strength and power quickly enough to save ourselves if our country were attacked?

We have underestimated the North Koreans, as has been, and will be, admitted by U.S. soldiers

One of four American soldiers of the 21st Infantry Regiment, 24th Division, found midway between the forward observation post and the actual front line. Most of them were shot through the head and had their hands tied behind their backs.

and generals alike. We are fast losing the early contempt we had for the North Koreans.

The withdrawals and losses out here have affected the morale of the soldiers who, like all Americans, hate to lose a fight. In their outcries against what has happened here this past week, men and officers complain:

Our force is not strong enough.

We are outnumbered.

The Air Force has let them down by failing to halt every Red tank on Korea's roads.

We are being committed in a piecemeal and haphazard fashion. This campaign is in its infancy, however, and as it develops so will our strength and power.

Everyone here is confident the North Koreans are in for the jolt of their lives when we get set and start moving north.

Our soldiers, generally speaking, seem to have no stomach for this war. This is a personal opinion, but I doubt if many of them believe that in fighting the Reds here they are fighting for themselves.

An occasional soldier mentions Russia and communism, of course, and some of them wonder if the third world war has started here.

Many of them think, however, the South Kore-

ans should fight their own battle and seemingly would little care if this country fell to the Reds.
July 11, 1950

By William R. Moore

NEAR THE FRONT IN KOREA, JULY 11 (AP)—I saw two dead American soldiers Monday. Their hands were tied behind them. They had been shot through the head.

The two soldiers lay just off a main road which carried the vital, frantic traffic supplying front line fighters. They had been there since Monday morning, I was told later by infantry officers at rear command posts.

These officers said three Americans had been tied and shot in the head, but I saw only the two bodies.

(Yesterday, Lt. D.C. Gates, Joinerville, Texas, reported seven American soldiers, their hands tied behind, had been shot to death by North Koreans. There was no indication whether the three reported today were some of those, or additional atrocities.)

I found no one who witnessed these slayings. Based on what was known of the fighting at this point early Monday, the belief was held generally that the soldiers, riding in a jeep in the morning mist, suddenly found themselves only 20 yards or so from a North Korean tank. With the tank guns raised upon them, they jumped out and surrendered.

Their bodies showed what happened afterward. One of the green clad corpses lay face downward, the other on its side. Cloth bands about three inches wide, like the bandages each American soldier carries in his first aid kit, were tied so tightly around the wrists of each that the hands showed purplish brown. The arms above the thongs were much lighter.
July 11, 1950

By Roger D. Greene

WASHINGTON, JULY 19 (AP)—The nation moved swiftly toward partial war mobilization tonight after President Truman asked Congress for a $10,000,000,000 down payment on the struggle to halt Red aggression.

The armed services announced they will begin immediately calling up limited numbers of reservists—chiefly specialists—to active duty.

Mr. Truman also authorized the calling of National Guardsmen and free use of the draft law.

The president called on Congress this noon to gear the United States to a virtual war footing. He called for: Anti-inflation controls, a swift step-up in war production, additional huge sums to arm non-Communist nations and, later, a sharp boost in taxes.

Then tonight he spoke to the nation over all major radio networks and television channels and read a dramatic last-minute report on the Korean War from Gen. Douglas MacArthur declaring:

"The issue of battle is now fully joined and will proceed along lines of action in which we will not be without choice.

"Our hold upon the southern part of Korea represents a secure base. Our casualties, despite overwhelming odds, have been relatively light.

"Our strength will continue to increase while that of the enemy will relatively decrease. His supply is insecure. He has had his great chance, but failed to exploit it."

That was the gist of MacArthur's dispatch—perhaps the brightest news of the war—as read by the president before a battery of radio microphones and TV cameras in the White House movie room.

But the president warned the nation that it must undergo some belt tightening to provide the sinews of war, and he condemned scare buying and hoarding as foolish and selfish. Coupled with his recommendations, the president voiced a stiff warning obviously aimed at Soviet Russia, in these words:

"The free world has made it clear, through the United Nations, that lawless aggression will be met with force. This is the significance of Korea, and it is a significance whose importance cannot be overlooked."
July 19, 1950

By Hal Boyle

POHANG AIRBASE, KOREA, AUG. 12 (DELAYED) (AP)—A column of American tanks—lost for a time because they lacked maps of the area where they were operating—saved this vital airstrip after smashing an ambush to get to it.

They spent 45 puzzled minutes last night under sniper fire laid down by Red troops in the enemy-held city, six miles northwest of the airfield. Then the tanks found their way out of town in a sort of Paul Revere type of ride.

"We rode through a solid wall of flame in the city," said Lt. C.D. Courtney, of Houston, Texas, a tank platoon commander who held up slightly burned hands.

"It singed everybody and caught fire to a piece of baggage on the rear end of one tank," he added. "It was that hot."

Some 70 or more Negro doughboys riding on the rear of other tanks escaped the blistering ordeal unhurt. They were part of the survivors of a central part of the column, which was ambushed the evening before some 10 miles south of Pohang.

It was at the same spot that the enemy tried a second ambush with machine-gun and mortar fire. The surprising appearance of tanks—unseen by them before—caught the Reds flatfooted. They couldn't face mass fire by the Army and broke and ran.

The story was told by Capt. Joseph Parrigo of Noroton Heights, Conn., a farmer, officer and professional engineer who rejoined the Army "because of a sense of adventure."

Parrigo, unshaven, dust-caked and shirtless, said he had joined the tank column just before it started its march after it was held up for several hours to build a bridge that would take the weight of the tanks.

The column lost its way in enemy-occupied territory and burning Pohang because the emergency nature of the movement hadn't given it time to get fresh maps.

Capt. Parrigo said he had brought a native boy from Pohang to guide the column through the city to the airport but that he disappeared after the leading tank fired a smoke shell down the main street to discourage snipers. The tank had run out of high explosive shells. Parrigo said he finally found the boy under a piece of fabric under the rear end of the tank.

"By then we had made three wrong turns in the town. But the enemy was afraid of tanks—and the boy steered us the rest of the way to the airport."

"We came to the ambush point and the enemy made the mistake of opening fire on us," he said.

"Apparently they had gone into a small village to pick up food. One tank caught a group of 60 or more as they ran under some trees, and it slaughtered them."
Aug. 12, 1950

By Hal Boyle

IN A FIFTH AIR FORCE PLANE OVER WAEG-WAN, KOREA, WEDNESDAY, AUG. 16 (AP)—A force of 98 B-29 bombers striking the mightiest air blow of the Korean War is turning a 21-square-mile target north of here into a gigantic smudge pot. That's how it looks from a grandstand seat in this transport plane—or as if the earth had parted in a sudden volcanic burst.

It is now 12:30 p.m. and the great Superforts have been coming over in waves of eight for an hour and a half. Not one single flak shell has been thrown up against them here where ack-ack is ordinarily reported heavy.

The enemy appears stunned and paralyzed by the shock of the massive air attack. The bombers, glinting like sleek swans as they swim with lazy grace through a blue sky flecked with light clouds, have dropped to 7,000 feet now to unload their bombs—10 tons for each plane. And still there is no enemy challenger of any kind.

Somewhere hidden in that inferno of smoke, flame and concussion below are some 40,000 North Koreans massed for a knockout blow at Taegu. But today they are keeping their heads down.

As another flight lets go its cargo, our pilot, Capt. James R. Young, of 2150 Lowell St., Denver, Colo., calls:

"Look—right on the nose!"

As the bombs strike the ground they unleash a series of bright flashes like tremendous firecrackers. The flashes stair-step to a village in the foothills and blow it apart as though it were a town of paper.

Then great columns of dirty gray brown smoke mushroom up and merge into a vast pall that covers the hills and fills the valleys and still keeps rising. Hardly a dozen flaming villages add to the pall—and some of the smoke is deep and black. It comes from burning enemy vehicles and fuel dumps.

On ridge lines east of the Naktong River, scat-

U.S. Air Force B-29 Superforts release their explosive cargos over a chemical plant during a raid on Konan in North Korea.

tered American infantry patrols cheer and wave at the B-29s. It isn't every day the doughboy sees these big bombers ride to his help and blast the enemy with the equivalent of 30,000 heavy artillery shells in two hours.

As our plane turns homeward, the pilot swoops down to within 50 feet of the sandy Naktong River and races down the eastern bank in an area where the enemy has put across troops repeatedly in an attempt to force a beachhead.

Suddenly Lt. Jim Bradley of Van Nuys, Calif., pointed out some pinpoint flashes coming from the hillside and our plane swings up and away.

"Small arms fire," says Bradley.
Aug. 16, 1950

By Don Whitehead

WITH U.S. MARINES, KOREA, AUG. 17 (AP)—The Marines were fighting the bloodiest battle of the Korean War today against Reds desperately trying to spread their bridgehead across the winding Naktong River.

Under a searing sun the leathernecks advanced behind a hail of steel. But it is a slow and costly advance—this battle of the Obongi Ridge.

The fighting was close-in and savage. The

Marines hit the North Koreans with everything they have except flame-throwers.

The Marines first went into action last week on the southern flank of the American attack toward Chinju. They pushed deep into Red territory in that drive. But then they were pulled back and rushed to this sector to help the 24th Infantry Division wipe out the Red penetration across the Naktong on the central sector of the front. Marine units got their marching orders late yesterday.

Last night they were on the move into the line, their convoys growing across dusty roads under a sky that sparkled with stars.

At 4:10 a.m. the 2nd Battalion was in the line ready to attack with "D" and "E" companies in the spearhead. Their objective was Obongi Ridge—a steep swayback hill covered with scrub growth and rock.

Their move had been swift. Shortly after dawn, the attack began. Artillery and Marine Corsair fighter planes plastered the enemy-held ridge with explosives and machine-gun fire. But when the leathernecks started up Obongi Ridge, the enemy cut loose with mortars, machine-guns and small-arms fire. They even lobbed grenades down the ridge into the faces of the Marines. On the road below was the blackened hulk of a burned-out Russian-made tank.

"We were dug in up here when three Red tanks came up the road at night with their lights on," said Pvt. Edmund Niper, of Riverdale, N.J. "They must have been lost.

"Some of our guys started taking hot chow to the crew thinking they were our guys. But all they got was hot lead."

He said three tanks escaped after the first one was knocked out.

I went over to one side and sat down beside two Navy corpsmen who had been carrying wounded in from the battlefield. They were John Stanley, 19, and Lynn Blethen, 20.

John leaned back wearily. "I respect the Marines a helluva lot more since I've seen them in action," he said. "The Reds threw everything at us. If it hadn't been for these planes, they'd have killed everyone of us."

Lynn said, "The worst thing was the mortars.

They can teach us something about mortars. They can lay one right in your hip pocket, if the pocket is open."

A padre (chaplain) walked among the wounded, chatting to them and comforting them wherever he could.

A wounded man—shot through the hand—said, "I could not run bending over, and they got me through the hand. That's a helluva place to be shot. I've got men laying with their brains shot out. We have to get corpsmen up there."

The padre listened to the man, walked through the gate and headed toward the front.

One of the young Marines, holding a cigarette in a hand that trembled with fatigue, called after the padre: "Be careful, father. They've got guns, you know."
Aug. 17, 1950

By Tom Lambert

WITH U.S. FORCES IN SOUTH KOREA, AUG. 30 (AP)—The road lay warm and yellow in the mid-afternoon sun, winding alongside rich green rice paddies on the floor of the valley.

On the gray sandy ridges above the valley, ridges laced with erosion ruts and sparsely covered with scrubby undergrowth, were the Reds.

American tanks and infantry began moving at 4 p.m., flanked by South Korean allies, to clear the hills.

In single file the tanks edged along the road with "Belle Starr" commanded by Staff Sgt. Ernest W. Belcher of Hazy, W.Va., in the lead.

"Belle Starr" is a Pershing tank, 46 tons of steel with a 90 mm gun. The other Pershings, "Bama Belle," "Bucket O'Bolts" and "Bewildered" followed.

The GIs commanded by 2nd Lt. Henry E. Davis, (943 S. Magnolia), Los Angeles, stalked warily along the flanks of the steel monsters or edged gingerly up the slopes of the ridges. The tanks' machine-guns hammered harshly at a few Reds who fled their approach, or at targets pointed out by the tense doughboys.

"Belle Starr" had just rounded a twist in the road when the Reds reacted first. There was a ripping burst of machine-gun fire, and a lieuten-

Under guard of U.S. MPs, dejected North Korean prisoners squat in an improvised barbed wire enclosure after their capture during the Red drive on Yongsan on Korea's Naktong River front. U.S. tanks move along the road in the background.

ant and two men on the slopes staggered, slumped and fell. The tanks and the soldiers halted.

While angry eyes scanned the hillside and the shallow ravines which scarred them, soldiers slid cursing down the shale slope, carrying the wounded men.

The fire and the blood halted the action, except for quick sniping shots by GIs and the occasional hasty stuttering rat-tat-tat of a Red burp gun.

Then the Marines flew in, four of them in Corsair fighters, laden with bullets, rockets and napalm bombs of jellied gasoline.

They circled the area once, carefully, then for approximately 20 minutes lashed viciously at the Reds.

One of them poured one short burst of machine-gun fire into our men—and elicited harsh cries of outrage—but that was their only slip.

The flying leathernecks circled the Red-held hills like riders on a merry-go-round. Each time

they swung past the Red-held positions, they strafed. The napalm bombs dropped lazily, bursting into flames and towering columns of smoke.

High on a slope, Sgt. First Class Bert Hensley of Commerce, Texas, said the Reds "had jumped up like quail, just like a covey of quail" as U.S. riflemen moved into a draw.

Lt. Davis clawed his way up the hill and asked Hensley about those casualties.

"One of them was that new kid, that replacement," replied one sergeant.

Davis grabbed up a handful of scrawny grass and threw it down fiercely in a gesture of anger.

Then the command to "move out" came out of the valley road and 2nd Lt. Dennis H. Hunter of Capac, Mich., tank platoon commander, outlined the plan of attack.

"Belle Starr" took the lead again. She lumbered up the road threateningly. A cluster of riflemen crouched on her back.

Then came "Bama Belle," "Bewildered" and "Bucket O'Bolts."

The tanks rounded one turn, then another. They were still in view of the infantrymen behind them on the slopes.

Suddenly "Belle Starr" opened up—and jolted with the effort. Dust spurted from her cleated tracks.

The shell burst on the hillside, to the right of a saddle on which we could see the Reds running up a ridge.

Then the rear tank began backing down, back toward us. Three of them came back, then "Belle Starr."

The attack was stalled for the moment. Red automatic weapons gunners had brought the tanks under fire and pinned down their accompanying infantrymen.

Aug. 30, 1950

TOKYO, SEPT. 14 (AP)—U.S. doughboys will get a free can of beer every day at the front in Korea.

Gen. MacArthur ordered it today.

Front line troops had been getting a can of beer about every three days.

They set up a howl Tuesday when Washington outlawed all free beer for men at the front.

Beer for combat troops, under the new plan, will be paid for out of post exchange profits instead of taxpayers' money.

To keep the record straight, Maj. Gen. William A. Beiderlinden, assistant chief of staff to Gen. MacArthur, said the free beer will be for combat men only.

Rear echelon troops may buy their own at the PX.

Sept. 14, 1950

The Tide Turns

Of the Inchon landings in September 1950, Gen. Omar Bradley later wrote in his autobiography: "I had to agree that it was the riskiest military proposal I had ever heard of. Inchon was probably the worst possible place ever selected for an amphibious landing." With harbor tides possessing among the greatest swings in the world, it was such an unlikely place for invasion that an amphibious landing could take the enemy by nearly complete surprise.

And that is precisely what Gen. MacArthur's attacking forces achieved on Sept. 15, 1950.

MARINES STORM INCHON

TOKYO, SEPT. 16 (AP)—American Marines and infantry stormed ashore at the big Korean port of Inchon Friday, 165 miles behind the lines of the North Korean Communists, in a bold nutcracker operation intended to crush the life out of the Red invaders.

The Americans knifed quickly eastward towards Seoul, the Red-held capital 22 miles inland.

Gen. MacArthur, who personally supervised the assault, called Seoul the key to the whole enemy machine.

"When the enemy is caught between two wings of our forces, his forces will sooner or later disintegrate and cease to be a coordinated fighting army."

The North Korean radio said the Americans already had advanced half the distance to Seoul, or 11 miles.

Covered by bombardments from British and American warships, the Marines landed first—at 6:30 a.m. The Navy said the Marines suffered only "negligible losses."

Eleven hours later the U.S. Tenth Army Corps went ashore, led by tanks.

Gen. MacArthur himself was off Inchon, touring the difficult mudflat and seawall landing areas in a launch while naval gunfire screeched overhead. He declared:

"The Navy and Marines have never shone more brightly than this morning."

These coordinated thrusts deep in Red territory were the kickoff of the long-awaited United Nations offensive.

This was the day of turning tide, coming after a series of bitterly-fought allied withdrawals that began with the tank-led North Korean assault across the 38th parallel June 25.

With warships slamming heavy shells into concealed Red shore positions, the Marines landed on Wolmi Island. It is connected to Inchon proper by a half-mile causeway.

Carrier planes slammed rockets at the shore guns, too, but the Marines still were under heavy fire. But they planted the American flag on Wolmi's highest hill within 32 minutes after landing.

The infantrymen were held back to take advantage of Inchon's exceptionally high tide. At 5:30 p.m. (3:30 a.m., EST), they went ashore. They drove two miles into Inchon, a city of 300,000, within 30 minutes.

Associated Press correspondent Relman Morin, with the forces, reported brown pillars of smoke billowed into the overcast sky, sent up by the shells of the warships. Then a light rain fell.

Morin described the Marine landing as "a gem of military precision." He reported U.S. tanks were fighting less than 15 minutes after the first leatherneck crossed the bombed-out beach.

Gen. MacArthur told AP correspondent Russell Brines and other newsmen accompanying him that the amphibious attack might break the backbone of the Korean Red army.

The main objectives: To cut Red communications in the Inchon-Seoul bottleneck, and then crush the Communists in a giant nutcracker—between the jaws of the Inchon Expeditionary Force and the American Eighth Army in the southeastern beachhead.

The Inchon beachhead was softened up by a two-day naval and air bombardment in midweek.

While the Inchon landings were in progress, the mighty U.S. battleship *Missouri* boomed back into hostilities. Her 16-inch guns whammed away at Samchok, Communist-held seaport on Korea's east Sea of Japan coast 70 miles north of Pohang port. The mighty *Mo* cruised into the Sea of Japan on the tail of a typhoon, after an 11,000-mile dash from Norfolk, Va. The shells she shot at Samchok were aimed at disrupting Red traffic north and south on the east coast rail line and highway. *Sept. 16, 1950*

By Russell Brines

WITH GENERAL MacARTHUR ON THE INCHON FRONT, KOREA, SEPT. 15 (AP)—Gen MacArthur—and the United Nations forces at his command—were back on the offensive today.

Marines and Army units of the Tenth Corps under the personal leadership of the 70-year-old United Nations commander, with two bold strokes assaulted the port of Inchon. A second front had been opened 165 miles northwest of the U.N. beachhead in South Korea.

It was part of a two-month old plan MacArthur conceived about July 12 to relieve pressure on sorely pressed Americans and South Koreans then battling on the Kum River line, some 85 miles south of Seoul.

Today, as on 11 previous landings he personally led during World War II, MacArthur had no qualms about exposing himself to enemy fire.

Wearing his familiar sweat-stained, braided campaign cap and crisp sun-tans, MacArthur watched the first phase of the joint sea and land operation open at dawn.

Seated in the lookout chair aboard the flagship of Rear Adm. James H. Doyle, commander of the assault force, MacArthur watched the beaches tremble under the bombardment of American and British warships.

Then, three and one-half hours after Marine units seized little Wolmi Island in Inchon Harbor, MacArthur and his staff boarded a launch. They cruised within rifle range of the North Koreans off a second beach on the edge of Inchon.

Shells thundered over the launch as allied warcraft bombarded the beach. There was no return fire.

Later in the afternoon, Marines landed on the second beach. MacArthur was smiling and confident as the operation proceeded like clockwork.

He had outlined his strategy to correspondents aboard the flagship two days earlier. It was this:

"Everything the enemy shoots and all additional replacements he needs have to come down through Seoul.

Gen. Douglas MacArthur (seated) and members of his staff view pre-landing bombardment and air strikes from the flag bridge of the USS Mt. McKinley in Korean waters off Inchon, as U.S. forces begin their offensive in that section. Left to right: Brig. Gen. Courtney Whitney; Gen. MacArthur (foreground); Brig. Gen. E.K. Wright, asst. chief of staff; and Maj. Gen. Edward M. Almond, Tenth Corps.

"We are going to try to seize the distribution area, so that it will be impossible for the North Koreans to get any additional men—or more than a trickle of supplies.

"When the enemy is caught between two wings of our forces, his forces will sooner or later disintegrate and cease to be a coordinated fighting army."

MacArthur realized the landing at Inchon involved a calculated risk. He gambled:

1. That highly-developed American techniques of amphibious landings could overcome the hazard of mudflats and seawalls—the toughest landing areas some of MacArthur's veteran officers ever had seen.

2. That Soviet Russia and Communist China would stay out of direct participation in the war.

The first risk appeared to have been won. It was too early to tell what the Russian and Chinese reaction would be.

Sept. 15, 1950

By Stan Swinton

MASAN FRONT, SOUTH KOREA, SEPT. 15 (AP)—Optimism swept this front tonight as word spread of the landing in Communist-held territory in and around Inchon.

"We are that much nearer home," exulted tank Lt. Donald Barnard of Richmond, Calif.

"This might mean the end of the war. Gosh, I hope so," exclaimed Pfc. Charles Fabiszak of (903 Alice Ave.) Beloit, Wis.

The weary infantrymen on the southern front were more pleased than surprised. The landing plan had been one of the worst-kept secrets of the war.

Nearly everyone from recruits to generals had been expecting it.

The general reaction was: "We're over the hump, boys, but there's a tough fight ahead." *Sept. 15, 1950*

By Relman Morin

ABOARD THE FLAGSHIP OF TASK FORCE SEVEN, OFF INCHON, SEPT. 15 (AP)—A D-day diary:

4 a.m. breakfast. There's a queer feeling in your stomach, but you discover it isn't hunger. All you want is coffee, coffee as black as the sky outside.

5 a.m. Ship creeping so slow up the channel motion is imperceptible. Other ships invisible but you know they are there. On either side, shore lights are winking, tiny cold points in darkness. They are channel lights, operated by South Koreans, believe it or not. Inchon is enemy held but they seem not to have bothered to grab these little islands and extinguish the channel markers.

5:30 a.m. Ship anchors. It's deathly quiet. On deck sailors unconsciously honor the stillness by talking in whispers. A faint silver glow of dawn outlines a hill on your right.

5:45 a.m.—This ship's 3-inch guns swivel toward Wolmi Island. Soon Marines will be hitting that island. It's an ugly hump-backed chunk of wooded rock, setting squarely in channel leading to Inchon.

It's badly scarred too, shaved clean of shrubbery on one shoulder. The Navy's been firing heavy shells into that shoulder, groping for North Korean defense positions.

5:50 a.m.—A burst of orange flame, then the slamming shock of sound and concussion. An instant later a furious puff of heat on your face, the hot breath of the guns. In the darkness you can see the shells white hot, almost floating, like well-hit golf balls. Seconds later the bumping thud comes back and the ship shudders—nine miles from Wolmi Island on which the shells landed.

6 a.m.—The morning hush is gone. In the elbow of the channel ships are rapid firing, the deep baying of the 8-inchers and the wicked, ear-shattering crack of the 5-inch guns. A dirty, brownish-gray pall mushrooms over Wolmi.

6:30 a.m.—Marines hit the beach. Counter-battery fire reported from the southern end of Inchon. Big gunfire has ceased and your ears strain for sounds of small arms fire. Not a sound from over there.

6:50 a.m.—Reports coming in fast from Wolmi now. First landing craft were off the beach in 30 seconds. That's fast, even for Marines. Thirty men per boat. One man on the beach every second.

7 a.m.—Things are moving fast now. Marines have red and yellow panels—to identify their positions for planes still hovering overhead—on high points of Wolmi. Word from their commander: "Landings successful. Losses negligible." You look at your watch. Only 30 minutes.

7:07 a.m.—"We have planted the flag on the highest point of the island." Nothing more said and nothing more needed.

10:30 a.m.—Gen. MacArthur, wearing familiar leather jacket, sunglasses and battered old cap, jumps nimbly into a launch. Its owner, Vice Adm. Arthur Dewey Struble, commander of joint task force, follows him. Officers, correspondents crowd in behind.

11 a.m.—They go first towards Wolmi, strangely quiet now. A tank is bulldozing rubble off a shore road. Marines wander aimlessly, looking at shattered revetments and dug-in defenses. Capturing of the island closed phase one of this operation. The main attack on Inchon will come later. Marines sit munching K rations and candy.

12:30 p.m.—MacArthur insists on taking a close look at North Korean main defenses fronting Inchon. The little gray launch noses up to within 400 yards of one main area—it's easy rifle shot and still five hours before "H" hour. His face is blank as his eyes search the position. It's first time a supreme commander ever did that and got away with it.

1 p.m.—Not a shot is fired. Maybe the North Koreans too were looking at Old Glory, waving on top of Wolmi, instead of the easy target in front of them. *Sept. 15, 1950*

ACROSS THE HAN

By Don Whitehead

WITH U.S. MARINES OUTSIDE SEOUL, SEPT. 20 (AP)—A pale three-quarter moon was sliding below the horizon when the Marines came out of their foxholes and started trudging toward the Han River today.

Ahead of them, somewhere on the dusty road, were the big amphibious tractors the assault waves would ride into the battle for the Han River bridgehead on the Seoul side.

The men came out of their holes unwrapping themselves from blankets and shelter halves and cursing softly. The night was cold and damp.

Maj. Mike Erhlich of San Diego yelled at his men, the heavy weapons company of the Fifth Regiment's first battalion:

"Get ready to move. Assemble in boats."

The men shouldered heavy machine-guns and mortars and ammunition and radios as they came stumbling out of the cotton patch onto the road. The assault was set for 4 a.m., and Erhlich's men were to ride with the assault.

The river crossing didn't look so good now. We knew the enemy would be waiting for the main attack.

Then I noticed the sergeant carrying the cardboard box—Master Sgt. Anthony Kent of 115 South Third St., Salina, Kan. He noticed my curiosity and opened the top. Inside were three fluffy white rabbits sleeping soundly on a bed of straw.

"Bought them with a package of cigarettes," Kent grinned. "Now they're our mascots." Rabbits going into battle with the big tough Marine! Suddenly, I realized how young these warriors were.

Dawn had broken when the amtrack column lurched forward and roared down the road toward the river. And in the bowels of each were sealed a unit of Marines, ready to begin fighting when the amtrack doors opened on the Seoul side.

The artillery thundered. We could hear the rush of shells and feel the shudder of explosions as our artillery pounded the enemy shore of the Han. The amtracks bounded and jerked down the road, and then we were in the river.

Bullets began to slam against the side of our amtrack. Through a slit in the rear door I could see little spouts of water jumping up as bullets hit the water. But the steel sides protected us, and the Amtracks plowed ahead.

Then we were ashore and climbing a steep sandy bank. The machine guns were rattling. Our amtrack pulled away from the river about 1,000 yards and swerved through a rice paddy to an embankment. The men were tense. They tripped their weapons, ready for the dash through the door.

Slowly the door opened. Sgt. Kent was first out, carrying the box with the rabbits. As he hugged the shelter of a bank he put them down carefully beside him.

I dashed after the sergeant and then the man behind me screamed and pitched forward. At the same time we heard the crack of the rifle.

Then another Marine screamed and fell from the amtrack.

The enemy on the hill above us was shooting straight down into our men as they came out the door.

The Marines hugged the embankment as the bullets cracked into the vehicle. The driver fell wounded.

Mike Erhlich thundered at his men to get out of the vehicle. Then he coolly sent a rifle squad around the ridge and ordered an amtrack machine gunner to swing his gun around and open fire.

Above us crackled rifles and machine guns as the fighting moved up the ridge. Our amtrack had gotten ahead of the infantry, and for a brief time, there was no infantry between us and the enemy.

Down the hill came frightened, whimpering civilians. Two women carried rosaries clutched to their breasts. The children were sobbing and frightened, their eyes wide with fear.

Sgt. Kent looked at the children and then he went back down the hill. When he returned he carried the box with the three white rabbits. He sat down and slowly opened the lid and took one of the rabbits out in his big ham-like hand. He smiled at the children.

The fear went out of their eyes and tears stopped. Then they smiled and came over to peek into the box and exclaim over the mascots of the Third Battalion.

The sergeant grinned and put the rabbits back in the box and went back to his job.

Rubble litters streets and smoke from burning buildings fills the sky as tanks lead U.N. forces in recapture of Seoul.

In a short time our mortars were thumping shells into the enemy lines.

This time the Marines had landed and the situation was well in hand.
Sept. 20, 1950

By Relman Morin

ON THE HAN RIVER, KOREA, SEPT. 20 (DE-LAYED) (AP)—This is a push, a big push, like those of the best days in the last war. Men, machines and guns streamed across the Han River all day and pushed on toward Seoul. Behind them, on the left bank of the river, an iron glacier was piling up. More tanks, amphibious tractors, artillery pieces, trucks and jeeps and every conceivable weapon and instrument of war were moving over the rutted roads raising columns of swirling dust.

There is so much amphibious equipment that the buildup behind the leading columns is moving smoothly.

It could be called a breakthrough except that there was very little Communist opposition to break through.

By late afternoon, some 200 prisoners had been rounded up and were sitting impassively on the river bank with no more fight left in them. They ranged from boys of 14 and 15 to grown men. American planes flew cover over the whole area. The North Koreans apparently have very little, if any, air power.

At this point it is all mud and dust, heat, sweat and blood. The great clanking engines of war are rumbling along toward Seoul. Yongdungpo is burning, with mounting columns of black smoke rising to the sky. The ambulances are coming back, while the main stream rolls forward. There are lifeless bodies, American and Korean, all along the road between the river and Seoul.

It is a big push. And it looks like the big ones that came near the end of the last war.

The Communists said they had been brought down from North Korea five days ago. They had some machine guns and mortars but not much other equipment.

They said they were told to hold the Han line at all costs, that reinforcements were coming from the south.

But they did not attempt much resistance. They opened up on the amphibious tractors full of Marines on the river at dawn. When the bullets bounded off the sides they stopped shooting and fled.

Americans were wounded and killed on the right bank of the river, however, long after the fighting apparently ended. As the main body of the Reds retired, scores hid in thatched-hut villages and waited patiently in the high corn and rice fields. All day long there were bursts of fire from places of concealment.

South Koreans who came in after the Marines wanted to kill the Reds on the spot whenever any were flushed out of hiding. Before they pulled out of one village, the North Koreans shot a number of civilians—apparently for purely political reasons. One old woman, wrinkled and thin, was shot through the thigh. She sat all day beside a smoldering stack of thatch.

Sept 20, 1950

By Don Whitehead

SEOUL, SEPT. 26 (AP)—This is a flaming, smoke-filled city of horror today. Great fires are raging, and a black dome of smoke hangs in the sky as a fearsome signal of destruction.

Street by street, the Marines are nearing the heart of the city behind flame-throwing tanks, heavy artillery and air bombardment and the rattle of machine guns and rifles.

Seoul is not being spared. It is a fight to the death, with the Reds defending from houses, ridges and rooftops in a desperate stand.

At 4 p.m., the Marines had pushed up Mapo Street almost to the French Consulate, only a short way from the American Embassy, and they had captured the Seoul railway station and yards.

On their right flank, Seventh Infantry Division units were cleaning up Namsan Hill, the big south mountain park heights that dominate all of Seoul.

Not in two wars have I seen anything to equal the battle for Seoul. This fighting through smoke-filled streets is eerie and unreal, with flames leaping from buildings and licking out at the Marines as they dash down the debris-filled streets and past buildings crashing to the ground after the fires have gutted them.

At dusk, the sky was aglow with the fires of Seoul—a great red flare that silhouettes the dark mountains for miles around. It is a bonfire of all the bitterness and hate of war concentrated on one city.

The Reds chose to defend Seoul. And the Americans are not sparing any building where the Reds had established defenses. Seoul is being scarred and battered terribly—but the allied high command is not sacrificing lives to save the face of Seoul.

And strange things happen in the battered streets. Such as the Marine racing down a street into battle with two live ducks strapped to his packs and quacking madly. Such as the Red platoon that marched out of the flames and smoke squarely into nuzzles of American guns. And such as the Red attack before dawn, which came as just the Marines were preparing to attack.

The Marines could not have ordered an attack by the enemy at a better time. American guns blasted four Red tanks, destroyed an anti-tank gun, and routed the Red infantry in a three-hour battle.

In that fight before dawn, U.S. artillery poured 1,096 rounds of explosives into the Red posi-

An American infantryman, his buddy killed in action, weeps on the shoulder of another GI somewhere in Korea. Meanwhile, a corpsman (left) goes about the business of filling out casualty tags.

tions—one of the most concentrated artillery barrages in this war. And the Marine lines held fast.

Lt. Col. Robert W. Rickert of 5649 Beaumont Ave., La Jolla, Calif., said: "By the grace of God and a long handled spoon, we were ready for them."

At 9 a.m. the Marines attacked. They moved up Mapo Street past the Seoul prison and toward the heart of Seoul.

Along the battered street civilians poured out of their homes to watch the Marines, even though bullets zipped overhead and occasionally Red shells whistled above them.

Every few hundred feet were thick earthen barricades across the street—thrown up by the Reds in the past few days for their defense of Seoul. One South Korean said the Reds forced American prisoners of war to help build the barricades. But I could never confirm this story.

Along with us came a sergeant with graying beard heavy on his face. He is Master Gunnery Sgt. William George Ferrigno, 43, of West Quincy,

Mass. And behind the sergeant was a South Korean carrying an American flag to be hoisted above the United States Embassy building when it is captured.

"We will have the flag flying before long," Ferrigno grinned. Up ahead a few blocks, a machine gun chattered and rifles cracked. Then the tanks moved up, Pershing tanks with 8 mm guns and some with flame-throwing nozzles jetting from their turrets.

The Marines moved between the burning buildings like wraiths. They were gray and tired. This was their 12th straight day of combat with little rest.

The troops were crouched against buildings on both sides of the streets—those buildings not on fire. And then the order came to move forward again.

We ran bending low up the street to an intersection and crouched behind the battered wall of a burned-out building. Another building burned fiercely across the street, and the heat was almost suffocating. The flames crawled and spread from one building to another.

Then something exploded and showered us with hot ashes and bits of burning wood, but no one was injured.

Further up the street—at a railroad overpass near the French Consulate—the commanders of two Marine companies planned their next attack.

"E" Company had made a wrong turn in the smoke-filled streets and wound up at the same place alongside "F" Company. But that was lucky, because "F" Company had hit a tough defense position.

The fight had been short but savage at this roadblock.

But before the attack could start, we saw one of the strangest sights of the war. Out of the flame and smoke ahead of us came a group of 30 to 40 Reds dragging an anti-tank gun. Down the middle of the road they came, head-on toward the barricade, to a point not more than 100 feet away.

Suddenly they saw the Marines, and the group halted in surprise. But before they could recover, Marines leaped to the barricades and poured a deadly fire into the Reds.

The concentrated fire blasted the little group of Communists to the road. Those who were not killed crawled into the doors of nearby buildings. But then the tanks opened up on them with heavy machine-gun fire.

Later we came back down the street. The smoke cleared for a moment and over a doorway—framed in flames—was a poster portrait of Josef Stalin, master of the Kremlin; and Kim Il Sung, the Red dictator of North Korea, who had hoped to rule all Korea.
Sept. 26, 1950

By John M. Hightower
WASHINGTON, SEPT. 27 (AP)—Gen. Douglas MacArthur has been authorized to send United Nations troops into North Korea, if necessary, as a military measure to destroy the power of the fleeing North Korean army.

This was reported today by responsible informants who said, however, that the longer range political question of establishing order in North Korea and occupying that area of the peninsula must be decided by the United Nations.

Thus the issue of "crossing the 38th parallel," as it is usually described, has been divided into two parts. On the one hand, is the necessity of defeating the Communist forces finally and completely. On the other, is the question of long term occupation policy.

According to this decision, authorities here said, MacArthur has the power to take whatever action may be needed to break up the Communist army. That, it was said, probably means sending troops across the 38th parallel in pursuit of Communist forces because otherwise all the North Korean divisions able to escape from the south would find refuge behind the parallel, regroup and again be in position to disturb the peace.

The basic idea underlying the current decision is that the restoration of "international peace and security in the area" is an objective which covers crossing the 38th parallel for purely military purposes. As for the long range question of what to do about North Korea—whether to create a U.N. commission to unify the country and hold elections—that is regarded as a matter on which more time can be taken without prejudicing the chances of a complete U.N. victory.

Authorities here said the speed with which Gen. MacArthur's forces succeeded in breaking

Left: First Division leathernecks advance single file through a street in Inchon, Korea, as they expand the bridgehead established by landing on the west coast near Seoul. Men were members of the 1st Battalion, 5th Regiment of the 1st Marine Division.

up the Korean Communist forces in the southern part of the peninsula was what made it necessary to split up the question of crossing the old dividing line between American and Russian occupation zones.

Sept. 27, 1950

RED CHINESE WARN U.S. ON KOREA

TOKYO, OCT. 1 (AP)—Communist China's premier said today that Chinese Reds will not "supinely tolerate seeing their neighbors being savagely invaded by imperialists."

Premier Chou En-lai said in a Peiping radio broadcast monitored here that the Chinese people were deeply interested in the progress of events in Korea. Chou expressed belief the North Korean Reds ultimately would win.

His remarks were contained in an 11,000-word statement issued on the first anniversary of the founding of the Communist regime in China.

Chou accused the United States of aggression in the Far East and charged it with "brutalities" in allegedly violating Chinese territory with its warplanes in Manchuria.

His assertion that the Chinese people would not tolerate invasion of their neighbors mentioned no country.

The statement, however, was the strongest made by an Chinese Communist official since the outbreak of the fighting in Korea.

"It is obvious," Chou continued, "that the Chinese people, after liberating the whole territory of their own country, want to rehabilitate it in peace."

Then Chou added:

"But if the American aggressors take this as a sign of weakness, they will commit the same fatal blunder as the Kuomintang reactionaries (Chinese Nationalists).

"The Chinese people absolutely will not tolerate foreign aggression nor will they supinely tolerate seeing their neighbors being savagely invaded by imperialists."

In today's English language broadcast of the anniversary statement, Chou again accused the U.S. of being mainly responsible for barring Communist China from the U.N. He said:

"Whoever attempts to exclude the nearly 500,000,000 Chinese people from the United Nations and whoever sets at naught and violates the interests of this one-quarter of all mankind and fancies vainly to solve any Eastern problem directly concerned with China arbitrarily, will certainly break his skull."

Chou described Gen. MacArthur as a central figure in the alleged plan to dominate the Far East. He said:

"MacArthur, commander-in-chief of American aggression, has long ago disclosed the aggressive designs of the United States government and is continuing to invent new excuses for extending its aggression."

Oct. 1, 1950

The Chinese Intervene

In the first stage of the Korean War, the North Korean invaders had driven the South Koreans and a few United States troops from the 38th parallel back to the Naktong River, a perimeter on the southeastern corner of the peninsula. But Gen. Douglas MacArthur's forces held on, and in September the general

opened a second stage in the war with a brilliant landing at Inchon, which cut the North Korean supply lines and set their soldiers to flight.

United Nations forces under MacArthur's command (mostly Americans and South Koreans, with troops from 15 other U.N. member nations) then drove the North Koreans back over the 38th parallel and almost all the way to the Korean-Chinese border. The North Korean army was virtually destroyed; almost half its men were prisoners. The end of the war seemed in sight.

But in the meantime, the Communists—who had seized power in China only a year earlier—viewed the northward movement of U.S. troops with alarm. Across the Yalu River from North Korea, battle-tested Chinese divisions were massing in Manchuria.

By the time of MacArthur's meeting with President Truman at Wake Island in October 1950, the Chinese had massed 800,000 troops in Manchuria, and 100,000 had slipped south of the Yalu into North Korea. But MacArthur did not appreciate the severity of the Chinese threat, and he underestimated the North Koreans' continued willingness to fight. Instead, he announced his plans for a campaign that would end the war by Christmas. On the western side of the peninsula, the U.S. 8th Army would push north from the North Korean capital of Pyongyang; to the east, another force would push north. The two would be separated, however, by a central mountain range protected by less effective South Korean troops. As the troops moved further north, their supply lines would grow longer and more exposed.

MacArthur made little effort to cover up his plans; he apparently did not believe they could fail. He was so confident of victory by Christmas that he did not even issue his troops winter uniforms.

The invasion of North Korea by hundreds of thousands of Communist troops swept the U.N. forces south, transformed the complexion of the war, and shocked an American public that had grown used to victory.

RED CHINESE ENTER WAR

By Tom Lambert

KUJANG, KOREA, OCT. 28 (AP)—A captured Chinese soldier said last night an attack unit of the Chinese Communist army crossed into North Korea 13 days ago with orders to battle the South Korean army.

The prisoner said that before crossing the Yalu River boundary between Manchuria and North Korea, his unit commander told his men:

"We are going to Korea and must fight against the South Korean army to guard our land and our nation."

And, after crossing the river, the 34-year-old prisoner, Li Tsu, said the same commander told his men:

"We are here under orders of a higher headquarters. So we must fight the South Koreans because if we are captured, we will be killed, and if we lose, we cannot return home."

In an interview in a South Korea intelligence office, Li, a private, said his unit crossed the Yalu River from Manchuria on Oct. 14.

He said he crossed by boat from Antung to Sinuiju and marched directly to the Onjong area. He was captured Oct. 25 by the Republic of Korea (ROK) Sixth Division.

Li said that the unit commander did not at any time mention U.S. or United Nations forces fighting in Korea.

Li apparently was unaware that they were here. A thin, frightened little man, he obviously is not a first line soldier.

This adds further to the mystery of reports of Chinese forces in North Korea.

Red China has plenty of battle-hardened troops. If she is sending soldiers here, why men like Li—and without air power or apparently without artillery?

Oct. 28, 1950

U.S. EXPECTS NO LARGER WAR

By C. Yates McDaniel

WASHINGTON, OCT. 31 (AP)—American officials, professing no surprise at the appearance of Chinese Communist troops in the Korean War, still do not expect any open, large-scale intervention against United Nations forces.

Pentagon officers cited to a reporter today two possible major reasons for the belated appearance of Chinese soldiers in Korea:

1. Red China's determination to protect the huge Suiho-Supung power dam on the Yalu River

Marines Pfc. Ralph Clifford (left), 21, of Pittsburgh, Pa., and Pfc. Dominic M. Bulgarella, 20, of Grand Rapids, Mich., hold their rifles at the ready as they hunt for North Korean stragglers and snipers in a war-torn building in South Korea.

which supplies electricity for Manchurian points as distant as Harbin and the Russian naval base at Port Arthur.

2. An apparently determined policy to keep Korea from working out its own non-Communist salvation by delaying United Nations efforts to pacify, unify and rebuild the war ravaged country.

Most of the Yalu power installations, toward which American troops are driving, are on the Chinese side of the river. But several of the big dams are anchored on the Korean side.

The U.S. Tenth Corps yesterday reported that

Chinese Communists were counterattacking near the Chosin Reservoir in north central Korea. Hydroelectric plants at this reservoir supplied power for the large scale industry on the east coast of Korea. American bombers destroyed most of this industry many weeks ago, but they left the dams alone.

The way in which Chinese Reds are appearing in Korea as individuals or in comparatively small groups suggests the pattern they followed in China until they had the Nationalists on the run.

Some American officials consider that the Chi-

nese Reds expect to reap propaganda dividends from their last-minute appearance in the Korean War. A Chinese propaganda machine could easily twist any clashes between their small units and American troops into charges that Western imperialists are assaulting the native defenders of Asia.
Oct. 31, 1950

KOREAN COLD

By Don Whitehead

WITH U.S. TROOPS IN NORTH KOREA, NOV. 15 (AP)—The winter winds are sweeping down from the Siberian plains, and this Army is fighting a battle to stay warm.

The winds slice down the valleys with a razor edge of icy chill.

They whip through open jeeps, moan across the foxholes in the mountains, and open the cracks and flaps of thin-walled tents. This country is in the hard grip of winter. There is a cold, desolate look to the land—a harsh and unfriendly look.

The earth has lost its softness and is frozen hard. The mountains have lost their tinted colors. They have the flat dullness that comes with wintry blasts from the north.

The men who suffer most, of course, are the infantry. Some of them are not yet equipped with all their winter clothing.

The winter gear is being rushed to them, some by special airlift. But men who live in holes in the ground can get little comfort, no matter how hard they try or what clothing they have.

It is just as cold and uncomfortable on the enemy side of the lines. But the Chinese and North Koreans know how to take care of themselves in such weather. They have lived with it from childhood. But most of the Americans are experiencing their first shock of winter warfare.

Some units are sheltered in Korean houses. They are the lucky ones because Korean houses have a 4,000-year-old method of central heating. It is primitive, but efficient.

The heat and smoke from the kitchen fires run through flues built underneath the floors and in the walls of the huts. Even in the coldest weather these floors are warm.

But very few Americans have this comfort. Most of the forward troops and headquarters units must live under canvas or in open holes. And these, at best, do little more than break the force of the wind.

With a long, costly supply line, fuel always is a critical item. And oil and gasoline for heating tents are strictly rationed.

Our press headquarters, for example, is a big drafty tent with two oil stoves. They do little more than take the chill off the air. The only time the tent feels warm is when one steps into it from the outside cold. After a few minutes this illusion of warmth wears off.

The veterans of World War II who fought through winter campaigns in Africa, Italy and Germany can appreciate what this army is enduring. But the winters in those campaigns were not as severe as the winter closing in over North Korea.

With relentless certainty the temperature is dropping toward the zero mark. And within a few weeks it will be falling well below zero, with an icy sheath laid over all the land.

And this army is not trained for fighting in such weather. It isn't the soldier's fault and it isn't the Army's fault. The fault lies within the military unpreparedness of the United States.

The big hope is that some reasonable and acceptable settlement of the North Korean question can be found. Because if that is not done, then this army will fight one of the bitterest winter campaigns ever fought by any American army.
Nov. 15, 1950

By Stan Swinton

WITH THE U.S. MARINES AT CHANGJIN RESERVOIR, NOV. 15 (AP)—A Marine patrol today gazed out over Changjin Reservoir—a sapphire blue lake in a setting of milk-white ice—their goal in two weeks of bitter fighting.

First they fought the Chinese Communists. After the Chinese faded away, they fought sub-zero weather.

"It's a beautiful sight. We worked hard enough to see it," said Col. Homer L. Litzenberg, Seventh Regiment commander. Litzenberg personally led six Marines of the Seventh Division and three correspondents to the lake side this afternoon, up the long twisting road through the river gorge. It was a road littered with the debris of burned,

Troopers, on a mop-up action, move through burning shacks.

Soviet-made tanks, a road skirting mountain precipices, scarred with shell marks. But the reservoir, heart of North Korea's greatest hydroelectric complex, was like a page torn from a tourist folder.

Below, on its east side, glistened the tan board shacks of a hamlet. Marine patrols have been in there, but found it empty. Only at night do a handful of half-frozen Chinese Red stragglers sneak into the village, scavenging for food and hunting warmth.

There is no sign of the enemy anywhere around the south end of the reservoir.

But so far as is known the 3,000-man enemy garrison has pulled far to the north and west.

The Marines captured a lone Chinese Red soldier yesterday from a division not previously known to be on the front lines. Intelligence officers regarded its presence as a new ominous sign of growing resistance ahead.

Back in Hagaru Town, three-fourths of a mile to the southwest, campfires make a crazy quilt of rose in the dusk.

"I decided it was more important to keep the men warm than to maintain a blackout," Litzenberg said. "The enemy knows our positions pretty well anyway."

Although the Reds gave up the reservoir without a fight, it was surrounded by great log-covered dugouts and lines of trenches, where a last-ditch stand could easily have been made. The main enemy now is the cold. But even with the chill misery that goes with life here, the men of the Seventh are jubilant as they look over the reservoir.

Pfc. Robert D. Kozkowski of St. Paul, Minn., commented:

"We sure should have brought our ice skates along."

Nov. 15, 1950

TRUMAN ASSURES CHINESE

By John M. Hightower

WASHINGTON, NOV. 16 (AP)—President Truman solemnly assured Communist China today that the United States has no intention of invading Manchuria.

His declaration, at a news conference, was the latest in an urgent series of moves by top American officials to remove any real fear the Chinese Reds might have about American intentions. The aim is to persuade them to pull their troops out of North Korea and thus remove the danger that the conflict may expand into World War III.

The president said the Chinese have cited fear of American invasion as a "pretext" for "taking offensive action against United Nations forces in Korea. Nevertheless he held out the possibility that they might really believe what they say. They might have been deceived, he said, "by those whose advantage it is to prolong and extend hostilities in the Far East"—an evident reference to the Soviet Union.

The seriousness with which the American government views Chinese Communist operations "from the safety of a privileged sanctuary" north of the Korean border was also emphasized by the fact that the president devoted a section of his statement to this subject. There has been some speculation that if the Chinese persisted in their present course the United Nations forces would have to decide whether they would bomb Communist supply centers north of the Korean-Manchurian border, which is the present limit of U.N. operations.

Nov. 16, 1950

BULLETIN

By William Jorden

WITH GENERAL MacARTHUR ON THE NORTHWEST FRONT, KOREA, NOV. 24 (AP)—

Gen. MacArthur said today, "I hope to keep my promise to the GIs to have them home by Christmas."

Visiting Maj. Gen. John Coulter, commanding the Ninth Corps, MacArthur added that he wanted to "finish this off as quickly as possible."

Nov. 24, 1950

CHINESE REDS ATTACK

By Tom Lambert

WITH U.S. SECOND DIVISION, KOREA, NOV. 26 (AP)—Chinese Reds halted abruptly today the U.S. Eighth Army's three-day-old "end-the-war" offensive in northwestern Korea.

The Red attack began last midnight and was continuing late this afternoon at renewed pace. Some Reds waded the partly frozen Chongchon River and attacked on signals from bugles and whistles.

They surrounded and cut up units of the Second Division and forced others to withdraw.

The Reds struck with coordination and power along more than 25 miles of the front where 110,000 United Nations troops opened an offensive Friday aimed at ending the war in short order. Forward elements of an estimated 100,000 Chinese and Korean Reds in northwest Korea struck back at the end and center of the U.N. line. More Red troops were reported east moving up for a possible showdown battle.

Other Reds drove between the 25th and U.S. Second Divisions and reached the Chongchon River.

Another enemy force hit Second Division forces near Sinhung, five miles northeast of Kujang. One American company was overrun and a second surrounded.

Air observers reported a concentration of enemy tanks in the Namsi area in extreme northwest Korea on the main road to the border town of Sinuiju. That road leads up from American-held Chongju where enemy opposition has been negligible. A Red force of about 3,000 was reported between Chongju and Namsi.

It was a different story in northeast Korea where U.N. forces were slowed only by sub-zero temperatures and snowy mountain terrain.

The Tenth Corps said Sunday the 32nd Regiment of the U.S. Seventh Division has gained six

The 'Off Limits' sign posted at a U.S. Ninth Corps headquarters in Korea obviously didn't apply to Gen. Douglas MacArthur during his visit to the battle area, Nov. 24, 1950.

miles and is almost at the border near Hyesanjin. That border city was reached last week by the division's 17th Regiment, which since has extended its hold for 10 miles along the Yalu River across from Manchuria.

But the estimated 100,000 Chinese and Korean Reds in the northwest showed fight against a U.N. offensive which Gen. MacArthur himself said was intended to get the Americans home by Christmas. *Nov. 26, 1950*

By William J. Waugh
ON THE CHONGCHON RIVER LINE, KOREA, NOV. 26 (AP)—Indirect censorship has settled like a fog over this heretofore freely reported war.

It is hard to say who ordered it, but any public information officer—the connecting link between the free press and the Army—will shrug and explain that the generals want tighter security.

The Army insists there is no censorship. There isn't so far as editing dispatches is concerned. The Army can and apparently is accomplishing the same result by withholding information at the operational command level.

The heat was greatest about two days ago. At one corps headquarters, correspondents reported that for one day the press telephone was disconnected and then for a short time their calls were monitored.

One PIO who asked that his name be withheld said:

"You can expect to find it that way all along the line, from regimental commander on up the line to Corps. They have been told to screen the news." *Nov. 26, 1950*

U.S. EIGHTH ARMY HEADQUARTERS, KOREA, MONDAY, NOV. 27 (AP) — A battalion of the U.S. 25th Division was still cut off today on the northwest Korean front after an attempt to air drop ammunition and supplies was thwarted.

The isolated battalion was five miles northeast of Kujang, in the area where Communist forces Sunday launched a counterattack.

Plans to drop ammunition and supplies from planes were canceled because the drop zone was occupied by Communists.
Nov. 27, 1950

Editor's Note

Relman Morin and Don Whitehead received the Pulitzer Prize for international reporting in 1951 for their coverage of the Korean War.

By Don Whitehead

WITH U.S. 25TH DIVISION, KOREA, NOV. 27 (AP)—The big United Nations offensive to bring an early end to the Korean War was threatened with complete collapse today.

This was the stark reality of the situation after 48 hours of savage fighting. Chinese and Korean Reds have dealt a stunning blow to U.N. forces.

The offensive that rolled forward for two days has been stopped cold. U.N. troops are on the defensive after giving up most of their gains.

The reversal in battle fortunes came with startling suddenness, and the Eighth Army is battling to hold the southward surge of Red troops. There is no chance of offensive action on this front until the Red attack has been halted and a firm new line established.

American artillerymen and infantrymen have piled up hundreds of Chinese and North Korean dead but still the enemy is attacking with large reserves of manpower.

Prisoners of war have identified the 66th and 39th Chinese Communist armies in this area. It is believed the Reds still are bringing reinforcements across the Manchurian border. One prisoner said his unit left Antung, just across the border, three days ago. He was captured in his first fight. Gen. MacArthur came to North Korea Friday morning to launch the big offensive. He expressed the hope his troops would reach the Yalu River quickly and that the Yanks could be home by Christmas.

But the Reds struck back Saturday night. They hit units of the U.S. 25th and Second Infantry Divisions and also units of the South Korean First and Seventh Divisions.

The Reds surged in again Sunday night, lashing the U.N. forces with mortar, machine-gun and small arms fire. They infiltrated behind the lines and shot up convoys, command posts and artillery positions.

This attack forced Americans and South Koreans to fall back all along the line to new positions. Some units were cut off and were fighting their way out of enemy pockets. It is not clear yet whether the Reds have started an offensive of their own.
Nov. 27, 1950

By Relman Morin

TOKYO, TUESDAY, NOV. 28 (AP)—Gen. MacArthur's words "Home by Christmas" spoken last Friday in Korea have been drowned out by the roar of a tidal-wave Chinese counteroffensive. Unless the Chinese break as suddenly as they struck—a wholly unlikely possibility—the general's statement cannot be fulfilled.

On the contrary, the Chinese appear prepared to commit more and more divisions from the inexhaustible reservoir of a subcontinent.

The short war seems likely to last indefinitely.

For the record, these were the circumstances of MacArthur's statement:

He flew to northwest Korea last Friday morning to supervise the kickoff of a grand offensive. His special communique, issued at 10 o'clock that morning, said "if successful" the drive should "for all practical purposes end the war."

He went by jeep from Sinanju airfield to First Corps Headquarters. From there he drove across country to Ninth Corps.

MacArthur and Lt. Gen. Walton H. Walker, commander of the Eighth Army, went into a wooden building where Maj. Gen. John B. Coulter, commander of the Corps, was waiting.

A huge war map blazing with blue and red squares, circles and arrows and other symbols covered the whole wall of the room. The blue represented Ninth Corps units and positions. The Red denoted the Communists.

MacArthur said to Coulter: "Just tell me what you are doing now."

Coulter quickly sketched deployment of his

troops and their movements. MacArthur obviously had a complete knowledge of the smallest details. He asked some questions about minor terrain features, like a platoon leader who had seen them personally. Walker then interjected: "I notice you haven't mentioned any objectives, Jack. I don't like the word objectives. I think we should just keep pushing as hard as we can go."

Coulter answered: "That's what we are going to do. We are not thinking in terms of objectives."

MacArthur smiled and said:

"That's right. Jack, you tell the boys that when they get to the Yalu they are going home. I want to make good on my statement that they are going to eat Christmas dinner at home."

Several days earlier, MacArthur was reported to have told the members of the United Nations Commission on Korea that he expected the war to be over by Christmas.

This could not be confirmed in Tokyo. But it may have been the "my statement" to which he referred in his remark to Gen. Coulter.

The offensive moved out. It was on or ahead of schedule for about 60 hours. Sunday night the Chinese hit back. By Monday field dispatches reported the drive was stalled.

Nov. 28, 1950

WASHINGTON, NOV. 30 (AP)—Possible use of the atomic bomb by the United States in the Korean fighting kept the world nervous tonight.

President Truman declared today this country will fight on in Korea, with every means at its disposal—including the atom bomb if necessary—to keep Red aggression from spreading to American shores.

With United Nations troops battling against strong forces of Chinese Communist troops, Mr. Truman's words provoked an uneasy stir. However, the odds were against use of the atomic bomb in Korea unless the situation there becomes much more desperate.

Some members of the United States Congress meantime expressed belief that use of the atomic bomb would touch off World War III, or would prompt Russia to retaliate with an atomic attack against this country. Communist China and Russia have a treaty of friendship.

There seemed little prospect of European support for any drastic American steps against Communist China, such as using the atom bomb.

Public reaction in the United States to President Truman's words brought a rush in messages to the White House. No immediate check was available on the percentage of those against use of the atomic bomb.

One leading churchman, Dr. O. Frederick Nolde of Philadelphia, liaison officer for the World Council of Churches to the United Nations, said the atom bomb should not be employed until "all other means have been explored and found impossible."

Mr. Truman made his comments about the bomb with the exasperated air of a man near the limit of his patience.

This country, he said, has made every possible effort to head off a third world war.

But he declared in a formal statement that "we are fighting in Korea for our own national security and survival," and he told a tense, crowded news conference we will use every weapon that is needed.

"That includes the atom bomb," the president said crisply in answer to a newsman's question.

And thus he touched off a flurry of confusion that didn't end until the White House, three hours later, issued a statement saying the use of the bomb has not been authorized so far and that the president's comments "do not represent any change in this situation."

Mr. Truman said, and repeated, in answer to questions hurled by some of the 208 reporters present, that the use of the A-bomb in Korea always has been under active consideration. In a voice charged with emotion, he said he doesn't want to see it used. It's a terrible weapon, he said—one that doesn't spare innocent men, women and children.

Asked if the use of the bomb would depend on United Nations permission, the president said no, he didn't mean that at all. He said the military commander in the field—Gen. Douglas MacArthur—will have charge of using all weapons, as he always has.

This remark, which seemed at first to mean that MacArthur would have the say on whether to use the bomb, led British officials in London to express shock and astonishment. MacArthur's political judgment has been questioned in some British quarters in recent days.

The White House statement made it clear, however, that MacArthur has not been empowered to use the A-bomb.

Nov. 30, 1950

By Don Whitehead

WITH U.S. EIGHTH ARMY, KOREA, NOV. 30 (AP)—Collapse of the United Nations offensive has drawn sharp criticism here of the divided command in Gen. MacArthur's military forces in Korea.

Many military men are questioning the setup in which the U.S. Tenth Corps is operating in northeast Korea entirely independently of the Eighth Army on the northwest Front.

The Tenth Corps, commanded by Maj. Gen. Edward M. Almond, frequently is referred to in this theater as a "special police force."

In effect, MacArthur has two forces fighting in Korea—one labelled as an army and the other as a corps. The coordination of these forces is not handled in the field but from GHQ in Tokyo.

This sharp separation of command responsibilities in the field has been one of the puzzles of the Korean War. No one yet has given an official explanation of why Tenth Corps is divorced from Eighth Army.

Associated Press correspondent Stan Swinton, who has covered Tenth Corps since Almond's men went ashore in the northeast, pointed out today there was a physical reason for the separation of commands. He said the north-central Korean mountain mass splits North Korea in half so Eighth Army and Tenth Corps could not operate as a single unit.

Lt. Gen. Walton H. Walker commands the Eighth Army. But actually he is responsible for only half the fighting front despite his three stars. The other half of the responsibility rests on the two-star command of Almond.

Right now, Eighth Army is fighting for its life against hordes of well trained Chinese Red troops. But Walker has no power to shift any positions from the east to bolster his western front. He cannot order Tenth Corps troops to bolster his

battered line. This would have to be a GHQ decision.

This situation developed when MacArthur organized the Tenth Corps for the amphibious landing at Inchon on Sept. 15. He gave the corps command to Almond, who had been his chief of staff in Tokyo.

At that time, there seemed nothing unusual in having the Tenth Corps operate as an independent force. The Eighth Army was fighting on the southern front and had no communications lines with the Tenth Corps except by way of Tokyo. These operations obviously could best be coordinated from GHQ.

But many military people thought that when the Eighth Army and the Tenth Corps linked up at Seoul on a one-front war, the Tenth Corps could become a part of the Eighth Army.

This would have given Walker direct command of all field forces in Korea. The entire responsibility of field operations would have rested in his hands.

But Gen. MacArthur did not merge the two. As soon as Seoul was captured, he pulled the First Marine and Seventh Infantry Divisions out of the line. These divisions were loaded aboard ships at Pusan and Inchon. The ports were tied up for 10 days by the loading, and then the divisions were at sea another two weeks.

These two powerful divisions were taken out of action at a time when the enemy was on the run northward. The pursuit halted while the two divisions pulled back to be loaded.

There are some who say the Eighth Army did not have sufficient supplies to keep driving north after the fall of Seoul on Sept. 27. But others argued that supplies would have been available if the ports and the shipping had not been tied up with loading these divisions.

A large fleet of ships was diverted from supply lines to carry the troops to northeast Korea. Since then the Tenth Corps has been reinforced by the Third Infantry Division and South Korean divisions.

For days there was a gap in the U.N. lines in the area dividing the Eighth Army and the Tenth Corps. For a time this invisible dividing line was almost wide open. Neither the Eighth Army nor the Tenth Corps had any sizable force in this area.

Finally this breach was closed, but the enemy obviously knew it was a weak spot—for that was where the Reds heavily hit the South Korean Second Corps early this week and collapsed the defenses.
Nov. 30, 1950

By Hal Boyle
IN A 5TH AIR FORCE PLANE OVER KUNU, NORTHWEST KOREA, NOV. 30 (AP)—The last American troops protecting the retreat of the U.S. Eighth Army across a key ferry point on the Chongchon River withdrew safely today through a flaming Kunu village.

A dozen fires sprouted in Kunu shortly before noon as fighter planes dived and strafed Chinese Red troops moving in to take it.

After pulling out of Kunu, American vehicles moved in a packed column westward along the river bank to Anju. There they could join other allied column retreating south.

A group of tanks was stationed behind the vehicles at a roadblock two miles out of Kunu to smash any Red pursuit attempts.

There was none.

The Chongchon River now is the dividing line that separates the bulk of the advancing Chinese Reds from the bulk of the retreating Eighth Army.

It is a winding, shallow stream about halfway between the former North Korean capital of Pyongyang and the Manchurian border. It isn't much of a military barrier.

The land beyond the Chongchon looked dead and brown and bare, except for huddled groups of refugees, some wading the ice-patched waters.

Every main road in a 1,600-square-mile stretch between Pyongyang and the Chongchon River was alive with U.N. troops moving south.

Thousands trudged slowly and painfully in long columns down the twisting yellow roads. Thousands more rode in trucks and jeeps in this forced migration. Our plane dropped to 500 feet to observe them, but the tanks and bounding artillery pieces stirred up such clouds of dust we had to rise higher to keep from running into the mountainsides they obscured.

At Sinanju air strip, pilots and ground crews were evacuating the most advanced air base in southwest Korea. It lies just south of the Chongchon River. Six planes were still left on the field. Airmen were burning equipment they couldn't fly away.

As we swept down again, crossing the river, a sharp explosion beneath us shot our observation plane up sharply.

"We just blew up the main highway bridge," said the pilot, Maj. Edward Ingram, of Fieldon, Ill.

Looking down we could see the brown debris settle in the slate gray river. The engineers had done a neat, clean job. The bridge would be of no use to the Chinese for some time.

We flew on to Anju, which in the last few days played the same role as a ferrying point on the American west flank as Kunu did on the east flank.

Our plane turned south. We flew over Sunchon, which is on one of the main supply routes from Pyongyang to the front.

Two retreating columns were snarled where the roads converged. And that was a measure of how the situation has changed in the last few weeks. The first time I flew over Sunchon, Gen. MacArthur was circling overhead watching his parachute troops land and seize the town.

Moving north against the tide of Eighth Army troops and mobile weapons retreating methodically toward the Pyongyang area was a long column of slow moving vehicles. They got the right of way on their trip back toward the old front.

They were ambulances—going up to salvage the broken human debris of a lost battleground.
Nov 30, 1950

Editor's Note

Associated Press writer Charles Moore was among the war correspondents at Hagaru. He interviewed survivors from their hospital cots, and filed this report.

NORTHEAST FRONT, KOREA, DEC. 2 (AP)—Survivors of a Communist ambush said today that fanatical Chinese burned wounded American prisoners alive and danced around the flames, "like wild Indians," while the GIs screamed in pain.

Other men of the U.S. 7th Infantry Division said the Chinese threw some wounded soldiers onto a highway and ran over them with halftracks, bayonetted others in the face and machine-gunned their flag of truce when they tried to surrender.

The 7th Division men made a bloody retreat down the east side of the Chosin Reservoir in northern Korea to Hagaru at the southern tip. From there, U.S. Marine and Air Force pilots in probably the greatest mercy flight in history flew 1,000 casualties to rear area hospitals.

One of the three survivors with whom I talked was Pfc. Benjamin Butler, 19. He said his group of trucks was attacked around midnight, after it ran into a roadblock in the snow-covered hills.

"When some of our guys tried to surrender, the Chinese bayonetted them in the face," he said. "Others waved a flag trying to surrender, and the Chinese opened up on them with submachine guns.

"After my ammunition was gone, I played dead in the truck. If a man was shot in the leg, they would shoot him again and again and kill him. They took most of the men's clothes and guns.

"They threw about 10 or more into a truck, some naked, some still alive, threw blankets and gasoline over them and set them afire. This bunch took off and we dragged some of them out of the fire."

Butler said while he was playing dead in a truck, a Chinese climbed in and stomped on his face, which showed bruises.

The other survivors with whom I talked were Pfc. Dayle Logan, 19, of Smithers, W.Va., and Pfc. Jackie Brooks, 18, of Richmond, Va., both of the 31st Regiment. The soldiers, interviewed separately, said the Chinese also bayonetted their own wounded.

Brooks said he was riding as guard on a truck loaded with litter patients.

"We had fought through three roadblocks," he said. "Some trucks made it and some didn't. Just after midnight, the trucks ahead of us were shot up and blocked the road. The Chinks started down off the hills blowing trumpets and whistles.

"Most of them had Thompson submachine guns. A few had .30 caliber carbines with bayo-

nets. The guy in the next truck had a .50-caliber machine gun and I had an M-1 rifle. They killed the machine gunner with a grenade. I got down in the truck body and fired at them. I stayed there till almost dawn.

"They poured gasoline over the truckloads of wounded men and set them afire. I actually saw them do it to four trucks. There must have been about 40 men in each one. Some of them had already been killed by bullets.

"I could hear the men on the trucks screaming 'Help me.' I couldn't do anything. I was out of ammunition by then and there were Chinese between me and the nearest truck.

"They would pour gas on a truck and set it afire and run around it yelling like a bunch of wild Indians. I could see their faces in the light from the flames, and they were all grinning and laughing.

"They turned over one truckload of wounded men and ran over several of them with halftracks."
Dec. 2, 1950

By Jack MacBeth

WITH U.S. MARINES, KOREA, DEC. 9 (AP)— American Marines walked out of 13 days of freezing hell today, full of fight after a gory nightmare of death in Korea's icy mountains.

The U.S. 1st Marine Division was rolling slowly into the northeastern Korea plains of Hamhung. The men's eyes and bearded faces, their tattered parkas and the strangely careless way they carried their rifles, showed the strain. These thousands of leathernecks did it on guts. They turned their encirclement into one of the fightingest retreats in military history. It was the longest pullback in Marine records—50 tortuous miles.

They broke out of a death trap sprung by many thousands of Red Chinese and Koreans that converted what looked like certain disaster into a moral triumph, if not a military victory.

I watched the retreat.

The story began in the flea-bitten village of Yudam, on the western edge of the Chosin Reservoir.

Three Red Chinese divisions and one Chinese regiment attacked two Marine regiments in a surprise offensive the night of Nov. 28.

The pressure was overwhelming. The Marines

A vanguard of fighting Marines makes up this convoy of trucks and other equipment rolling along plains, 20 miles north of Hamhung. In the background are the mountains the Marines fought through for 12 days after starting their retreat from the Changjin Reservoir area.

struck right back. When orders were given to pull back, the leathernecks responded—with an offensive.

I was in Koto when they came in. It was a gruesome sight—wounded men with their blood frozen to their skins; their clothes stiff with ice; grotesque dead men lying across trailers and stretchers; live men stumbling along, grimacing from frostbite, using their rifles as crutches.

The dead count is high. Two days ago, I watched nearly 200 bodies nosed into a single grave by a bulldozer. There was no time for more elaborate arrangements.

The leathernecks inflicted casualties on the enemy many times those suffered. The weather also took a heavy toll on the Chinese.

Tension greeted the order for all the Marines to break from Koto.

One senior officer wept.

A grizzled Marine blurted, "These kids are too good to have this happen to them."

Saturday at sunrise, patrols struck out from Koto. Intelligence reports had said the enemy was in this area in strength. There were fears another bloodbath was in store similar to that on the Hagaru-Koto road earlier.

But the patrols reached their objectives on schedule. One suffered moderate casualties, the other made it almost without incident. Immediately after these groups had left, the vehicular columns began to move. Equipment considered more of a burden than its actual value was destroyed.

By noon, the column was stretched about two miles south of Koto.

Dismal little Koto lies on a plateau 3,500 feet above sea level. For two miles south, the narrow road, if anything, goes up. Then it twists down a narrow gorge 12 miles to the valley below. It was covered with ice. The temperature was 25 degrees below zero.

For four hours, the column stood motionless. A bridge had been blown by the Reds.

Before the engineers could work on it, a company of Marines had to drive off a pocket of Chinese guarding it. This was done.

Then the column started to roll, but road conditions made progress slow. By nightfall Saturday, some 100 vehicles had moved across the new bridge.

Throughout the night, there was sniping from the hills overlooking the winding road.

Four Marines on the truck I was riding huddled in blankets. All chewed gum and spoke occasionally in soft tones. They knew they dared not sleep. A machine gun was mounted on the back of the truck, but was not needed.

These kids mainly had two thoughts uppermost in their minds: their families and their determination to whip the enemy.

"I'm still carrying a small hunk of steel in my ankle," said one. "When I get home, that will make me think of this damned place."

Just before daylight, the mountain grade became less severe and the turns less harrowing. We were nearing the bottom.

For some reason, I thought at this point of the dramatic 1st Cavalry Division sweep which I had accompanied across country toward Seoul in victory-flush September. The contrasts of this now-successful retreat quickly dispelled such pleasant reminiscences.

Dec. 9, 1950

By Tom Lambert

PYONGYANG, KOREA, DEC. 4 (AP)—They were trudging south across the Taedong River this morning—North Koreans to whom escape anywhere was better than life under the Communist-indoctrinated men who seem certain to rule this city again.

They came from the northeast part of the city, down the poor and silent roads and alleys to the north bank of the river. There they halted briefly in the shadow of the Communist-erected "liberation" monument, a great white shaft dedicated to communism's "liberation" on these people from the Japanese.

They looked briefly for boats, and a few managed to find places in the frail craft being poled across the river. But there was not room in the boats for the thousands of them. So they started to wade.

The river's edges are crusted with ice, and the people crunched gingerly across that, then stepped into the cold, swift water.

They were all sizes and ages. But all were bound by the desire to leave this Red-threatened city and make their way south.

So they walked into the water, silent and shivering. The children broke the silence first, with wails of pain and misery.

The people walked on in a long and steady file. Water rushed against their legs and the underbellies of the bullocks some were leading. A harsh wind whipped at them every step of the way.

We stood on the south bank, warm in our clothing, and watched them cross. We were reminded of the biblical picture of Moses leading his people through the Red Sea. But these people had no leader. Then they came up on the south bank, the water slushy, with ice lapping at their ankles.

Some sat down at once to dry their feet, purple with cold. And in the great confusion at the river's edge some became separated from their families or their friends.

Then the shouting began, mournful and half lost in the bitter wind.

But some did not stop then to dry their feet or put on their socks and shoes. They walked painfully across the sand and over the shallow, crumbling ponds of ice in the backwashes of the river.

They passed us, and our misery for them was added to their own.

There was no accusation on their faces, and this was the greatest pain of all for me. I had the feeling

An infantryman dashes for cover as members of a unit of the 3rd Infantry Division are pinned down by enemy small-arms fire.

that their misery was our fault, because we had not been able to halt the force which drove them across the river.

One man came up to me and took my arm in his mittened hand. "I am sorry," he said, and I could not answer him.

The barefooted people walked on to a dike and stopped there in the cold sunshine and the bitter wind to dry their feet. The faces of children were pinched with the cold.

The men and the women took socks or cloths from their pockets and whipped the water off the children's legs, then their own. Then they put on the socks and stood up. The men hoisted the packs on their backs, and some of the women put great bundles on their heads.

Then they walked on the top of the dike,

sharply etched for a moment against the sky, in which towered columns of smoke from demolitions.

They walked down to the road, and many of them hesitated there, debating which way they should go.

Then they started away, heavy laden and silent and resigned. The bitter wind went with them.
Dec. 4, 1950

RETREAT FROM PYONGYANG
By Don Huth

WITH U.N. FORCES RETREATING IN KOREA, DEC. 5 (AP)—I rode 165 miles with an American army in retreat—from Pyongyang to Seoul, the uneasy present capital of South Korea.

This was the greatest retreat of any American army in modern history.

I hope I never see it again.

For 18 hours I rode through biting winds, snow and dust with convoys of trucks, jeeps and other vehicles. All were headed south to Seoul or other points below the 38th parallel from Pyongyang, the captured capital of Red Korea, which U.N. forces abandoned Tuesday.

There are no favorites in a retreating army. Officers in jeeps and GIs in trucks jockeyed for positions in the endless train of convoys rolling southward. Everyone seemed intent upon getting there first—without knowing exactly where they were going.

I pulled our jeep into the first convoy a few miles outside Pyongyang. Before long, I was dodging in and out among the trucks, trying to speed along the icy road. Our jeep had poor brakes, and at times we barely slid into an open space before a truck came thundering northward.

The dust, billowing up from the wheels, cut under my eyelids until I thought my eyeballs would pop out. The more I tried to see, the less I could see.

Associated Press correspondent Bill Waugh, riding beside me, had to stand up for an hour with the wind beating in his face and tell me when I was coming too close to the vehicle ahead. Waugh's face looked like a mask when he finally sat down. The light gray dust gave him a deathly pallor, and his eyes were narrow slits.

While I watched the ditch on the left, Waugh would call out, like an old Mississippi steamboat captain, "You have about four inches on this side. You're getting too close. You're clear—barrel ahead."

Throughout the drive Waugh kept feeding us cigarettes. Few words were spoken. He seemed to know instinctively when I wanted a cigarette. Automatically he'd reach in his pocket, put two cigarettes between his chapped lips and light them. As time went on, my hands got so numb he had to set the cigarette between my lips.

The dust was still biting when the snow came, first a few flakes flicking against the windshield and then a steady fall. "I can't see through the glass," I told Waugh. He switched on the wind-shield wiper in the gathering dusk. We still couldn't see.

A few miles ahead of the convoy we ground to a halt. The MPs said traffic was jammed at a pontoon bridge ahead. Traffic already was fouled up on both sides of the road, and we could not pass. GIs were building fires along the roadway. I got out of the jeep to stretch my legs.

The feeling had gone from my feet during the long drive. The big toe of my right foot, frostbitten during a recent trip to the Yalu River on the northeast front, throbbed, and I kicked my feet against a jeep tire to restore circulation. Then I ran up and down the road for a short distance to drive off the chill.

An ambulance driver who saw me asked, "Would you like to come inside and get warm?" I mumbled gratefully and got inside. He started the motor and turned on the heat. I couldn't stop shivering. Waugh, reconnoitering along the road, had met a colonel with a bottle of whiskey. He brought me the bottle, and I took a drink. I stopped shivering.

The whiskey, the warmth of the ambulance and the weariness of 12 hours' driving crept through me. I suddenly began to burn from head to toe. I struggled out of the ambulance. Waugh found me sweating in the jeep, with both of my coats off.

The next thing I remember was waking up on the top tier in the ambulance. Below me a soldier snored rhythmically. I ached from head to foot, and my head was throbbing. Until Waugh poked his head through the door, I didn't know where I was. Thinking of the hundreds of drivers who had been through the same thing I had, I felt ashamed.

The bottleneck at the bridge finally was broken, and we continued south. Soon the trucks thinned, and as we dropped farther below the 38th parallel, the road became desolate.

The retreat had ended, and the army was moving into its new positions.
Dec. 5, 1950

By John Randolph

AT THE 38TH PARALLEL, KOREA, DEC. 31 (AP)—There is a hill in North Korea, just over the 38th parallel, which becomes a tiny part of allied territory every night.

During the day it is just one of a thousand hills in the no man's land between the Communist hordes and the outnumbered soldiers of the United Nations.

At dusk, whatever the weather, a little band of Americans from a famous infantry regiment steals across the frozen rice paddies and takes possession of the hill. Instead of a flag, the patrol plants a couple of Browning automatic rifles, unslings Garands and carbines, loosens pistols, tunes in a field telephone and a two-way radio.

Then for 12 hours, the enemy willing, these men crouch and freeze and curse in the zero temperature, waiting. They are what the Army calls a listening post. They are the eyes and ears that will warn of the long awaited Red rush down the opposite slope that will throw whole armies of Chinese and Korean Communists into the final battle for South Korea.

If these men can fall back and escape after doing their duty, well and good. If not—the job still has to be done.

At about a quarter to six each night, the leader of "I" Company's First platoon stands up and breaks off the joking talk around the watch fire.

He is 1st Lt. Solomon L. Hay Jr., of Johns Island, S.C., 21, and slight, but a leader and well liked.

"Okay, boys, it's time to get going," he says.

The seven-man detail then stumbles and slips down the slope to the icy rice paddies that stretch ahead for a quarter of a mile. Through the field runs the 38th parallel.

The squad crosses the invisible border and approaches the observation hill.

MAX DESFOR

By December of 1950, North Korea was a land of chaos and confusion, with families fleeing for fear of their lives, evacuating their land as hordes of Communist Chinese and North Korean troops pushed south.

AP photographer Max Desfor had hitched a ride with other correspondents in a crowded jeep for the trek across one of the few bridges still intact over the icy Taedong River at Pyongyang. When he got to the other side, he looked back at the stunning sight of thousands of refugees crawling across the skeleton of the bridge with their meager bundled belongings. He jumped out of the jeep and on to the slippery bridge as far as he dared and shot four pictures.

This one was published Dec. 5, 1950 and won a Pulitzer Prize in 1951.

A Marine (foreground) ducks flying rubble as an enemy bunker is blown up by grenades and charges set by comrades on the central Korean front.

At the bottom of the hill, everyone crouches low. Chinese or North Koreans may be up there, also waiting.

Two men start up the slope, while the others get ready to blast.

Cautiously, they reach the top. The rest begin to ascend the 300-foot ridge. Two men fan out to a foxhole on the right for fire support.

Two more crawl out on a bare bluff that juts northward where the enemy are concealed in the mountains.

Battalion headquarters had spotted a light from a higher hill to the rear, and wonders what it means.

The squad leader, Cpl. George J. Williams, 23, of 9932 Morgan St., Chicago, says mortars can't reach it, but howitzers can.

Moments later, battalion takes over, and there are quick flashes all along the Front as 105-mm howitzer shells go over.

The light remains, and the guns worry at it, off and on all night.

Thus begin the long 12 hours of watching, waiting and freezing.

There is a cracking sound in a paddy at the foot of the hill.

Williams hears it too. He goes to the radio and almost immediately from the rear "I" Company's mortars send three high explosive shells, followed by nine of white phosphorous.

The noise in the paddy field ceases.

The men, hurting through and through from the cold, curse Army clothing with overflowing bitterness. Some curse their rubber bottom shoe pacs. Some their leather combat boots. Others curse the shortage of wool garments. These men definitely have the best, but they are still cold. Their feet are in agony after the first few hours, from lack of movement. "God, what I'd give for a cup of coffee," murmurs one voice.

"God, what I'd give for a blonde," echoes another.

"Ah, you ain't gonna see a blonde for 10 years. The Chinese will get here first."

"Well, I wish some of 'em would come right now—about five would be just right—so we could pass the word and fall back off this damned hill. I'm freezing to death."

Dec. 31, 1950

By Robert Eunson

TOKYO, JAN. 1 (AP)—Masses of Chinese Reds unleashed a powerful New Year's Day offensive against Seoul, which rolled back United Nations defenders for several miles.

One veteran United Nations division was shattered, AP correspondent Jack MacBeth reported in a field dispatch from the fighting front.

The long-awaited offensive exploded along a 20-mile sector north and northeast of Seoul. Some Red waves were attacking within 28 miles of the menaced South Korean capital.

Gen. Matthew B. Ridgway, new commander of the U.S. Eighth Army, was at the front directing resistance against onrushing vanguards of a Chinese army exceeding 1,000,000.

Blowing bugles, the Chinese hurled themselves in hordes at barbed wire entanglements and across mine fields. They appeared oblivious to heavy losses.

Near the west end of the 150-mile U.N. line across Korea along the 38th parallel, the Reds crossed the frozen Imjin River at two points. One crossing was in battalion strength. It occurred near Korangpo, 23 miles north of Seoul.

MacBeth said he saw 300 members of the routed U.N. division straggling southward. He said the division had a reputation for tenacity under attack.

Jan. 1, 1951

BULLETIN

U.S. ABANDONS SEOUL
By Olen Coments

TOKYO, JAN. 4 (AP)—Chinese Red hordes took Seoul today.

The flame-swept South Korean capital was abandoned by United Nations troops. They blew up the last bridge across the frozen Han River south of the city at noon.

At about the same hour, the last U.N. plane left big Kimpo airfield, 10 miles northwest of Seoul.

The big air base was yielded to the advancing Chinese only after 500,000 gallons of aviation gasoline and 23,000 gallons of napalm (jellied gasoline for bombs) were set aflame.

A swiftly increasing menace east of Seoul was disclosed today by Gen. MacArthur. He said 120,000 Chinese and about 60,000 North Koreans were driving toward the vital rail and highway hub of Wonju, 55 miles southeast of Seoul.

This big force was seeking to cut across escape roads leading south from Seoul and pin the U.N. forces against the west coast.

A United Nations fleet stood off the west coast, ready to evacuate troops, if necessary, for redeployment.

Jan. 4, 1951

By Jim Becker

ON THE WESTERN FRONT, KOREA, JAN. 24 (AP)—War is death and wounds and danger and dirt. War is all of these, but mostly war is waiting. That's what the cold, dirty but surprisingly cheerful American, British, Turk, Canadian, Siamese and South Korean troops are doing on the western front today—waiting.

They sit in their fox holes, which they have

made into little homes with bits of stray wood and metal, and they wait in the cold.

They patrol constantly in front of their lines. And they wait for the blow the higher headquarters tells them the Communists are mounting to throw at them.

While the soldiers wait and stare across the snow-dusted Korean valleys and hills, looking north for the Chinese, they talk. Mostly they talk about the cold.

"The only gripe I've got is the cold," said Cpl. Robert A. Lallish.

"But I figure if it's hard on us, it's harder on them. They don't have the equipment we have. And cold or no cold, we started this job and might as well finish it. We're here for a purpose."

Some of the frontline soldiers are talking about the United Nations cease-fire efforts.

"Some of the guys are for it and some against it," said Pfc. Donald Crouch of Tipton, Ind. "Personally, I figure we've got a job to do, and we ought to see it through."

Sgt. John W. Lucas of Philadelphia put down his canteen cup of steaming coffee on a tree stump which was severed neatly by a shell the last time U.N. and Red troops battled over this ground.

"The only thing that burns me up is the attitude of the people in the States," he said. "We don't get much news up here, but from what we can find out, they're trying to ignore the whole thing back there.

"I figure if they don't want to go to war in the States, we ought to get out of here and go someplace where it gets warm once in a while."
Jan. 24, 1951

BULLETIN

By Stan Swinton

OSAN, KOREA, JAN. 15 (AP)—United Nations forces suddenly went over to the offensive on the western Korean front today.

By nightfall, tank-infantry teams had rolled up to 12 miles northward toward Seoul. They recaptured the ash and ruins of Osan, Kumyangjang and Chon.

Frontline morale soared as weary fighting men

realized—at least locally—that the allies had grabbed the military initiative back from the Reds

There was a strange lack of Chinese resistance

The Reds made their first serious stand from dug-in positions north of Kumyangjang at dusk They opened up on Third Division doughboy from the hills with automatic weapons.

Troops jumped off on a nine-mile front. Thei mission was to re-establish contact with the enemy and destroy as many Reds as possible.
Jan. 15, 1951

By Robert Eunson

TOKYO, SATURDAY, JAN. 27 (AP)—Two power-packed allied corps rolled north today along a 40-mile front in western Korea afte hurling back a strong Chinese Communist attack

Backed by bombarding warships and swarm of planes, United Nations troops and tanks punched within less than 15 miles of Seoul on the third day of their drive.

They seized a vital hill with the biggest bayone charge of the war. An actual count showed 47 dead Chinese on the field of battle.

Last night, the U.N. assault groups had to overcome heavy Red resistance before resuming the advance this morning. Red resistance also wa being encountered at points east of Suwon.

AP correspondent Jim Becker, on the western front, said U.N. troops were slugging it out with two Red battalions near Ichon, 23 miles east of Suwon.

The bayonet charge was made five miles south of Suwon in capturing hill 156.

AP correspondent Stan Swinton, reporting the cold-steel action, said the Chinese 50th Army of three divisions—possibly 30,000 men—was in line opposite the advancing allied forces but made no move to counterattack.

In a 12-mile northward advance Thursday and Friday, men of the First and Ninth Corps recaptured the airbase town of Suwon, 17 miles south of Seoul, and Kumyangjang, 11 miles southeast o Suwon.

Both places were empty of the enemy. Infantry patrols roved on two miles north of Suwon Friday and armored spearheads were set to follow.

Suwon once held a large part of an estimated 100,000-man Chinese Communist force massed on the western front for an expected all-out assault on the U.S. Eighth Army.

Air reconnaissance reported withdrawing Reds had dug in two to five miles north of Suwon. Air spotters also said about 15,000 Chinese were massed in the Ichon sector, 13 miles east of Kumyangjang.
Jan. 27, 1951

BATTLE CLOSEUP
By Jim Becker

WESTERN FRONT, KOREA, JAN. 29 (AP)—"They're firing on us from that hill," said Sgt. J.W. Hardin of Watertown, Tenn.

That hill was a dust-covered mound 600 yards away. The men of King Company had just laboriously pried 150 Communists off the hill on which we were standing.

Now they were to press forward to the next one.

We were eight miles north of Suwon. A spring-like sun shone down on the grimy foot soldiers. The doughboys were slugging it out with a fanatical enemy.

"They don't just get in their holes and die," said Lt. Arvine Eyer, company commander. "You have to go in and kill them."

Lt. James Oliver of South Portland, Maine, a platoon leader, said, "you run by those holes and they jump up behind you and shoot. You put three bullets in them and they keep right on firing. They shoot until they're dead.

"I shot one and was sure he was dead. When I walked up to the hole, he started firing. I felt the muzzle blast of the first one and the second parted my hair. I got out my .45 and emptied the clip into him."

There was more of the same waiting for the GIs on that hill.

A thin file of dirty doughboys moved slowly down the road that flanked the hill. Tanks limped behind, their rate of advance geared to the pace of two grim faced men searching the road for mines. Five hastily planted mines already had been unearthed in a quarter mile stretch of the road.

On the hill, a big recoilless rifle pounded the next ridge, trailing a fiery stream each time it sent more death across the small depression between the two hills.

A machine gun hemstitched the ridge, its chatter echoing down the valley. Suddenly there was a high whining scream and a shell pounded into a dugout. Soon there was another. It was only 50 yards to the right of where Capt. Sam C. Holliday of Houston, Texas, and I watched the action.

"Some guy back there is probably saying 'I must have left the charge off that one,' " Holliday said. "Luckily they don't do that too often."

An impassive group of GIs, crouching in the mud, were even closer to the burst, but seemed to ignore it entirely.

Soon "that hill" was silent, and the little band of soldiers continued to press north—the farthest spearhead of the U.N. offensive.

Once the action was over, Eyer said, "there are about 50 Chinese bodies on that hill. The Chinese are 10 times as determined as North Koreans."

Other company commanders said they were reaping about the same harvest of Reds.

An example of the fanatic resistance offered by the Chinese was told by Sgt. Arnold Missildine of Fairfield, Texas:

"This guy was sitting in a beautifully camouflaged hole watching us walk down the road. He had only grenades, no rifle. When we began to position our men we put a South Korean soldier near that spot. He saw the Chinese soldier move and shot him. The wounded Chinaman pulled the pin of a grenade but before he could throw it, the grenade went off and blew a big hunk out of him."

Two other Reds stayed in their holes, waiting to detonate a dynamite charge in the road as soon as they saw a target worthy of their scarce supply of explosives.

A soldier who had gone right by them spotted the pair and riddled them with bullets. One of them had a hole gouged from his skull that a dollar bill would not cover. The other struggled to heave a hand grenade, but it blew both his hands off before he could get it away.
Jan. 29, 1951

BACK INTO SEOUL
By Jim Becker

YONGDUNGPO, KOREA, FEB. 10 (AP)—A little more than a month ago, a dejected and apparently defeated army straggled south from this factory-jammed suburb of Seoul.

Today, a cheerful, victorious American Army slogged back into the town. It was the same army—the U.S. Eighth.

Just across the frozen Han River, the dirty soldiers of the 35th Regiment of the 25th Division could see the buildings of Seoul—the symbol of political victory in South Korea.

To the naked eye from this distance, the buildings of the capital city looked serviceable, but field glasses disclosed shattered roofs and windows and doors hanging askew. Not a living thing moved through the streets. The GIs were elated at gaining this vantage point over the city they were forced to abandon Jan. 4, but they were tired, very tired. Many had not slept on a cot for three weeks. Their eyes were bloodshot, and they slumped wearily. They sprawled on the ground, which a night-long snow had covered more than an inch deep. Then some of them began to gather wood from the demolished houses of Yongdungpo for warming fires.

The doughboys heated their C rations within easy sight of the Chinese Communists officers' mess hall in Seoul, across the river.

The rubbled streets of the town were nearly deserted. Signs which welcomed the Chinese Reds a little more than a month ago still hung from buildings.

Task forces, which had spearheaded the last six days of the 17-day-old U.N. offensive along the extreme western end of the front, drove to the northwest of captured Yongdungpo in an armored smash aimed at Kimpo airfield, 15 miles northwest of Seoul.

American artillery hammered the rude plank bridges the Communists had thrown across the ice-jammed Han. A tank commander with Task Force Dolvin today described the six-day hammering that allied armored forces had dealt the Reds:

"We hammered them the first two days and pulled back. They were fighting fiercely then. The third day we smashed right into their main defenses and they started to crack. The fourth day we had them on the run. It's just been a turkey-shoot the last two days."

One of the banners the Chinese Communists and their North Korean allies left in their hasty retreat from Yongdungpo urged the Koreans:

"Cement the ironclad unity of China and Korea. Make friends with your brothers who are carrying on the peoples' war for independence."

Another sign in Korean declared: "We (Chinese) are fighting for independence. Long live the people's army and the people's war for independence."

Giant railroad and highway bridges that led from Yongdungpo into Seoul still lay twisted and useless a few hundred yards from where GIs warmed themselves around their fires.

Later, some of the grimy, hollow-eyed men wandered down the almost deserted rubble-strewn streets of Yongdungpo. Now and then, a Korean civilian would appear from a battered building and shout a greeting.

Some civilians waved dirty South Korean flags, apparently the same flags the same civilians had waved at allied troops who marched this same way in September.

There were surprisingly few people, however. Most of this once-thriving suburb had long since fled south. Now the people are straggling north again, behind the advancing allies.

They stumble along the road under incredibly heavy burdens of household equipment.

Soon these people will be back in Yongdungpo and perhaps even Seoul. They will not find their homes as they left them. Constant struggles over this area have battered and beaten and ruined them.

Feb. 10, 1951

By Olen Clements

TOKYO, WEDNESDAY, FEB. 14 (AP)—Red hordes today pounded in human waves against the United Nations' front in the snow-mantled mountains of central Korea—striving for a breakthrough.

They poured banzai attacks at an allied force surrounded in Chipyong, 35 miles east of Seoul.

Their tanks and self-propelled guns menaced Wonju, the key to all highways in South Korea—including those behind 100,000 allied troops around Seoul.

The Reds cut the north-south road between Chipyong and Yoju. An allied division spokesman

Gen. Douglas MacArthur points across Han River toward Seoul during his 10th visit to the Korean front since the start of the war. At MacArthur's left is Lt. Gen. Matthew Ridgway, 8th Army commander.

said the central front's streams "turned red with Chinese blood" as artillery hit the enemy. Some shells hit enemy pack animals loaded with ammunition.

Red strategy was to cut off U.N. forces massed against the bridgeless Han River just across from Seoul.

Feb. 14, 1951

'WONJU SHOOT'

By John Randolph

ON THE CENTRAL FRONT, KOREA, FEB. 16 (AP)—Chinese blood ran down the side of the hill in rivulets. It flowed into the winding Som River, turning it red.

It was the most dramatic battle of the Korean War.

For years, artillerymen will tell the story of the "Wonju Shoot" that turned the tide of battle Tuesday on the central front.

No firing in this war has been so suddenly murderous or so decisive.

In most actions, the guns only serve and protect the infantry. Tuesday the artillery was queen of battle. It was the allies' weapon of surprise, destruction and pursuit.

The infantry fought and fought hard, but it was the guns that broke the back of the deadly Chinese thrust down the Chipyong-Wonju mountain corridor in central Korea.

If the Red gamble had succeeded, the allied front would have been split wide open and there might have been a real disaster in Korea.

At 4 a.m. Tuesday, the Allied position was grave. The Chinese Reds, with overwhelming numbers, had shattered a South Korean regiment and driven the Americans and Dutch back from Hoengsong in some confusion.

Another Red force swept through a thin curtain of defenders and encircled Chipyong, northwest bastion of the central front.

The Chinese strategy was obvious—to neutralize Chipyong and Wonju, then strike down the gap between them.

At 4 a.m., a call came from a forward artillery observer with the infantry. The enemy was four miles northwest of Wonju and heading south down the Som Valley.

It was up to the artillery to stop them, for the infantry was already at full strain.

Four battalions of artillery, nearly 60 guns, were firing and eating up ammunition at a frightening rate.

"I was with the Divarty (Division Artillery) liaison officer when he asked why the guns weren't firing faster," said Lt. Charles T. Burch, of Red Oak, Ga.

"I explained that they had to conserve their ammunition, that they were running low.

"'Conserve be damned!' he said, 'Give them everything they want!'"

The bombardment picked up speed until the whole valley rocked with the rolling blasts. "Beautiful shooting!" one pilot called into his transmitter, "You're really clobbering them!

"Look, there's another bunch of them, just beyond that stream of blood running down the bank!"

But the Chinese kept coming on.

Seconds later, a new storm of flame and steel broke upon the terrified Chinese from the east.

It was the artilleryman's dream, a cross fire.

The Chinese dissolved in a maelstrom of torn limbs, blood, earth and steel. Their pack animals carrying ammunition blew up like firecrackers all up and down the valley.

The Chinese fled north and northwest with shells exploding at their heels.

At 10 o'clock it was all over. In six hours the four battalions had fired 5,000 rounds of ammunition, killed an estimated 3,000 Chinese, shattered two divisions, and won the battle.

No Chinese masses crossed the allied lines that night. But the blood of thousands flowed down the winding Som between the snowy mountains and lost itself in the wider streams of South Korea. *Feb. 16, 1951*

CHIPYONG

By John Randolph and Tom Bradshaw

CHIPYONG, KOREA, FEB. 17 (AP)—The Communists almost had enough men and time to buy Chipyong.

For three days the Chinese Reds threw overwhelming numbers of troops against the iron perimeter of this western bastion of the central front. They surrounded it, and twice on Thursday they almost won it.

The first time was in the morning. The Reds surged up the southern ridge that dominates the town in the greatest of their 24 "banzai" charges. The American-French line sagged but didn't quite break.

The second time was Thursday afternoon, just as American tanks hammered through the encircling Reds and put them to rout. At that climactic moment of the battle, the ammunition of the garrison was all but exhausted.

Now that this battered little hill town remains firmly part of the United Nations front, its two most desperate moments can be described.

Take the story of the valiant garrison first:

The Reds' biggest suicide charge crashed into George Company, worn by two solid days and nights of fierce combat. The Reds rushed up the hill. The Americans were forced down.

A break in this thin line and a Red tide would have poured through on the unprotected back of the hard-fighting French on the west.

That would collapsed the defense. But George Company held. Chipyong's last reserves — the Ranger Company and two platoons of Baker Company — rushed in to bolster the sagging line.

All day the Chinese hammered at the perimeter. By the hundreds they were burned and blown to pieces.

It began to snow. Chipyong was cut off from planes that would have rained destruction on the enemy. It also was cut off from the supply-dropping planes on which it lived.

Despite the great numbers of Chinese and the snowstorm, the Americans battered part way back up the hill. Every artillery piece, mortar and machine gun was pointed up the slope.

The tremedous barrage staggered the Reds, but it could not last.

Ammunition melted away at a terrific rate. As the battle raged into the afternoon, the guns fired slower and slower.

By 4 p.m., Chipyon's defenders had only 650 rounds of mortar ammunition—10 minutes worth at heavy firing. The 105-mm howitzers had only 700 shells. The 81-mm mortars already were out of ammunition.

The second battalion, then counterattacking, messaged the command post: "Out of rifle and machine gun ammunition: Scratching the hillside for stray cartridges."

Just then the snow clouds parted.

F-80 Shooting Star jets dived on the Chinese positions, searing them with flaming napalm and blasting with rockets.

At almost the same moment, 22 American tanks of the relief force began nosing around a hill only one mile to the south, their guns belching death.

To get to beleagured Chipyong, the tanks had drilled through a five-mile valley of death.

Near Koksu, four and one-half miles south of Chipyong, the Reds fired mortars from ridges on both sides of the road.

The tanks fired back with their guns and with machine guns manned by 120 men of the U.S. Fifth Cavalry Regiment, who rode atop the tanks.

Ten times, the tanks stopped in that five-mile stretch and blasted out Red concentrations.

As the tiger-faced tanks wormed toward Chipyong, Reds carrying satchel charges and explosives fastened on poles jumped from overhanging ledges onto the tank turrets. The GIs bayoneted them off.

Halfway to Chipyong, the lead tank was struck by a bazooka charge, which burned to death two of the five-man crew and left only one unhurt.

GIs riding the backs of the tanks took a terrific beating from the Red crossfire on the ridges.

But the bodies of more than 500 Reds lined the road after that murderous hour was over.

Then the tanks burst in on Chipyong.

The Reds attacking the garrison broke and ran.

"They were so completely demoralized that they herded together in front of our guns," said Col. Marcel G. Crombez, of Portland, Ore., commander of the armored column.

The siege was broken. Before dark, planes got through and dropped ammuniniton. By next morning, all positions around Chipyong had been regained, and the supply route for trucks was open.

The three-day assault by elements of five Chinese divisions had failed. Some 30,000 Chinese had been beaten off by an American-French force about one-eighth as large.

Feb. 17, 1951

'MASSACRE'
By John Randolph

ON THE HOENGSONG FRONT, KOREA, MARCH 3 (AP)—"It was a massacre."

Still shaken at the sight, a tough frontline Marine officer thus described the burned-out remains of an allied Army convoy that was ambushed and wiped out by the Chinese three weeks ago, two miles northwest of Hoengsong.

"It hit them without warning. Some of the GIs were dead in their trucks, cut down by the first shots," the officer said. "Some of the others had grabbed up machine guns to fire from the hip without tripods. We found the guns by the bodies. None of them had been mounted.

"It must have been all over in a matter of minutes."

For a mile and a quarter nearly 40 American trucks and several field guns were scattered along the road.

In, under and beside them were burned and decomposed bodies. There were many dead Americans, a number of South Korean soldiers and 112 Red Chinese bodies. Several South Korean civilians apparently were caught and killed in the line of Chinese fire.

Some of the dead Americans had their feet tied together and had been shot in the head.

The convoy was ambushed when American elements of the Second Division were trapped north of Hoengsong after the Eighth (Republic of Korea) Division fell to pieces Feb. 12 under the Chinese central front offensive that was stopped a week later. To the Marines moving up the road from Hoengsong today, the sight of the smashed convoy came as sickening surprise.

"There were bodies scattered everywhere," said Lt. W. R. Abell.

"You could see how the Chinese had done it. On one side of the road a dike went out at almost right angles. On the other side there was a wall that served the same purpose. The Reds had got behind these barricades and simply waited for the convoy to come by in the night.

"Some of the Americans were killed in fair fighting. They and the Chinese they had killed lay together in small heaps around the trucks.

"But other Americans apparently had been murdered. They must have been the wounded ones. I saw two GIs who had been hit with mortar shrapnel but probably not fatally.

"Their trousers had been taken off and their ankles tied together. They had bullet holes in their temples."
March 3, 1951

By Jim Becker

SEOUL, KOREA, MARCH 15 (AP)—Old men wept unashamed. Women hugged and kissed us. And squealing children fought to touch us as the first 19 United Nations men reached the heart of fire-blackened Seoul today.

Six were U.S. Third Division infantrymen. One was a Korean interpreter. Eleven were an assortment of correspondents and photographers. The 19th was a British 29th Brigade Corps driver. A police dog named "Buck" completed the party.

We were the first to penetrate to the center of Seoul after abandonment of the ancient capital by North Korean Reds. And we walked there without a shot being fired.

Lt. John Hougen led the infantry patrol.

The streets were deserted as Hougen's squad

moved cautiously from the outskirts. But the news began to spread.

At first, small groups of Koreans waved flags and shouted "banzai," the Korean equivalent to victory.

Then tiny children came scurrying from the houses like ants at a picnic.

Aged men and women with children on their backs clustered about.

Some of the women threw themselves at our feet and sobbed hysterically. Tears coursed down the cheeks of bearded old men. Most citizens wore tattered clothing.

Other children gave me a ride on a flat car down the streetcar tracks of Seoul. It was the only vehicle that was running. It required dozens of the children to push it.

The British Corps driver was John Blackwell of Luton, Bedfordshire.

Seoul was a sorry sight. Buildings were demolished. Many were destroyed during the three previous times the capital changed hands. During the past month, it was pounded daily by 1,600 rounds fired by allied artillery into Red positions.

Civilians said some North Korean soldiers still lurked in the town in civilian clothes. But not a shot was fired in the first hours of Thursday.

Yesterday, allied outposts had noted civilians looting the foxholes of the defenders. That was the first tip that Seoul was being abandoned by the Reds.

Hougen's group proceeded toward the city's heart. And the some 200,000 civilians left of Seoul's one-time 1,500,000 population came to life.
March 15, 1951

U.S. BACK ACROSS 38TH

By Robert Eunson

TOKYO, SATURDAY, MARCH 31 (AP)— American tank forces smashed across the 38th parallel into Red North Korea today.

The crossing by U.S. troops north of Seoul came just a week after South Korean forces on the east coast punched over parallel 38 without opposition.

The Republic's forces (ROKs) are more than eight miles above the parallel, beyond Yangyang village, and meeting some opposition now.

The Americans crossed where the fighting is heavier and met stiffer resistance from Red forces, who apparently are building up for a spring counter-offensive.

Once again a massive Red buildup appeared definitely under way. Allied commanders anticipated a spring drive sometime during the first three weeks of April from as many as 270,000 fresh or well-rested Chinese of the Third Field Army.
March 31, 1951

GEN. RIDGWAY

By Leif Erickson

U.S. 8TH ARMY HEADQUARTERS, KOREA, APRIL 11 (AP)—Lt. Gen. Matthew B. Ridgway, successor to Gen. MacArthur as United Nations commander in Korea and occupation chief of Japan, is a lean, hard-bitten soldier.

The 56-year-old paratroop veteran of Sicily and Normandy garnishes his uniform with a live grenade. Worn taped to his shoulder, it has become as much a trademark as the late Gen. George Patton's pearl-handled six-shooters.

But Ridgway has more than color. In less than four months since he took command of allied ground forces in Korea Dec. 27, he has whipped a defeat-ridden army into a winning team. Ridgway is no rear echelon general. He has been bitten by the frontline flea. Moving back and forth across the front with a compact staff, he has directed his drive against the Reds from forward command posts.

Allied forces were near their lowest ebb in Korea when Ridgway took command. And only a few days later, the Chinese launched their massive New Year's Eve offensive across the Imjin River north of Seoul.

Ridgway ordered a fast retreat, deliberately withdrawing to regroup his disorganized divisions.

The paratroop general whipped new confidence into troops stunned by Chinese intervention in the Korean War as they were on the threshold of victory. He generated fresh vigor and confidence.

American and French soldiers in a bloody stand held the Wonju mountain passes against a Chinese drive to cut Allied supply lines.

That turned the tide.

Then, in late January, Ridgway launched his first drive—a limited offensive aimed to kill Reds, not win ground.

His tactics paid off. Allied troops piled high the Communist dead along ridgelines and hilltops and in the valleys of South Korea.

They gained ground too, moving steadily to the Han River near Seoul.

Then in February, the Chinese struck fiercely in a new offensive aimed at the center of the line near Gongchon and Wonju. Allied artillery and bayonets checked that last Red thrust into South Korea.

While the Chinese attack was under way, Ridgway planned and ordered a new offensive. It jumped off Feb. 21 and has pushed steadily northward since.

Today, most of the front is once again in North Korea. Ridgway has been careful to express his cordial relations with MacArthur.

Ridgway's classmates at West Point knew him as a man of energy. The yearbook called him "the busiest man in the place."

He is still like that in Korea. When the 197th Airborne Regiment dropped near Munsan in an attempt to trap Communists north of Seoul, Ridgway landed in a liaison plane in the drop zone less than two hours after the first wave jumped.

Ridgway's personality outside of direct command is quiet. He is notably courteous and polite to junior officers. He sets visitors at ease with quiet humor and twinkling eyes. His style of talking is in staccato phrases and in a low quiet voice.

On a point of special conviction, however, he puts volume and ringing feeling into his words and his eyes flash.

One command characteristic of Ridgway has been a conservative caution in claims of victory and damage inflicted on enemy forces.

The great shift in Eighth Army morale from a "bug out" defeatism to a winning confidence has aroused discussion of comparison in Walker and Ridgway.

Ridgway had proved a capacity to grasp and understand questions and issues beyond soldiering. He is more careful and considerate in his public statements than Walker.

Walker is a strictly military man who had had

scant experience with the press and public before the Korean War.

His staff remains loyal to Walker's memory. But officers concede Ridgway's leadership is more dynamic and that it extends to civilian public opinion as well as to the men in the ranks.

Ridgway called on an experienced press adviser soon after taking command in Korea. He is Lt. Col. James Quirk, former press relations officer to Gen. Patton and now on leave from the *Philadelphia Inquirer*.

It is apparent that Ridgway closely follows Quirk's advice.

The news that MacArthur was replaced by Ridgway was a shocking surprise at Eighth Army Headquarters.

But the men who have worked closely with Ridgway knew he was a man on the way to the top.
April 11, 1951

Right: Upon his arrival at Kangnung, Korea, Douglas MacArthur, commander-in-chief of United Nations forces in Korea, is greeted by Lt. Gen. Matthew B. Ridgway, U.S. 8th Army.

Chapter 7

President Truman greets Gen. Douglas MacArthur upon the president's arrival at Wake Island.

Stalemate, Confrontation and Negotiation

Gen. Douglas MacArthur, addressing a joint meeting of Congress in the House chamber, April 19, 1951, said the U.S. cannot appease communism in Asia "without simultaneously undermining our efforts to halt it in Europe."

On Christmas Day 1950, with U.N. forces in Korea still reeling from the Chinese onslaught, Gen. Matthew B. Ridgway took command of the U.S. 8th Army. He was met at the airfield in Tokyo by the Supreme Commander, Gen. Douglas MacArthur.

"General, if I get over there and find the situation warrants, do I have permission to attack?" Ridgway asked.

"Do what you think is best, Matt. The 8th Army is yours," MacArthur replied.

Ridgway's optimism—the notion of turning retreat into attack—seemed misplaced. Observing the war from Washington, Secretary of State Dean Acheson detected "the stench of spiritless defeat." But under Ridgway's inspired command, the "stench" lifted. U.N. forces held their lines and gradually regained lost territory.

Gen. MacArthur, however, was in no mood for gradual advances. Having led the longest retreat in U.S. military history, he was determined to broaden the war if that was what it took to defeat the enemy. In the process he caused a severe constitutional crisis, bearing directly on the president's authority as commander in chief.

Truman and MacArthur

The need for a face-to-face talk between Gen. of the Army Douglas MacArthur and his commander in chief had been developing for months before a meeting finally was arranged on Wake Island in October 1950.

In July, MacArthur had visited Nationalist Chinese leader Chiang Kai-shek, who had fled with his government to the island of Formosa (Taiwan) following the Communist military capture of the mainland. MacArthur told reporters that U.S. warships patrolling the waters between Formosa and China were "leashing" Chiang and should be withdrawn.

MacArthur had sent a message to the Veterans of Foreign Wars in which he seemed to propose an American defense line in the Pacific stretching from Vladivostok to Singapore, and including Formosa. Administration officials thought the statement likely to aggravate the Chinese Communists and make them more inclined to intervene in Korea. Truman told MacArthur to withdraw his statement, and the general did.

After the diplomat Averell Harriman had journeyed to Tokyo to convey the administration's concern about the Chinese Communists and its reservations about Chiang's Nationalists, he returned to Washington feeling the general hadn't gotten the point. Now it was Truman's turn to try.

WAKE ISLAND, OCT. 15 (AP)—President Truman and Gen. MacArthur met on Wake Island Sunday (Saturday, U.S. time) and both voiced confidence that the Communist perils in Asia could be overcome.

Before starting back for Hawaii from the historic conference, Mr. Truman issued a statement saying he was confident "we can surmount these dangers."

Arriving back in Tokyo from Wake, MacArthur released a statement which declared:

"The president's visit to the Pacific cannot fail to arouse great enthusiasm throughout the Far East, where it will be interpreted as symbolizing a firm determination that peace shall be secured in the Pacific and that Asia shall be free, not slave."

Mr. Truman said the two had covered a wide range of momentous subjects in the brief, two-hour meeting.

The primary topic was Korea, where MacArthur is putting United Nations forces deep into the Communist North in a drive designed to end Red aggression and unify the nation.

The president said he had found MacArthur's view "most helpful" and concluded with this:

"We are fully aware of the dangers which lie ahead, but we are confident that we can surmount these dangers with three assets which we have:

"First, unqualified devotion to peace; second, unity with our fellow peace-loving members of the United Nations; third, our determination and growing strength."

The first meeting of the president with MacArthur was shorter than had been expected. The conference had been expected to run into the afternoon. It was over in about two hours.

The presidential statement said that the "very complete unanimity of view which prevailed enabled us to finish our discussion rapidly" so MacArthur could return to Tokyo as soon as possible.
Oct 15, 1950

By Ernest B. Vaccaro

WAKE ISLAND, OCT. 15 (AP)—This tiny barren island, having played its part in history again, is quiet this afternoon.

The president of the United States, Gen. MacArthur—and the brass and bigwigs who came with them—are gone.

The sunbathed airstrip is empty now, save for the big airplanes that move through on their way to and from Korea. Only a few hours ago, the attention of all the world was focused on this little strip of land far out in the Pacific.

For here, in a rough, one-story block cement and frame office building, two of the most influential men of these times sat down together to assay the threat of war and draft a formula to preserve the peace. The gray-haired, blue-suited, 66-year-old president had flown more than 7,200 miles to spend five hours with the 70-year-old supreme commander of all United Nations forces in Korea.

But no one who was here today will ever forget the drama of that first face-to-face meeting of the colorful five-star general and the matter-of-fact Midwesterner.

Their meeting, in this scrubby land of Quonset huts, seemed strangely out of place.

MacArthur, who had flown in the night before from Tokyo, walked up to the ramp of the presidential plane to grasp Mr. Truman's hand and half embrace him.

"I have been a long time meeting you, General," the president said.

"I hope it won't be so long next time," the general replied. After much handshaking for photographers, they entered a battered and dented 1948 Chevrolet sedan and drove away together.

The car, with the presidential flag and the stars and strips waving bravely in the breeze, rattled along the coral road to a Quonset hut where the two men sat down together.

There, in a crude living room strangely in contrast to the White House, the president sat in a wicker chair, MacArthur on a settee.

For a full hour, they talked alone—animatedly, said those who peeped in from time to time.

There were no advisers, no staff of experts.

Suddenly the president and the general got up, strode out to their unglamorous car, the only sedan on the island, and rode to the little office where the others awaited them.

This formal conference lasted less than another two hours.

Then it was all over.

It was for this that the president made his spectacular flight from Washington.

It was for this MacArthur was summoned from his Korean War duties.

They agreed upon the language of a statement by the president. It was initialed by MacArthur and rushed to White House reporters.

If the statement didn't answer all the questions they had in mind, it did speak bravely.

It was the president's show.

It wasn't even noon by the time the president and the general met again on the airstrip as both returned there to fly away. The president had a medal for the general, who already had more medals than he probably could enumerate. This one was a fourth oak-leaf cluster to the Distinguished Service Medal.

They shook hands warmly, if not effusively, and within minutes both were winging their way outward through peaceful Pacific skies.
Oct. 15, 1950

Editor's Note

According to a stenographer who took notes of the Wake meeting, MacArthur apologized

A serious-faced President Truman listens as Gen. Douglas MacArthur speaks at an impromtu meeting on the airstrip at Wake Island after the general and the president held their historical two-hour meeting. At right is Brig. Gen. Courtney Whitney, Gen. MacArthur's civil government section chief.

to Truman for his VFW message. He also told him that the Communist Chinese were not likely to enter the Korean War, and that if they did they would be slaughtered. But as the U.S. military position in Korea deteriorated after the Chinese entered the war later that year, the relationship between Truman and MacArthur deteriorated, too.

MacArthur felt hamstrung by his inability to bomb Communist staging bases in China; he wanted Chiang "unleashed" to participate

in a diversionary attack; and ultimately he wanted to invade Manchuria and use atomic weapons against the Chinese.

But the world had changed since Mac-Arthur stood on the deck of the battleship **Missouri** to accept the Japanese surrender five years earlier, and so had war. "In war," Mac-Arthur would claim, "there is no substitute for victory." But that was before the Cold War, before 'The Bomb.' "In a world with weapons capable of inflicting megadeaths,"

William Manchester wrote, "war was no longer the last argument of kings and presidents."

There were more specific grievances against MacArthur. His harsh warning to Peking in March seemed designed to sabotage the administration's plan for cease-fire negotiations. Meanwhile, there was no support for MacArthur's own program. No one who counted wanted a wider war—not the military, diplomatic and political powers in Washington, nor the other nations with troops in the U.N. force.

By the end of 1950, the Joint Chiefs of Staff in Washington had lost confidence in MacArthur's generalship. He seemed overconfident, out of touch with the realities of the battle theater. The enemy had taken him by surprise, and now he seemed unwilling to admit it.

The incident that actually ended MacArthur's brilliant career—his letter to Joseph Martin, the Republican leader in the House of Representatives—was merely the last straw.

Mac BLASTS 'POSITIONAL WARFARE'

By Russell Brines

TOKYO, FEB. 13 (AP)—Gen. MacArthur said in effect today that military and not political factors will keep his United Nations troops south of the 38th parallel for the present.

He emphasized, however, that the allies must cut down Chinese numerical superiority considerably before the U.N. troops can thrust across the old border in force.

The implication was also that a far greater toll of Chinese life must be taken before the allies can expect a military decision. MacArthur is known to believe the campaign can be won only with full control of North Korea.

MacArthur said his command was "doing everything that could reasonably be expected of it" until international decisions are made on how the campaign is to be fought.

For the fourth time in a public statement, he appeared to be asking for permission to bomb Chinese bases. He spoke again of the "sanctuary protection" given the Chinese by halting allied air

power at the Yalu River, the border between North Korea and Manchuria.

In the meantime, he said, his forces are fighting the only kind of war they can. This is "a war of maneuver" designed to inflict maximum losses on the Communists, to keep them off balance and to deprive them of the initiative.

Any effort to throw a line across the peninsula and "enter into positional warfare is wholly unrealistic and illusory," he said. This concept ignores Korea's rugged terrain and the "relatively small force" employed by the allies. To try it "would insure the destruction of our forces piecemeal."
Feb. 13, 1951

By Leif Erickson

SUWON, KOREA, MARCH 7 (AP)—Gen. MacArthur said today continued "limitations upon our field of counteroffensive action" means the Korean War "cannot fail" to end in a stalemate.

MacArthur read his carefully-worded statement at a news conference in the tent beside Suwon airstrip. The conference followed a three-hour tour of the front with Lt. Gen. Matthew B. Ridgway, Eighth Army commander. It was MacArthur's 12th wartime flight to Korea. He then flew back to Tokyo. MacArthur said the Chinese Communists have no more than "an almost hopeless chance of ultimate military success."

He said on the other hand, the United Nations, barred from attacking Communist war production in China and without reinforcements, can achieve no more than continuing stalemate. MacArthur seemed to suggest to the United Nations to put more strength into convincing the Communists they should seek a peaceful settlement in Korea.

For the Reds to continue "this savage slaughter" amidst almost hopeless chances of victory, MacArthur said, was to display "contempt for the sanctity of human life" and "wanton disregard of international decency and restraint."

He warned "there should be no illusions" about the allied campaign of maneuver. As allied battle lines shift north, he said, the enemy's supply situation will improve and allied planes will have less chance to hit the Reds' shortened lines this side of the Manchurian border.
March 7, 1951

By Leif Erickson

SUWON, KOREA, MARCH 7 (AP)—Gen. MacArthur said in effect today that no one can win the war under present conditions.

But MacArthur said in a statement that the Chinese Reds have no more than "an almost hopeless chance of ultimate victory." He was no more hopeful of allied chances for victory.

As the war is being fought now, MacArthur said, "The battlelines cannot fail in time to reach a point of theoretical military stalemate."

After the front reaches a stalemate, MacArthur added, "Our further advances would militarily benefit the enemy more than it would ourselves."
March 7, 1951

By John M. Hightower

WASHINGTON, MARCH 24 (AP)—The administration disassociated itself today from Gen. Douglas MacArthur's declaration that if the United Nations want to expand their military operations into attacks on the Chinese mainland, they can destroy Red China.

The hands-off attitude—indicating some disapproval but falling short of real disavowal or rebuke—was expressed in two ways:

1. State Department officials said in response to reporters' inquiries that so far as they could determine MacArthur's statement was not cleared in Washington before he released it in Tokyo.

2. A department press officer, Reginald P. Mitchell, issued a carefully worded statement, which had been under preparation for several hours. It offered no support to anything MacArthur had said and emphasized that political issues beyond his responsibility as military commander are being dealt with through the United Nations and through talks between governments.

Secretary of State Acheson is reported to have conferred with President Truman today about the MacArthur statement. The comment finally issued is understood to have been cleared with the president. What Mitchell said was that as military commander, MacArthur is operating in Korea under directives issued through the American Joint Chiefs of Staff which, "as the president stated in a recent press conference, are fully adequate to cover the present military situation in Korea."

The reason for the administration's sensitiveness appeared to be a feeling here that MacArthur's statement as he left Tokyo for the battleground along the 38th parallel had somewhat the look of an ultimatum, although it was not that. MacArthur expressed readiness to meet the enemy commander in the field, while emphasizing that the Chinese had proved incapable of waging successful modern war and warning that if the United Nations decided to assault Chinese bases and coastal areas, Red China would be doomed "to the risk of imminent military collapse."

The implication that the United Nations might undertake such action goes far beyond any step which the U.N. coalition has recently been willing even to consider seriously.
March 24, 1951

By Willard H. Mobley

WASHINGTON, APRIL 5 (AP)—Gen. Douglas MacArthur kicked over the administration traces again today by applauding a Republican leader's demand for the use of Chiang Kai-shek's Nationalist troops to open a second front against the Communists in Asia.

He declared the demand made by Rep. Martin of Massachusetts, Republican leader of the House, is logical and in accord with the American tradition of "meeting force with maximum counterforce."

The administration is opposed to use of Chiang Kai-shek's troops, now penned up on Formosa. The official position here is that they are needed for the defense of Formosa. Officials also say they want to prevent a spread of the present war beyond Korea.

In a letter to Rep. Martin, MacArthur declared:

"It seems strangely difficult for some to realize that here in Asia is where the Communist conspirators have elected to make their play for global conquest, and that we have joined the issue thus raised on the battlefield; that here we fight Europe's war with arms, while the diplomats there still fight it with words; that if we lose the war to communism in Asia, the fall of Europe is inevitable. Win it, and Europe most probably would avoid war and yet preserve freedom. As you point out, we must win. There is no substitute for victory."

This placed MacArthur squarely in conflict with the theory held by administration officials that Europe, not Asia, is the major theater in the worldwide conflict with communism.

MacArthur's letter was in reply to a letter from Martin, asking for the general's reaction to Martin's Brooklyn speech Sept. 12. The Republican leader called for a second front on the Chinese mainland and use of Chiang's forces to set it up. Martin's letter to the general was marked personal, but the general's reply carried no such restriction. Martin read it to the House.

It was the latest in a series of developments showing a marked conflict of thinking between the administration here and the American high command in Tokyo.

What the administration would do about it was not immediately clear. But some officials did not conceal their resentment, feeling that MacArthur was trying to go over the president's head to carry his case to the people.

The MacArthur letter was dated March 20, a few days before reports circulated in Washington that the Far East commander had been directed to get clearance here for any future pronouncements with political significance.
April 5, 1951

John M. Hightower

WASHINGTON, APRIL 5 (AP)—Gen. Douglas MacArthur's dramatically disclosed desire to throw Chinese Nationalists forces into the battle against the Chinese Communists drastically widened today the split between the Truman administration and the U.S.-U.N. commander for Korea.

The views which the general expressed to House Republican leader Joseph Martin of Massachusetts are sharply at odds with the declared policy of the administration, which was reaffirmed at the State Department today. This policy opposes the use of Nationalist troops either to open a second front or to join the fight in Korea itself.

The MacArthur letter to Martin was considered by administration officials as but the latest of

many efforts by the general to bring a change in the policies which lay down the overall strategic limits of the Korean conflict and dictate the way in which MacArthur must broadly employ his forces.

State Department officials have said privately he is within his rights in pointing out that the limitation of his efforts to Korea itself—and particularly the bar against bombing Red supply bases in Manchuria—imposes great handicaps on his forces. He is considered to be equally within his authority in pointing out that his forces are limited, and that any great new effort would require additional forces, which thus far the U.N. governments fighting in Korea have been flatly unwilling to contribute.

But when MacArthur contributes his views, as the commander on the spot, on matters of domestic or international political controversy, he is considered by both State Department and various White House authorities to be seeking to promote policy changes by going over the president's head to the people. The officials who resent this contend it is not proper conduct for a military officer subject to the orders of the president as commander-in-chief.

The latest incident has renewed speculation in some quarters of the administration that Mr. Truman may consider removing or recalling MacArthur. Some authorities have also talked informally about sending an emissary to Tokyo to see whether affairs between MacArthur and Washington can be straightened out.

Mr. Truman is believed to be reluctant to take any drastic step involving MacArthur because (1) his assignment may end in a few months with the completion of a Japanese peace treaty, (2) he has great political prestige which could prove embarrassing, (3) he has excellent accomplishments to his credit, (4) any decision to alter his status radically might set off a big controversy which would divide the country.
April 5, 1951

Editor's Note

For his reporting of international affairs in 1951, John Hightower was awarded the Pulitzer Prize in 1952.

MacARTHUR vs. TRUMAN

By John Hightower

WASHINGTON, MARCH 26 (AP)—The dispute that rages between Gen. Douglas MacArthur and the Truman administation over how to win the Korean War has reached fever heat again. The administration may shortly ask the general to clear with Washington anything he says involving broad foreign policy issues.

This may or may not prove acceptable to MacArthur, but State Department officials as well as some others with great influence at the White House privately say something must be done to prevent a repetition of last week's exchange of shocks and harsh words between Tokyo and Washington.

President Truman circulated last December a firm, government-wide directive declaring that any statement on foreign policy by any official or employee of the government in a speech, article or other public utterance, should be cleared with the State Department. Informants said today that order was called to MacArthur's attention at the time.

Friday night, Washington time, MacArthur left Tokyo for the 38th parallel area of Korea to order United Nations forces to cross into North Korea as tactical requirements made necessary. Before leaving Tokyo, he issued a statement to the press.

In this statement, he made a bid for peace talks with his opposite number on the Communist side, said the Chinese Reds were licked and incapable of waging modern war and warned that if the United Nations launched attacks on Chinese bases and coastal areas, the Red nation would probably suffer military collapse.

This statement, a check showed, caught the State Department completely unawares. It apparently also caught President Truman without advance notice. After several hours of parleying, including a talk between Secretary of State Acheson and Mr. Truman, a rather meaningless statement was issued, designed to say on Saturday that Washington has had nothing to do with what MacArthur declared Friday night.

The statement said MacArthur had authority to conduct military operations but that political issues which "he has stated are beyond his responsibilities" are being dealt with in the U.N. and by the governments having troops in Korea.

The key MacArthur clause which set off the alarm here was that the United Nations could probably succeed in forcing a military collapse of Red China by a limited coastal attack and base-bombing war. A Tokyo dispatch yesterday suggested MacArthur probably was trying to divert the Chinese Reds' attention from Korea to the danger of a coastal attack.

Whatever his objectives, any statement he makes—even hedged with "ifs"—about extending the war in the Far East always sends huge shudders among the Canadian, French, British and other friendly governments. When the Europeans come in to the State Department wanting to know "what does MacArthur propose to do," Acheson and his aides get upset about the problems of holding together the political side of the coalition of which MacArthur is military commander.

The basic difference between Washington and MacArthur, however, goes back a long time. It involves the relative importance of the Far East and Europe and MacArthur's constant emphasis on the former. It involves how to deal with the peoples of the Far East and what forces will eventually win there. And it has exploded in a sensational manner twice before.

The first time came last August, about a month after war started in Korea. MacArthur was instructed to find out what Generalissimo Chiang Kai-shek needed for the Chinese Nationalist defense of Formosa. Instead of sending an emissary, he went personally. He thus identified the American cause with the Chinese Nationalist leader on Formosa, which was at that time about the last thing the Truman administration wanted to have happen. His action, in a roundabout way, was repudiated.

Then came the Chicago meeting of the Veterans of Foreign Wars late in August. By invitation, MacArthur sent a message; the president ordered him to suppress it, but it got out anyway. It pictured the defense of Formosa as of permanent vital importance to America's security in the western Pacific and advocated strong-handed methods in dealing with the peoples of the Orient. Again, MacArthur's views were repudiated.

President Truman told radio and television audiences that he fired Gen. Douglas MacArthur because the Far Eastern commander's policies carried a "very grave risk" of starting a general war.

Since the Chinese entered the war in Korea, MacArthur has repeatedly hammered two points in public statements. One was that Chinese Reds were operating from a "privileged sanctuary," Manchuria, which could not be bombed even though its bases fed the Communist front in Korea. The other was that he needed much more power forces to deal with the new situation.

There was a time when serious consideration was given here to waging a limited war against China. But Washington policy now rules this out. Reasons include the fact that Britain and other allied countries are dead set against it; also the fear that action against China might bring in Russia or the Communist air force based in Manchuria; also the probable diversionary drain on materials which would otherwise go to Europe. *March 26, 1951*

MacARTHUR FIRED

WASHINGTON, APRIL 11 (AP)—President Truman early today forced Gen. Douglas MacArthur from all his commands.

The president said he had concluded that MacArthur "is unable to give his wholehearted support" to United States and United Nations policies.

Mr. Truman immediately designated Lt. Gen. Matthew B. Ridgway as MacArthur's successor.

Mr. Truman asserted that "military commanders must be governed" by policies and directives of the government and "in time of crisis, this consideration is particularly compelling."

Announcement of the almost unprecedented dismissal of the hero-general was made at a rare news conference at the White House at 1 a.m. (EST). The time was fixed to coincide as nearly as possible with the delivery to MacArthur at Tokyo of the order relieving him of his commands, "effective at once." The White House released, with the president's statement, a memorandum purporting to show differences between MacArthur's statements and action and presidential policy.

The president's order, telegraphed to MacArthur over the Army network, was brief and pointed:

"I deeply regret that it becomes my duty as president and commander-in-chief of the United States military forces to replace you as supreme commander."
April 11, 1951

By Don Whitehead

WASHINGTON, APRIL 11 (AP)—President Truman solemnly declared tonight that Gen. MacArthur's proposed policies in Asia carried the grave risk of a third world war.

He said he had to fire the general to make clear this nation's "real purpose and aim" of peace.

"Our aim is to avoid the spread of the conflict," the president said in a speech broadcast from coast-to-coast.

The president went to the radio and television to defend his drastic action which had touched off a worldwide uproar and brought demands in Congress for his impeachment.

MacArthur remained silent in Tokyo. But earlier he let it be known through Republican leaders who called him by telephone that he is ready and willing to defend his views before a joint session of Congress.

President Truman flatly rejected MacArthur's views that the United Nations should bomb Manchuria and China and aid Chinese Nationalist troops to invade the Chinese mainland.

"If we were to do these things," he said, "we would be running a very grave risk of starting a general war."

Mr. Truman did not mention Gen. MacArthur's name until he reached the tag-end of his speech. Then, in three paragraphs he delivered his punch. He said:

"I believe that we must try to limit the war to Korea for these vital reasons: to make sure that the precious lives of our fighting men are not wasted; to see that the security of our country and the free world is not needlessly jeopardized; and to prevent a third world war.

"A number of events have made it evident that Gen. MacArthur did not agree with that policy. I have therefore considered it essential to relieve Gen. MacArthur so that there would be no doubt or confusion as to the real purpose and aim of our policy.

"It was with the deepest personal regret that I found myself compelled to take this action. Gen. MacArthur is one of our greatest military commanders. But the cause of world peace is more important than any individual."

The president's speech capped a hectic day in which Republicans thundered angry criticism of his firing of MacArthur while Democrats defended the president in a new "great debate" which has become an issue in many countries.

The president's ouster of MacArthur jarred the world into an emotional and political outburst unlike anything in modern times.

The man-in-the-street joined political leaders at home and statesmen around the world in choosing up sides in the bitter dispute that is certain to rage for months to come. Telegrams from across the country were beginning to flood into the offices of lawmakers. Congressmen lined up on the issue generally along political lines—the Republicans damning Mr. Truman for his action and the Democrats supporting him. European diplomats generally cheered the president's decision.

But in Tokyo, the news was received with dismay.

Republican cries for impeachment of President

President Truman just before he started his nationwide address, April 11, 1951, explaining that he fired Gen. Douglas MacArthur because the Far Eastern commander's policies carried a "very grave risk" of starting World War III. The President spoke from his White House study as he declared "We are trying to prevent a World War III, not to start one."

Truman today punctuated the furious argument over the firing of Gen. Douglas MacArthur.

The GOP leadership in Congress announced that the possibility has been studied at a private huddle of top party men from both houses. The group talked of "impeachments" in the plural and obviously had Secretary of State Acheson in mind too.

Then Sen. Jenner (R-Ind.) made a flat demand in the Senate for such action against the president. He got a burst of applause from the spectators' gallery that obviously encouraged backers of the idea.

Sen. Nixon (R-Calif.) used the word too, in telling reporters about reaction from his home state. He said when he reached his office this morning he had 378 telegrams on his desk and "90 percent of them urged the impeachment of the president."

Truman's firing was viewed today as "a blunder beyond belief" by Miss Louise Yim, South Korean delegate to the United Nations.

With the Chinese Communist Korean offensive in full swing, Gen. Matthew B. Ridgway, supreme commander (second from left), huddles with some of his top field commanders at an advance base in Korea.

The *Detroit News* quoted Miss Yim as saying in an interview here:

"The ousting of Gen. MacArthur is a blow to the whole world, a bitter defeat for democracy, and a direct play into the hands of the Communists.

"I cannot understand such an action at this time. It will be a shock to the whole eastern part of the world. I will be surprised if there is not a formal protest from Korea, from Japan, and from the Philippines. Gen. MacArthur is looked upon as democracy itself in those countries.

"I am sick with discouragement."

Miss Yim was interviewed while en route to visit nearby Windsor, Ont., where she was to meet officials of the Canadian city. She is touring the Midwest.
April 11, 1951

By John Randolph

ON THE WESTERN KOREAN FRONT, APRIL 11 (AP)—Gen. MacArthur's soldiers are sorry to see him go—but they like the general who takes his job.

A radio announcement of the change in supreme commanders hit the front in mid-afternoon today. The news spread swiftly. "Did'ja hear the news? MacArthur's been relieved!"

The invariable reaction was disbelief—"You're kidding."

It took repeated assurances that this was no joke, but an official fact before soldiers would believe that "Uncle Doug" no longer was in command.

"It's a shock," said Cpl. John Howell of Sioux, N.C., a 25th Division rifleman. "I don't know what to make of it. I hate to see us lose a good man like Mac."

Most soldiers were quick to praise Lt. Gen. Matthew B. Ridgway, the U.S. Eighth Army commander who succeeds MacArthur.

"Maybe it was time for a change, but MacArthur was a grand old man," said Lt. Medford Travers of Woolford, Md., an F-51 fighter pilot with 103 combat missions.

"Ridgway ought to do all right," Travers continued. "I've never heard anything but good of him. All the front line people I've met say he's a 'fat positive.'"

"Fat positive" is Air Force slang for the direct opposite of "negative."

"I'm sorry to see it myself," said Sgt. Joel Thrasher of Vance, Texas, who was loading rockets on a Mustang fighter. "I don't like changing horses in midstream, although Ridgway seems like a good guy."

Lt. Henri Deklerk of (60615 Eggleston) Chicago, put it this way:

"I don't know what to think of it. It's a surprise to everybody. I guess MacArthur did act like a big wheel sometimes. That probably had a lot to do with it. But Ridgway is a fine man. Either one of them can do the job."
April 11, 1951

By Russell Brines

TOKYO, APRIL 11 (AP)—Gen. MacArthur received the news of dismissal from all his commands today "magnificently and without turning a hair."

Maj. Gen. Courtney Whitney, military secretary of the United Nations command, told newsmen MacArthur would have no comment "for the time." He added:

"I just left the general. He received the word of the president's dismissal from command magnificently. He never turned a hair. His soldierly qualities were never more pronounced.

"This has been his finest hour."

The general with the dramatic touch went out under circumstances more like the stage than war. His notice came without warning, during a quiet luncheon at his home. MacArthur returned to his office at 5:30 p.m. where he remained until 8:55 p.m. He then left for home in a dismal rain.
April 11, 1951

HOLLYWOOD, APRIL 11 (AP)—A Hollywood producer today offered Gen. Douglas MacArthur a $3,000 a week acting job—playing a general on the stage.

In a cable to MacArthur, who was fired today by President Truman and has announced no plans, producer Tom McGowan asked the general to play the lead in "The Square Needle," which concerns a World War II officer whose operations were hampered by policy directives from Washington.

McGowan cabled:

"Renowned playwright Samuel Taylor will rewrite the role to be dignified and fit our beloved general perfectly. Please cable yes or no so script can be flown to you."
April 11, 1951

By Russell Brines

TOKYO, APRIL 16 (AP)—Gen. Douglas Macarthur left Japan today amid a great tribute from the Japanese people he ruled and Allied forces he commanded.

His Constellation plane *Bataan* roared into the spring sunshine at 7:21 a.m. (5:21 p.m. EST, Sunday), ending an epoch that remained dramatic and ironic until the last moment.

Fourteen minutes later, his successor, Lt. Gen. Matthew B. Ridgway, moved into the same plain headquarters office, from which MacArthur ruled Japan for five years and seven months. The Japanese gave their conqueror the greatest acclaim they have ever shown a foreigner.

Between 500,000 and one million people jammed the streets for a final glimpse of "Field Marshal Makas-Sar," as they call him. They paid tribute their own way, with reverent silence and polite bows, during the general's 12-mile motor trip to Haneda Airport.

Military associates gave MacArthur a 19-gun salute from stubby 105 mm howitzers. They said he was entitled to two more rounds than any other American general, because he had served as Supreme Commander for the Allied Powers in Japan.

And, finally, the air was cleared temporarily of busy military planes, so the *Bataan* could head directly for Hawaii.

The general could not have had a more triumphant exit. MacArthur was plainly moved. He held himself with extra erectness. His face wore a quick, tense smile. He was in a hurry to leave.

Mrs. MacArthur seemed on the verge of tears.

Thirteen-year-old Arthur MacArthur seemed bewildered and uneasy.

The epoch that has become associated with MacArthur in Japan and the Orient ended quickly. It took 30 minutes for the drive to the airport and out of the lives of the Japanese. In 14 minutes more, the general completed his military ceremonies, greeted the dignitaries on hand and was in his plane.
April 16, 1951

By Don Whitehead

SAN FRANCISCO, APRIL 17 (AP)—Gen. Douglas MacArthur arrived home tonight to a riotous welcome that almost became a mob scene when he stepped from his plane, the *Bataan*. Spectators, newsmen and photographers broke through greeting lines and swarmed around the general in a tumultuous welcome that almost swamped the ceremonies at the airport.

With deep feeling, MacArthur told the airport crowd of nearly 10,000:

"I cannot tell you how good it is to be home. In these long, long dreary years, Mrs. MacArthur and I talked and thought about home. We appreciate your marvelous hospitality and this great reception. We will not forget it."

He wore his familiar gold-braided cap and a trench coat buttoned high around his neck.

As the plane rolled to a halt before the crowd, a woman's high piercing scream was heard. A baby's thin wail rose about the shouting, and there was pandemonium.

Officers and friends formed a tight circle around Mrs. MacArthur and young Arthur to keep them from being crushed. There were several "MacArthur for president" signs in the crowd.

It was the first time in 14 years MacArthur had been in the continental United States. The intervening years had been spent on U.S. Army duty in the Philippines, commanding American forces in the southwest Pacific in World War II, as occupation commander of Japan since V-J Day, and as United Nations commander in the Korean War—until he was fired last week by President Truman.

The Bay area's greatest outpouring since V-J Day cheered the general's party from jam-packed streets throughout the 15-mile ride from the airport to the St. Francis Hotel in downtown San Francisco.

Smiling and waving, MacArthur paused at almost every intersection to acknowledge the wild reception. He required 100 minutes for the trip.
April 17, 1951

By Relman Morin

WASHINGTON, APRIL 19 (AP)—Gen. Douglas MacArthur, in a fighting speech before Congress, defended the whole of his Far Eastern strategy today and said he had understood that his views were shared in the past by "our own Joint Chiefs of Staff."

The speech drew mixed reaction—most of it along party lines. Republicans called it "noble" and magnificent." Democrats applauded MacArthur's eloquence, but some of them said the speech had not changed their view that his policies would lead to a third world war.

His address to Congress, while it was restrained in tone and manner, was a fighting speech all the way.

It drew wild applause at many points. MacArthur was interrupted more than 30 times by cheering. And at the end, just before the general said "Goodbye," tears were running down the cheeks of many of his listeners.

MacArthur retreated not an inch from the pattern of Pacific defense he has been advocating for many months—a set of policies that finally brought his abrupt discharge by order of the president.

He reviewed, and re-advocated the main points of that strategy again today. And then, in a voice that almost broke with his own emotion, he said:

"For entertaining these views, all professionally designed to support our forces committed to Korea and to bring hostilities to an end with the least possible delay and at a saving of countless American and Allied lives, I have been severely criticized in lay circles, principally abroad, despite my understanding that, from a military standpoint, the above views have been fully shared in the past by practically every military leader concerned with the Korean campaign, including our own Joint Chiefs of Staff."

These words, the core of his defense, seemed to strike like a thunderbolt.

For the briefest instant, the packed chamber, floor and gallery was silent. Then a deafening ovation exploded. Republicans and most of the spectators leaped to their feet, cheering and stamping. It was almost a full minute before MacArthur could continue.

He stood, motionless as a statue, his freckled hands gripping the sides of the dais where his manuscript lay.

When he was able to continue, he said—and his voice dropped lower—"I asked for reinforcements, but was informed that reinforcements were not available."

Then he said he made clear his belief that Chinese Communist air bases had to be destroyed, that "the friendly Chinese force of some 600,000 men on Formosa" should be used, and that the China coast should be blockaded.

Otherwise, he said, "we could hope at best for only an indecisive campaign with its terrible and constant attrition upon our forces if the enemy used his full military potential."

MacArthur said he had called for new political decisions to adjust policy to the fact of Red China's entry into the war. "Such decisions," he said, "have not been forthcoming." He continued, with great deliberation:

"Efforts have been made to distort my position. It has been said in effect that I was a warmonger. Nothing could be further from the truth."

General of the Army Douglas MacArthur, relieved of commands and returned to the United States, is shown as he addressed a joint session of Congress in April 1951. In the background is Vice President Alben W. Barkley.

MacArthur entered at 12:32. He received a rising ovation from everybody present, Republicans and Democrats alike.

He wore an Eisenhower jacket, without decorations. The silvery circle of five-star rank glittered on his shoulders. He shook hands with Vice President Alben Barkley and turned, placing a typed manuscript on the dais.

His face was an unreadable mask. His voice was low, but firm and emphatic.

Nearing the end of his speech, he paused. "I have just left your fighting sons in Korea. They have done their best there, and I can report to you without reservation that they are splendid in every way."

He paused to let pass another burst of applause. In the gallery, a woman's white handkerchief fluttered up to her eyes. Tears welled up in the eyes of a man nearby.

MacArthur recalled an old barrack room ballad,

quoting it: "Old Soldiers Never Die—They Just Fade Away."

By that time, people were weeping openly. He said:

"I am closing my 52 years of military service. And like the old soldier of that ballad, I now close my military career and just fade away—an old soldier who tried to do his duty as God gave him the light to see that duty.

"Goodbye."

A hurricane of emotion swept the chamber. The noise and swirling movement exceeded even the earlier demonstrations while he was speaking.

Hands reached out to grasp his hand. MacArthur turned away, looked up toward the White House gallery and waved to his wife. Stepping down from the dais, he waved to her again.

He passed through the chamber between a gauntlet of hands, reaching out from both sides of the aisle.

April 19, 1951

By Relman Morin

NEW YORK, APRIL 20 (AP)—With a wave of his gloved hand, Gen. Douglas MacArthur captured New York today.

He whipped the city's millions into a screaming frenzy of excitement and adulation, stirring the spectacle of a lifetime. Not even New York had ever seen anything like it. And MacArthur, seldom a man to show his emotions, showed them today.

His open convertible travelled a 15-mile route, from midtown Manhattan, up through Central Park, and along the waterfront to lower Broadway.

The general, buttoned to the chin in his familiar trenchcoat, seemed to be taking it all in stride during the first few miles, along Park Avenue. He managed a bleak, disinterested smile, once or twice. But, mainly, he acknowledged the cheers and clapping with a mechanical wave of his hand.

The chain of cars passed between lines of school children in Central Park.

Their shrill voices sounded like millions of crickets on a warm summer day. MacArthur's smile grew a little warmer.

In Times Square, a theater marquee announced:

"Held Over—The MacArthur Story." A gigantic electric billboard, usually alive with ingenious advertising antics, was stopped today and spelled out only two words, "Welcome Mac."

At that point, and in the garment district, the first heavy storm of confetti, snipped paper, pages torn from telephone books, and long, writing paper streamers began to explode from office windows.

The upsurge of wind in draught canyons caught the paper and carried it, swirling, up and then down, shimmering and glistening like the gold specks in those glass balls that you have to shake first.

A dentist had drawn up his blinds, and a woman—with the bib still around her neck—was sitting in the chair, turned toward the street. There was another, a block later, swathed in a white sheet and with a masseuse standing beside her.

The streets blazed with flags and banners, giant pictures of MacArthur cut from today's New York papers and tacked to a pole, and hundreds of home-painted slogans" "God Bless You Mac, Glad You're Back."

On the streets, surging against barricades of wooden horses, people screamed, wept, and waved in spasms of excitement as the General's car passed.

Somebody yelled, "Give 'Em Hell, Mac." And again, "Don't let 'em get you down, Doug. Keep hitting 'em."

A policeman, marching beside the car, gasped "This is the damnedest thing I've ever seen."

It was a frantic, roaring maelstrom of sound and movement. White-coated nurses and interns lined the East River Drive from nearby hospitals. Fish-cutters, in stained and grimy aprons, longshoremen, and booted ship's crews shoved and jostled each other along the waterfront.

In the river, the fireboats threw fountains of white water high into the air. A bright sun turned them into millions of glittering diamonds.

But the real storm broke on lower Broadway.

There, the fluttering paper and tape was so thick it blotted out the sky. A deafening, ear-crushing roar went up as MacArthur's car was halted to wait for an honor guard of blue-uniformed marchers to start.

Paper continues to shower on Gen. Douglas MacArthur as he stands in open car to salute the color guard of the 1st Army (left) during a parade in his honor in New York City, April 20, 1951. This view is looking south on Lafayette Street in lower Manhattan. Faintly showing in the background is the Woolworth Building.

Suddenly, he stood up in the back of the car. A tidal wave of cheering and shouting rocketed back and forth in the narrow street.

MacArthur began to wave and the roaring grew even louder.

He looked up at the office buildings, bulging with faces. He returned the salute of a GI in a battered uniform.

He smiled and his whole face was transformed. He waved again—and a city surrendered.
April 20, 1951

The Peace Talks

By mid-1951, the Korean War had settled into to what William Manchester would later call a "mad solution ... war with neither triumph nor subjugation—a long bloody stalemate which would end only when the exhausted participants agreed to a truce."

In a nuclear age, anything more or less was too risky. But to Americans, who only five years earlier had claimed the greatest of martial victories, the standoff was the height of frustration.

Despite the storm of praise that greeted MacArthur upon his return from Asia, there was no support for a wider war, which would only kill more soldiers and endanger the consumer's paradise that was forming at home.

But arranging a truce was complicated by several factors, including a lack of a reliable go-between and a complete lack of trust on both sides.

SOVIET PEACE PROPOSAL

By A.I. Goldberg

UNITED NATIONS, N.Y., JUNE 23 (AP)—Russia's Jacob A. Malik urged in a nationwide broadcast today that both sides in Korea confer on a cease-fire, armistice and withdrawal of troops from the 38th parallel as the first step to peace.

The U.S. State Department in Washington quickly declared the United States is ready to do its share if Malik's statement "is more than propaganda."

The Russian United Nations delegate's proposal was the first Russian peace bid for Korea not hedged with conditions favorable to Red China.

It was met with wary skepticism in Washington, but with every indication it will get serious study. Several key congressmen, citing caution necessary to appraise any Russian statement, said Malik's new proposal must be considered carefully. Distribution of President Truman's speech Monday on the Korean anniversary was held up for possible revision in the light of the Malik statement.

Malik's speech—unusually short for any Russian policy statement—left a number of questions unanswered. The chief one was whether he could speak effectively for the Chinese Communists.

Malik said the belligerents on both sides should take part in discussions for an armistice and withdrawal of troops of both sides from the 38th parallel.

Malik's high policy statement, the first program speech he has ever made on a U.S. radio network, was contained in a broadcast of 14 minutes and 25 seconds recorded for a U.N. weekly program "Price of Peace." He was the series' 13th speaker.

Malik devoted much of his speech to attacks on the Western Powers, the North Atlantic Treaty, American military bases abroad, the armaments race, and U.S. policy in Germany and Japan.

He insisted that the Soviet Union and its people were devoted to peace and still believed in the peaceful coexistence of socialist and capitalist systems.

But after summing up his attacks and what he called the "profoundly vicious" policy of the West, he said the Soviet people felt the problem of the armed conflict in Korea could be settled. *June 23, 1951*

By Roger D. Greene

WASHINGTON, JUNE 26 (AP)—Secretary of State Acheson told Congress today the restoration of the old 38th parallel boundary between North and South Korea would satisfy U.S. terms for an end to the Korean War.

American troops and their United Nations allies are now operating as much as 20 miles north of the parallel after breaking the back of the latest Chinese Communist offensive.

Acheson said that if the Reds agree to remain behind the old frontier—and offer guarantees against further aggression—the United States would consider it "a successful conclusion of the conflict."

But he cautioned that the cease-fire proposal by Soviet Deputy Foreign Minister Jacob Malik might be "camouflage" to mask Soviet designs in oil-rich Iran in the Middle East and Burma in the Far East. Both are potential powder kegs in the troubled world situation.

"We are doing our best to obtain clarification of what was meant (by Malik's proposal)," Acheson said.

The Cabinet officer gave his views in appearing as the first witness before the House Foreign Affairs Committee to support President Truman's request for a new $8,500,000,000 program of foreign military and economic aid.
June 26, 1951

By Nate Polowetzky

SEOUL, KOREA, JULY 10 (AP)—Allied military leaders met Red generals in Kaesong today and told them the United Nations wants a real end of hostilities—but without strings attached.

The chief U.N. delegate, Vice Adm. C. Turner Joy, said the sole aim of his delegation was to achieve an end of hostilities under conditions which would guarantee they would not be resumed.

He told the five Red generals the U.N. group would not talk politics, obviously a reference to such matters as Red China's bid for admission to the United Nations.

He also said the U.N. five-man team would not talk about military matters not related to Korea. This obviously referred to such matters as Red demands for Formosa.

The two admirals and three generals representing the U.N. met with the Reds at a once sumptuous residence in Kaesong, 35 miles northwest of Seoul and three miles south of parallel 38. Today, it was disclosed that during Sunday's discussions, the Reds turned down an allied offer for a 10-mile wide neutral corridor extending 12 miles northwest to Kumchon and an equal distance southeast of Munsan. Allied sources quoted the Reds as saying they felt they could rely on the U.N. commander in chief not to launch an attack in the area, so no neutral corridor was necessary.

The Red liaison officers said they had ordered their troops in the Kaesong area to refrain from any military action.

While the negotiators met, the war—now in its 55th week—went on. There was sharp action Monday.
July 10, 1951

By Robert Eunson

TOKYO, AUG. 23 (AP)—The Reds called off the turbulent Kaesong truce talks today "from now on" after charging that a U.S. plane dropped bombs near quarters of the Red truce delegates last night.

Gen. Matthew B. Ridgway's headquarters announced the Red decision and said heatedly, "The whole incident is a frame-up staged from first to last."

A Red liaison officer, reading from notes which appeared to have been prepared well in advance, told Allied liaison representatives at Kaesong shortly after midnight that the talks were "off from now on."

The Allied officers asked the Reds if this meant no more meetings of even the liaison representatives who have met daily even when the main delegates stayed in camp.

The Reds emphasized "all meetings."
Aug. 23, 1951

Editor's Note

Although they continued for month after month, the truce talks went nowhere; the two sides could not even agree on how many Americans were held prisoner by the Communists.

Meanwhile, the combatants continued their limited conflict. If it was a war no one really wanted, at least it was not the war everyone feared. For all the lives it would claim, the Korean War in its last two years was little more than a fight for position, a war stripped of any real meaning for those who actually fought it.

HEARTBREAK RIDGE
By Nate Polowetzky

U.S. 8TH ARMY HEADQUARTERS, KOREA, OCT. 6 (AP)—American and French Infantrymen, charging with fixed bayonets behind flame-throwers, seized virtually all of bloody Heartbreak Ridge today.

The fighting flared up suddenly in the eastern Korea mountains as the Allied offensive in the west ground to a halt—with most objectives secured.

There was no new move toward reopening truce talks.

The western offensive along a 40-mile front by 100,000 men from nine United Nations countries gained up to five miles in four days. It was the biggest Allied drive in three months. Front line dispatches reported the U.S. First Cavalry captured three hills in a mile-long advance Saturday West of Yonchon, but was stymied in attempts to take a fourth. To the south, two Chinese counter-attacks shoved Northumberland Fusiliers off a hill the British took early in the day. One American patrol in the west central front fought its way out of a trap in a six-hour battle.

The Allies moved into the best positions they have held in the west in a year and sent patrols reaching out as much as three miles in front of their newly won hills.

The long stalemated battle of Heartbreak Ridge erupted suddenly in a surprise night attack by American and French troops.

Infantrymen of the U.S. Second Division's 23rd Regiment, charging with fixed bayonets and shouting "banzai," stormed to the top of a 3,000-foot peak. They captured it for the third time in a month.

They killed 100 Red Koreans in the predawn fight. Other Reds fled in disorder before the Americans' flamethrowers and white phosphorous grenades. United Nations forces now hold all but the extreme northern tip of four-mile-long Heartbreak Ridge. Patrols began moving down from the ridge, some 20 miles north of the 38th parallel, and probed Mundung Valley. It is believed to have been a Red assembly area.
Oct. 6, 1951

By Stan Carter

EASTERN FRONT, KOREA, OCT. 6 (AP)—The Communists lost control of Heartbreak Ridge because they had to divide their forces to meet anticipated thrusts elsewhere.

They evidently did not expect the night assault by the U.S. 23rd Infantry Regiment, which ended at daybreak today with seizure of the tallest peak on the long north-south ridge line above Yanggu.

It was the idea of Maj. Gen. Robert N. Young, new commander of the Second Infantry Division, to couple a surprise attack of the 23rd Regiment on Heartbreak Ridge with a division-sized feint against Communist positions in the mountains surrounding the Mundung Valley, west of the ridge.

Tank thrusts into the Satae Valley, east of Heartbreak, and movements toward the Mundung Valley gave the Communists the idea that the Allies were interrupting their costly 24-day assault on Heartbreak Ridge.

The Reds split their forces to defend their positions in the mountains surrounding the Satae and Mundung Valleys.

It was comparatively easy for the 23rd Regiment, attacking in the dark with flamethrowers and bayonets, to reach the top of the tall peak in the center of Heartbreak Ridge. They overran the few North Koreans left to defend it.

An Allied officer said, "They didn't know we were coming until we hit them."

As it turned out, the Communists wasted most of their artillery on a tank force which probed into the Satae Valley for the third day in a row to shoot at Communist positions.

As long as the Communists held the tall peak at the center of Heartbreak Ridge, they were able to call down mortar and artillery fire on American troops both north and south of the peak. In effect, they controlled the ridge line. "The only thing living up there was the enemy, and we got rid of him this morning," said Pfc. Anthony Tavilla, 24, of Arlington, Mass. Tavilla was standing at the foot of Heartbreak Ridge, describing the desolation at the top of the peak which he helped seize.

There were bodies of American and North Korean soldiers—bodies which had been there for days—and there was the barren, shell-pocked ground.

"There was nothing there. It was flat on top," chimed in Pvt. Roy Baxter, 18, of 3815 Toomington Ave., Minneapolis. "I was in between two guys who got it in the back from one of our own machine guns," said Baxter. "The gunner thought we were gooks. They were wounded, but I wasn't even touched."

One young squad leader was hit by Red small arms fire. While he was waiting to be evacuated, he opened his billfold and gave $20 to the men of his squad to buy beer.

"We were mostly new replacements and we hadn't been paid yet, so he decided to pay for our beer," said Baxter.

The new men in the 23rd Regiment, replacements for the dead and wounded in the first two weeks of the Heartbreak Ridge battle, found it hard to keep up with the veterans at first. But when the North Koreans at the top of the mountain began firing, the replacements charged to the top with fixed bayonets.

Baxter said most of the North Koreans apparently had deserted the peak Friday night, when Allied artillery bombarded it.

"I think they just left a couple of suicide squads there to make a last ditch stand," he said.

"There was a lot of fire coming in, but mostly it was going over our heads."
Oct. 6, 1951

By Robert B. Tuckman

MUNSAN, KOREA, OCT. 24 (AP)—Allied and Communist negotiators will re-open Korean armistice talks tomorrow. They will tackle first the knotty problem of where to establish a buffer zone.

The five-man delegations will meet at Panmunjom, a roadside village six miles east of Red held Kaesong where the search for a cease-fire agreement was suspended Aug. 23 by the Reds. Panmunjom is accessible to each side without having to travel through enemy territory.

The tiny town now has the appearance of an American carnival. Armistice activities are housed in circus-like tents. Huge, colored balloons and searchlights ring the conference area to warn warplanes away from the neutral zone.

Resumption of the conference talks was made possible when the Communists on Wednesday ratified security ground rules drafted by U.N. and Communist liaison officers in 12 meetings at Panmunjom since Oct. 10.
Oct. 24, 1951

By Robert B. Tuckman

MUNSAN, KOREA, OCT. 26 (AP)—The Allies today quickly rejected a Communist buffer zone proposal that the U.N. give up such bitterly won Korean areas as Heartbreak Ridge, Punchbowl, and the Iron Triangle.

The Reds wanted the United Nations forces to withdraw as much as 15 miles. Their proposal countered yesterday's U.N. suggestion for a buffer zone generally along present battle lines. Maj. Gen. Henry I. Hodes told the Reds their proposal bore "no relationship to the military line of contact and did not offer truce protections."

The Communists made no mention of their previous demands for a demarcation line along the 38th parallel. Apparently, they have abandoned the idea.
Oct. 26, 1951

By Robert B. Tuckman

MUNSAN, KOREA, NOV. 27 (AP)—Truce negotiators signed a cease-fire line agreement today and immediately developed two vital differences on how to supervise an armistice in Korea. United Nations delegates insisted on:

1. Joint Allied-Communist inspection teams with "free access to all parts of Korea."

2. Provision against military buildups by either side.

Neither point was included in a plan proposed by the Reds, who have never permitted outsiders in Communist Korea.

The differences developed in a session described by the top Allied negotiator as "short and sweet."

The full five-man negotiating teams—all in full dress except for two drably clad Chinese generals—approved a cease-fire line agreement, opening the way for an armistice within 30 days. Then they plunged into the next truce question. That is supervision of an armistice. Each presented its own ideas.
Nov. 27, 1951

TOKYO, NOV. 27 (AP)—Allied and Communist radios today claimed a great victory in the agreement reached at Panmunjom on a Korean buffer zone.

It was a question of which propaganda broadcast you listened to.

The "voice of the United Nations Command" (UNC) said:

"The provisional settlement of item two (the buffer zone) represents a triumph of persistence by the UNC and the productive results of an unwavering perseverance to produce an agreement that has been avoided by the Communists for more than four months."

The Communist North Korean Pyongyang radio said: "Our delegates not only succeeded in overcoming the difficult and evil intentioned obstruction to the adoption of item two, but, maintaining their basic methods, our delegates smashed the destructive intentions of the enemy against the conference agenda."

Each warned the agreement didn't mean peace.

Each blamed the other for the delay.

The "voice" said the Reds insisted on "fuzzy, vaguely-phrased proposals" and tried "to confuse the issue and to mousetrap the UNC into accepting a stand that would lead only to the prolongation of the talks, possibly for an indefinite period." Pyongyang said the delay "was caused by the shameless disruptive tactics of the American delegates and by their attitude of utter insincerity. The American delegates employed every tactic possible to delay the progress of the talks."
Nov. 27, 1951

MUNSAN, KOREA, NOV. 27 (AP)—The agreed cease-fire line, to take effect if a Korean armistice is reached within 30 days, leaves Allied troops entrenched in hard-won hills of North Korea.

The line is 145-miles long. It begins on the east coast 43 miles north of the 38th parallel and four miles south of Kosong.

It drops sharply to a point just north of the Punchbowl, 22 miles north of the parallel and 22 miles west of the coast. Then it runs westward north of Heartbreak Ridge through Kumsong and the Reds' former Iron Triangle. In this westward stretch, the line remains 22 to 25 miles north of 38.
Nov. 27, 1951

By Olen Clements

TOKYO, NOV. 29 (AP)—An unwarlike attitude—"Don't shoot me and I won't shoot you"—spread along the 145 mile Korean front today, while officials from Korea to Washington denied a cease-fire order was issued.

Gen. James A. Van Fleet said the attitude may have developed from "distortion of the meaning" of an Eighth Army military directive.

He did not disclose the context of the directive but said definitely "there is no cease-fire order in Korea."

Against these denials, frontline reporters ran across these facts:

1. Associated Press correspondent Milo Farneti on the western front said he had seen such a written order. He did not say by whom it was signed.

2. National Broadcasting Co. correspondent John Rich on the same front sent to Tokyo a tape recording of a lieutenant giving a cease-fire order to his men on Wednesday.

3. Communist newsmen outside the armistice conference tent in Panmunjom said the Red ground commanders may have decided not to shoot unless they were shot at.

4. Another western front officer said his men had been instructed not to do any offensive firing now, but to fire back five shells for each Red shell fired at them.

5. Pulitzer Prize winner Keyes Beach of the *Chicago Daily News* said he drove over 100 miles of the front Wednesday through three divisions and did not hear a rifle shot. He told of a British lieutenant opening the door of a frontline bunker and facing two Chinese inside. He said the British officer excused himself and backed away.

6. NBC's Rich sent a second recording to Tokyo in which the voice of a company commander, just returned to the western front at 11 a.m. Wednesday said:

"At ease, gentlemen, I have just returned with this first word of the cease-fire. I want to relay it to you so that you can immediately get it to your platoons. There are several notes here I want to cover. I'd like for you to take notes so that they will not be forgotten.

"There will be no more raids by us.

"We send out no more combat patrols.

"Prior approval on a combat patrol when they are sent out will have to be approved at corps level.

"Reconnaissance patrols will be utilized only to maintain contact with our enemy.

"We will fire only in self-defense and in defense of the main line of resistance.

"And in the event the enemy starts building up a troop concentration to our front, we will in no way let this lower our efficiency. We must be alert and ready to move on a moment's notice."
Nov. 29, 1951

TRUCE TALKS WIND ON

By Robert B. Tuckman

MUNSAN, KOREA, MAY 9 (AP)—The Allies and the Communists rounded out 10 months of negotiations for a truce in Korea today with a futile 10-minute session. There were indications that the Communists may be waiting for new instructions while harping on old issues.

The main delegations faced each other at Panmunjom only long enough for Gen. Nam Il, senior Red delegate, to accuse the U.N. Command for the third straight day of holding up a truce.

Nam, in a 9½ minute harangue at Panmunjom, described as "outrageous" the Allied refusal to repatriate prisoners unwilling to return to the Reds.

Vice Adm. C. Turner Joy, chief Allied truce delegate, told the Reds it "should be unmistakably clear to you by this time" that the United Nations Command position is firm and final. However, the truce delegations agreed to meet again tomorrow.
May 9, 1952

BUNKER HILL

By William C. Barnard

WITH THE U.S. MARINES, AUG. 18 (AP)—Two Marine sergeants, grimy and red-eyed, came off Bunker Hill after three days and three nights of fighting, full of bitterness of battle and thankful to be alive.

They were two of the many men who staved off seven fanatical Chinese attempts to recapture the scarred and barren hill. It's more a ridge than a hill, sprawling out between the battle lines. When you approach it from any direction you are exposed on both sides.

"I'll tell you how it was," said Sgt. Clarence Wilkins Jr., of Hartford, Conn. "We didn't eat much and we didn't hardly sleep any, and whenever we moved, the goonies could see us do it and they'd let us have it with their big guns. Once they threw 7,000 rounds on us in just a few hours. They came at us in all kinds of attacks. But our boys never griped about anything."

Even the wounded guys didn't gripe, according to Sgt. Howard Ryan of Hempstead, N.Y.

"The first guy I helped carry out was laid wide open under the stomach, but he was grinning and smoking a cigarette. He laughed and said, 'I wear a helmet and flak jacket and they get me below the belt.' He was so cheerful. The rest of us had a hard time keeping him from seeing how sick we felt."

What were the Chinese attacks like?

"You never knew when you were going to get one," said Ryan.

"One started when a goonie ran up a high ridge and fired three shot bursts on a burp gun. That set off the battle and every gun in the world went off. Everybody was waiting. That's the way it always was — everybody waiting."

"Most of the time they attacked at night," Wilkins said. "When we couldn't stand it any longer, we'd doze a few minutes at a time in the daytime, but it was 100 percent watch every night, all night. When they came up the hill, we'd wait 'til they got about 30 yards away and open up, firing at their gun flashes and lobbing grenades at them. Afterwards, we could hear them rustling and scratching around, getting their dead and wounded out. The wounded would moan, but they never hollered."

All night long, each Marine gun would fire sporadic bursts now and then, sweeping a certain sector, Ryan explained. "One night one of our boys didn't see a single Chink, but he kept firing bursts every once in a while. Next morning he was surprised as hell to find 75 dead in front of his gun."

Daytime temperatures reached 100 degrees, which inflicted a rash of sunstroke cases.

"Lots of guys passed out," Wilkins said. "The heat waves came right off the sand and you had your jacket and helmet and all that stuff on you, and you had to be going up and down the hill.

"When a man would pass out," Wilkens said, "we'd try to get some kind of shade over him. Some were so bad off we had to give them artificial respiration. If they didn't come around,

we'd ship 'em back to an aid station. But they'd always be back in a couple of hours."

"You got so hot and tense you couldn't eat," Ryan said. "We had some C rations. Mostly I lived on cocoa."
Aug. 18, 1952

Armistice

The Korean War contributed nothing to Harry Truman's popularity. During World War II, Franklin Roosevelt was able to win re-election for an unprecedented second and third time; during Korea, Truman did not seek re-election even a single time.

Dwight D. Eisenhower, another great general of World War II, was the Republican nominee for president in 1952. If elected, he said, "I will go to Korea." He was and he did, shortly after the election, with no immediate result. The new secretary of state, John Foster Dulles, let it be known through diplomatic channels that unless the Communists settled, they faced the risk of a major new U.S. offensive that might include nuclear weapons.

In March 1953, the Communists indicated they wanted to talk about prisoners of war. The next month, Eisenhower gave a speech to the American Society of Newspaper Editors entitled "The Chance for Peace." Its tone encouraged the Communists, and peace talks resumed with some vigor shortly thereafter.

The key issue was the status of about 22,000 North Korean and Chinese prisoners of war who said they did not want to go home. The situation reminded some in the West of Germany's Soviet POWs in the last war. The Western Allies had turned them over to their old commanders, with the result that many were mistreated or killed. In 1952, Truman had said, "We will not buy an armistice by turning over human beings for slaughter or slavery." Finally, a compromise was worked out allowing the soldiers a choice whether to go north.

The military demarcation line was set near

the 38th parallel, where it all started. South Korea gained 2,350 acres of North Korea; the latter gained 850 acres of what had been South Korea.

When the war ended after 37 months, nearly 1.8 million Americans had served in Korea. About 33,000 of them were killed, more than 100,300 were wounded and 8,200 were listed missing in action. In all, the war claimed 2 million lives.

BULLETIN

WAR ENDS

PANMUNJOM, MONDAY, JULY 27 (AP)—The Allies and Communists signed an armistice at 10 a.m. today to end the Korean War. The shooting will stop at 10 a.m. (8 a.m. Monday, EST).
July 27, 1953

ARMISTICE

By Robert B. Tuckman

PANMUNJOM, JULY 27 (AP)—The United Nations and the Communists finally signed the hard-bargained Korean armistice today, ending 37 months of war, but both top commands quickly warned their troops that a truce did not necessarily mean a peace.

These discordant notes sounded almost immediately:

The Chinese Communists in Peiping broadcast a claim that the Reds had won "a glorious victory."

Gen. Mark W. Clark, U.N. commander, pointedly stated that his forces remained "to defend the

Gen. Mark Clark, United Nations supreme commander in the Far East, affixes his signature to armistice documents at his base camp in Munsan, Korea. The documents were taken to Munsan after having been signed at Panmunjom by U.N. and Communist negotiators.

Republic of Korea against any aggressor," and "I cannot find it in me to exult in this hour."

President Syngman Rhee reminded the world that there was a six-month time limit on his compliance, and he still intended "to reclaim and redeem our provinces and our people in the North."

The main ceremony was a cold, 10-minute formality in Panmunjom attended by Lt. Gen. William K. Harrison, American representing the United Nations Command, and Gen. Nam Il of North Korea, representing the Chinese and Korean Reds.

Shortly afterward, Gen. Mark W. Clark, United Nations supreme commander, countersigned the 18 documents—nine copies for each side—and issued a warning statement to his forces. Clark said the armistice does "not mean an immediate, or even early withdrawal" from Korea.

"It does mean that our duties and responsibilities during the critical period of the armistice are heightened and intensified, rather than diminished," he said.

"The conflict will not be over until the governments concerned have reached a firm political settlement.

Gen. Maxwell D. Taylor, Eighth Army commander, warned similarly that the armistice was "just a suspension of hostilities, which may or may not be preparatory to permanent peace."

The formal signing ceremony by Harrison and Nam Il was a cold and silent one in this hamlet near the 38th parallel, where the war began and near which the stalemated armies have been locked for two years past.

Newsreel and television cameras hummed steadily and still cameras clicked at intervals throughout the ceremony.

The prisoners of war—all who want to go home—must be exchanged at this historic little mud-hut village where the armistice was signed. These include about 3,500 Americans, 8,000 South Koreans and about 1,000 from other Allied nations.

The exchange should start within the week.

Prisoners who refuse repatriation—there are about 14,500 Chinese and 8,000 North Koreans—will be given explanations by countrymen designed to allay their fears. Then if they still resist after 90 days, the political conference will be handed the problem.

Representatives of four neutral nations—Sweden, Switzerland, Poland and Czechoslovakia—are charged with observing the armistice.

The problem of what President Syngman Rhee of South Korea would do—after a period of six months grace he has granted the Allies—hung like a specter over the prospect for permanent peace.

The Republic of Korea, which opposes a truce that leaves Korea divided with Chinese Red troops in the North, was not represented at the signing.

The delegates met in a jerry-built but ornate structure with an Oriental pagoda roof in this war-ruined wayside village of Panmunjom, which the Koreans called, "The Inn with the Wooden Door."

They began at 10:01 a.m. and finished exactly 10 minutes later. They separated in silence, but not before exchanging one long, searching look.

Three hours later, at 1:01 p.m., Gen. Clark signed at the Allied Advance Headquarters in Munsan and sent the copies off to North Korea.

The Red chiefs, Chinese Gen. Peng Teh-Huai and North Korean Marshal Kim Il Sung, were to send their signed copies down to Clark. These were anticlimactic signatures.

Unable to agree on meeting at Panmunjom, the top commanders had agreed that Harrison and Nam Il would do the signing that set the armistice in motion.

The strokes of their pens on the 18 copies of the armistice document touched off reactions around the world, from the hilly battlefields of Korea where troops have fought in mud and dust and snow, to the world capitals where diplomats have pondered the Korean crisis and what to do about it.

President Eisenhower, in a radio-television address to the American people from Washington, hailed the armistice with thanksgiving. He declared the United Nations had met the challenge of aggression with "deeds of decision" and warned that the United States and its Allies must remain vigilant.

July 27, 1953

By George McArthur

WESTERN FRONT, KOREA, JULY 27 (AP)— Brilliant flares silhouetted the low hills of the western front tonight as U.S. Marines and Chinese soldiers signalled one another the shooting was over in Korea.

Just before the shooting stopped at 10 p.m., Marines and the Chinese began firing the signal flares into a clear, moonlit sky.

The Marines fired white flares. The Chinese fired red, green, blue and yellow flares. The flares might have signalled an attack before, but not tonight.

A few minutes before 10, Marine guns barked out their last few rounds. The deep-throated explosions echoed through the valleys.

The sound echoed along the Imjin River and into Panmunjom, where, 12 hours, before armistice negotiators agreed to stop the bloody conflict.

Then, at 10 o'clock, a sullen silence fell over the front and flares lit the sky.

Gen. William K. Harrison Jr., chief U.N. armistice delegate (seated left), and North Korean Gen. Nam Il (right), chief communist delegate, look up as they complete signing armistice documents at Panmunjom, Korea. With Gen. Harrison are Cmdr. J.E. Shew, U.S.N. (left) and Col. J.C. Murray, U.S.M.C. (right).

For half an hour or so, the Marines were silent. Then a few began to laugh. Personal jokes were exchanged. The Marines kept on their armored vests but began, ever so slightly, to cast off the strain of war.

"It looks like the Chinese mean it," said Pfc. Robert Harmon, Chattanooga, Tenn., as he peered out over no man's land at the ominous black hills held by the Reds.

On the Chinese hillside there were a few faint flickers of light.

The Chinese soldiers were smoking cigarettes and emerging from their bunkers for a respite of fresh air.

Even more than an end to the shooting, this small human sign demonstrated that hostile guns now were silent.

The Marines clustered in groups atop their outpost hills that just the night before were viewed as a risky home.

"I'm sure glad it's over," said 22-year-old Cpl. Walter Ratka. "I wish it was signed three or four days ago. We wouldn't have lost all those men."

Capt. James Landringan, Wakefield, Mass., had more reasons than most men to be thankful the shooting had stopped. He had fought in two wars, and has four small children waiting for him to return.

Landringan recalled the day when he heard the news that World War II was over. He was on Okinawa, and had just stolen a can of cheese from a major. He and his friends celebrated by eating the cheese.

"This time I am very skeptical," he said. "Last

time there was a hell of a lot more you could relax about. You knew it was an accomplished job. This time you don't."
July 27, 1953

By John Randolph
CENTRAL FRONT, KOREA, JULY 27 (AP)—I had promised Item Company I would bring them a bottle of whiskey the minute that agreement was reached on the armistice.

They didn't see me coming until the last 20 yards on the steep and muddy hill northeast of Kumhwa.

Under my arm, like a football, I was carrying the fifth of 100 proof Bond, wrapped safely in a dirty GI khaki towel.

Sgt. Ippolito spotted me floundering and gasping up the final slope. He looked a long moment—then he started to yell, his voice breaking with excitement.

"He's got it! He's got the bottle! It's an armistice, by God—they've got an armistice!" Helmeted heads craned out of bunkers and foxholes and dirty bearded faces turned my way and Ippolito ran down the slopes to meet me.

A horrible suspicion of doubt crossed his face and he stopped short.

"You wouldn't kid us, would you? It's true, ain't it?"

"I wouldn't kid you," I said. "It's true. It's official. The U.N. Command this afternoon announced an armistice had been agreed upon. They sign it tomorrow at 10 a.m. The cease-fire is 10 p.m. tomorrow."

Another and deeper shadow crossed Ippolito's face.

"Tonight? You mean we gotta sweat out tonight? Jesus Christ. I hope we make it." Then he shoved the awful fear out of his mind, brightened again and shouted:

"Lieutenant! Lieutenant! They got an armistice—he brought the bottle just like he said."

The others were crowding around now, maybe a dozen of them, and I was escorted to the muddy hole covered with logs that was the company command post.

Lt. Don C. Patton, the company executive,

leaned out from under the sandbagged logs. Patton is a bronzed young man with a big brown mustache and a sweaty, mud-stained face.

We shake hands. Ippolito explains our bargain. I hand over the bottle.

"Whenever you think best," I tell him.

Patton considers.

It is 5 p.m. now, Sunday evening. For 29 hours still these men will be at war—while all the world relaxes and rejoices. Twenty-nine hours, 29 eternitys, on a hill in North Korea, where death counts out the seconds, one by one.

"We'll drink it tomorrow night—at 10 o'clock," Patton decides, and he puts the bottle carefully in an old ammunition box underneath his field telephone and the mud-stained battle map.

"Thank you very much," he said.

I have come back to Item Company at a terrible moment. Only two hours before, in a tragedy almost beyond bearing in the last hours of the war, two rounds of American artillery have landed by accident in the middle of the company. In two seconds, a sergeant was dead and 10 other men were wounded, some very seriously.

Just the night before, this company and King Company, its neighbor, fought back a savage Chinese attack that was launched with 5,000 rounds of Communist shellfire.

These men are bone weary, filthy, dirty, soaked to the skin by unending summer showers. They have been living in holes like rats since the U.S. 3rd Division was jerked from only three hours of reserve and flung into the Kumsong front to plug the gap left by the collapse of the Republic of Korea's Capitol Division.

Now these men are told that the war is over—except that they must go through one more night of fear and terror on this hill position, less than a mile from Chinese lines.

The "krrrgump!" of a Chinese shell resounds from the hill where Love Company is waiting across the valley to our left. These men, with their angers, their bitterness, their hope, their fears, their terrible physical exhaustions, are at a peak of emotional strain that is rare among the infantry, where fatalism is cultivated.

"An armistice—it makes a man want to get

down on his knees and thank God," said Sgt. Sall Ippolito, 437th St., Brooklyn, N.Y., who has served for nine months in Korea.

"We'll stay in our holes tonight and pray to God we make it. It makes a man want to pray—make him want to cry and it was one of our own goddamned rounds that got the guys today. We had to police up 11 men today—all at the last moment. I don't think it was the gunners' fault, maybe it was just some bad ammunition."

The phrase "police up" is new Army slang the way Ippolito uses it. It always did mean "tidy up" but here it means gathering up the possessions of a dead or wounded comrade. A pile of those possessions is lying on the ammunition box beside the field telephone. There is a fountain pen, a New Testament, dog tag, a watch, and a few old letters from home.

Cpl. Walter W. Turner, a Negro squad leader from 1912 Orleans St., Baltimore, shook his head in deepest skepticism.

"We'll catch it tonight for sure. We can look for a lot of blank blank blank blanking hell tonight. It's all in the trust of the Lord—it'll be a long night till daybreak comes."

Lt. Patton, who comes from Dallas, shook his head slowly:

"If I ever get back to Texas I'll never bitch again. All I ever want to do is to forget I was ever here. I keep thinking of the old sergeant who rotated home and said all he wanted was his dog tags for medals and his backside for a souvenir."

Another officer, Lt. Francis J. Nester of Bell St., Middletown, Conn., a platoon leader, said:

"Everybody's thankful that it's going to end—but we can't help thinking of those who didn't make it. Why couldn't they have ended it just a little sooner?"

"If tonight goes OK we've got it made," says Pfc. James Piersal, 2118 Spann Ave., Indianapolis.

"It seems like it isn't true," says Pvt. Daniel W. L. Wines, 126 North "A" St., Lebanon, Ind.

Both men are from Mike Company, the battalion's heavy weapons unit. They handle a 57 millimeter recoilless rifle up on the front line with Item Company's riflemen.

Sgt. Cobert Mitchell, 443 W. 50th St., New York City, talked about the Chinese across the hill.

"You know, I don't think they want to fight any more than we do. I hope they stay in their holes tonight, just like we will. A lot of men here are going to be jumpy tonight."

Just then the battalion commander climbed up into the bunker area on the reverse slope. He is Lt. Col. Jesse D. Willoughby, 5125 Worthington Dr., Westgate, Md. He had learned about the tragedy of the short round and the armistice news and had come to his most forward company to tell the men: "Play it cool" in this final night, but take no chances and do not give the Chinese one last opportunity to attack.

Willoughby is not old, but he is fatherly compared to the young boys in the company. He goes from group to group. Here and there he pats a man on the back and you hear a faint "Play it cool, son," and he goes on to another group until he disappears down the trench on his way to the last outpost. "He's pretty good, the old man. A lot of colonels never come up to see you," says Mitchell. "He's up here all the time. He even came up the road last night, right in the middle of the shelling."

Pfc. Jesse J. Moore, Route 2, Fulton, Miss., a forward observer for Mike Company's 81mm mortars, woke up from a nap and was told the cease-fire would be Monday night at 10 o'clock.

"You guys can take 10 o'clock—I'll wait 'till 11. I want to give those bastards one more hour to play in."

On my way back I talked to Cpl. Manuel Ross, Route 1, Bessemer City, N.C., the company's senior medical aid man, who hands out pills and bandages cuts, and carries the dead and the wounded in battle.

"It's really wonderful—if it's only true," he said.

"I feel better tonight than I have ever felt before. All I want to do now is to go home to my wife—yesterday was our fifth anniversary."

Lt. William T. Loyd, 920 26th St., Newport News, Va., shook hands with me as I started to go.

"I hope it's true," he said. "I hope we get through tonight without some crazy attack. It would be shameful to have anyone hurt tonight."

One last look back—at the red cocoa colored mud, the primitive holes and bunkers on the reverse slope, the rocks, the torn scrub, the thin radio antennas trembling slightly on the skyline near the observation post, at a helmet here and there against the sky, and at the lush green hills beyond, rich and green in the rainy season.

A man always feel cheap to walk away from an infantry company on the line. On the way down, I meet an outpost patrol coming up the hill. We are talking in a ravine when the old terrible whistle shrills. We fling ourselves to the ground and two Chinese shells crash a hundred yards beyond us. The war is not over here. It is deep dusk when I reach the jeep at the bottom of the hill. The warm summer rains begin to fall in torrents.

I see men approaching—another outpost patrol from King Company.

They are marching single file, each man 50 feet apart, hugging the sheltered side of the road in case of artillery fire. I pass them very slowly, for it is an unpardonable crime to splash foot soldiers with mud. Then I stop and look back. The rain is driving, and already the night and the mist are closing in. Already the head of the little column has disappeared in the gloom and the rest are hastening away into the darkness.
July 27, 1953

Editor's Note

Released prisoners of war told grim stories after being released from Communist captivity. An Associated Press story from "Freedom Village" in August 1953 reported some of them:

RELEASED U.S. POWs

FREEDOM VILLAGE, KOREA, FRIDAY, AUG. 7 (AP)—The stories told by soldiers back from Communist captivity turned grim yesterday.

A relative of the chief Allied armistice negotiator at Panmunjom said his captors tortured him in a futile attempt to wring military information from him.

The co-pilot of a downed Superfortress said he was tortured for four days.

A U.S. Army corporal said he saw 1,500 of his comrades buried in the brutal winter of 1950-51, dead of starvation, freezing or neglect of wounds.

There was visual evidence, too, of Communist neglect on the second day of the exchange of prisoners. One South Korean soldier was dead on arrival at Panmunjom. Another South Korean died of tuberculosis as a helicopter took him away from Panmunjom. Many of the Allied prisoners were human wrecks. Some were terribly emaciated. Others could hardly walk. Most were South Koreans.

There were 70 Americans in the second exchange, 42 of them sick or wounded. Most appeared to be in good condition.

Lt. Col. Thomas D. Harrison, told of nine days of starvation and torture.

Harrison lost his left leg when his plane was shot down over North Korea in May of 1951. He said he was taken in September to a building near the North Korean capital of Pyongyang where North Korean civilian police tried to get military information from him.

"For seven days they cut off my food entirely, but at every meal they compelled me to watch others eat," he related.

In November, 10 police entered his room, stripped his clothes from him, wired him to a chair, and pulled his head back.

"They put a towel over my face and poured water on the towel," he said. "This cut off the air and I could not breathe. When I would pass out, they brought me to by stabbing me with [lighted] cigarettes.

"It was so cold the water they poured on the towels ran down me and froze. They didn't get any information."

Lt. Samuel E. Massinberg of Detroit, co-pilot of a Superfort shot down over Pyongyang last Jan. 11, said he was tortured for four days by North Koreans trying to get military information.

He said his frostbitten hands were bound behind him, he was given no food and was beaten. The beatings stopped only when part of his left hand rotted away from gangrene.

A pattern began to emerge from the soldiers' stories. Foot soldiers captured after the winter of 1950-51 told of somewhat better treatment, but they said food and medical care were inadequate.

On the other hand, airmen in the last two years of the war often were treated with utmost brutality, apparently in reprisal for the endless bombings.
Aug. 7, 1953

Editor's Note

The following story, written in 1953 by Associated Press war correspondent John Randolph, goes inside a Communist interview tent for an incisive description of the meetings with North Korean prisoners who rejected communism and resisted repatriation.

By John Randolph

INDIAN VILLAGE, KOREA, AUG. 24 (AP)—The tall, slender Communist lieutenant stood up yesterday, placed his fingers on a small table, and leaned toward the struggling North Korean prisoner. "Tung-moo," the North Korean officer began, "Comrade."

The word was like a whip across the prisoner's face. "Tung-moo," he screamed and hurled himself against the lean, brown arms of his Indian guards.

"Tung-moo, you filthy son of a dog, you dirty Communist trainer, you and your Russian Chinese barbarians. Don't 'comrade' me you dirty Chinese lover. I spit on your father and mother."

He spat straight at the officer only five feet away. It missed his face but soiled the crisp olive green uniform with its gleaming belt and gold and scarlet shoulder boards.

The officer stood quietly erect as the prisoner writhed and stomped and kicked to break away from his guards and rush his interrogator.

The Indian neutral chairman in the tent, a Capt. Garaya, looked inquiringly at the Red officer. The Communist shrugged in resignation and started to sit down.

But before Garaya could wave the raging prisoner out of the south door of the tent—where anti-Communists go—the latter hurled himself forward with a supreme effort. He kicked viciously at the little table and sent it hurtling into the Communist's lap.

Then the Indians, patience exhausted, lifted him off the floor and carried him bodily out of the tent. The interview had lasted nearly 40 seconds.

The next prisoner was led in, struggling and sullen, and Garaya read the required preliminaries.

The Red lieutenant stood up, placed his fingers on the table, and leaned forward.

"Tung-moo"" he began, "Comrade."

The prisoner remained silent but struggling.

"Tung-moo," the Communist repeated. "As a representative of the government of the Republic I can guarantee your personal safety on my own word. You are safe now, and free if you go home now."

"I don't want to be repatriated—I want to stay in South Korea!" the prisoner said.

The North Korean officer did not ever seem to hear him.

"You must think how great the grief of your father and mother will be if they cannot see you," he went on.

The prisoner looked appealingly at the chairman Garaya and pleaded, "Let me go—I don't want to be repatriated." But he did not show the implacable hatred of the first man.

So began a strange duel that lasted for 123 minutes more.

The duelists, apart from their common language, were distinct contrasts.

The Communist political officer, resplendent in his colorful uniform and black leather Russian boots, showed steady nerves. The stocky prisoner, wearing olive drab American Army woolens and muddy boots, clenched his hands tightly and tried to wrench out of the grasp of the Indian guards.

The Red officer talked almost without interruption for an hour and half, delivering each word with full force.

The prisoner appeared like a bird hypnotized by a snake, wanting, but unable to get away. More clever men might have argued. The prisoner just put his head down like a balky mule and let the words roll over him.

"You must come home," pleaded the officer, alternately an orator tense with emotion and then an elder brother, kindly and confidential. "You must think of your father and mother—we are building a new Korea."

"Let me out of here," the prisoner shouted each time the officer paused for breath.

At 9:58 a.m.—"I don't want to be repatriated!"

At 10:04 a.m.—"I refuse to return!"

At 10:13 a.m.—He whimpered and squirmed.

At 10:15—"I want to go back to my compound!"

At 10:20—"I don't want to go back!"

At 10:21 the Communist broke the rules and

threatened, "You must come back—you know that the Peoples Republic will occupy the southern half of Korea."

Garaya barked the Communist to a stop.

"Tell him," he told his interpreter, "that he will not use this threatening language."

At 10:30, more than an hour after the interview began, the weary prisoner turned pleadingly to Garaya:

"I have listened to the explanation and I have said I want to go out that door to South Korea. Can I go now?"

Garaya answered that he must listen until the Reds were finished. The prisoner moaned and slumped back in the guards' arms.

At 10:57, the prisoner shrieked, "I want to go out."

"Isn't there any time limit?"

Garaya shook his head in the negative.

The prisoner sat down wearily and his head hung low.

Finally, at 11:13, he surged to his feet.

"I refuse to go," he said.

"I have listened to the explanations.

Now I want to go out of that door."

He pointed to the one leading back to the Allied side.

"Have you finished?" Garaya asked the Red officer.

The orator reluctantly nodded.

The dazed prisoner was allowed to go.

Another prisoner was brought it, screaming, "You sons of dogs."

The Red officer leaned toward him.

"Tung-moo," he began.

Aug. 24, 1953

Index